Coming Together

Coming Together

The Bible's Message in an Age of Diversity

Curtiss Paul DeYoung

Judson Press ® Valley Forge

Coming Together
The Bible's Message in an Age of Diversity
© 1995
Judson Press, Valley Forge, PA 19482-0851

Unless otherwise noted, Bible quotations in this volume are from the New Revised Standard Version of the Bible, copyrighted 1989 by the Division of Christian Education of the National Council of the Churches of Christ in the USA. Used by permission. All rights reserved.

Other quotations are from *The Holy Bible,* King James Version. Revised Standard Version of the Bible, copyright © 1946, 1952, 1971, by the Division of Christian Education of the National Council of the Churches of Christ in the USA. Used by permission. HOLY BIBLE: *New International Version,* copyright © 1973, 1978, 1984. Used by permission of Zondervan Bible Publishers.

Library of Congress Cataloging-in-Publication Data
DeYoung, Curtiss Paul.
    Coming Together : the Bible's message in an age of diversity / Curtiss Paul
DeYoung.
        p. cm.
    Includes bibliographical references.
    ISBN 0-8170-1226-5
    1. Christianity and justice. 2. Jesus Christ—Afro-American interpretations.
3. Multiculturalism—Biblical teaching. 4. Race relations—Religious aspects—Christianity. I. Title.
    BR115.J8D48 1995
    261.8'34—dc20   94-41664

Printed in the U.S.A.

95 96 97 98 99 00 01 02   8 7 6 5 4 3 2 1

To my children, Rachel Maria DeYoung and Jonathan Paul DeYoung

may you be among the artisans of reconciliation in the twenty-first century

In memory of Samuel George Hines (1929-1995) And in honor of James Earl Massey

my mentors in the ministry of reconciliation

And in gratitude to Cain Hope Felder

my mentor and inspiration
in the pursuit of biblical truth that responds to all of the voices emanating from the rich mosaic of the human family

Contents

Foreword

by Cain Hope Felder

In the 1990s, we may be witnessing one of the most profound sociopolitical revolutions in biblical interpretation that the world has seen since the Protestant Reformation. Instead of the Bible being presented to the world as a compelling compendium of ancient European spirituality designed to "civilize" pagan cultures and preserve European cultural domination, increasing numbers of contemporary interpreters are breathing new life into ancient biblical texts no longer accepted as tools for oppression but as divine promptings for human liberation. It is striking that the decade that is closing the twentieth century is apparently reopening an almost forgotten vision of racial and ethnic pluralism and reconciliation that dates back to events that culminate in the first century.

The signs of extraordinary changes are in evidence the world over—the fall of the Berlin Wall; the stepped-up pace of nuclear disarmament; the long-overdue championing of the rights of women; the end of the Cold War; remarkable handshakes between the leaders of Israel, Palestine, and Jordan; the drama of Nelson Mandela's release from prison and ascent to the presidency of South Africa; American troops being deployed on three continents on almost unprecedented missions of mercy and humanitarian relief; the prospects of a rapport between North and South Korea as well as the almost unimaginable prospect of reconciliation between Britain and the Irish Republican Army, Sinn Fein! Yet, amidst such hopeful sociopolitical changes there have been the strong negative undercurrents of those forces always resistant to change in order to protect the presumed privileges of the rich and the powerful. The soul of a nation and a civilization is in utter turmoil and the stakes are high indeed!

With all that the Bible has to say about divine reversals, profound judgment, and depth spirituality, one should never forget that it fundamentally is the definitive ancient book of Western culture. It has arisen from ancient cultures and groups whose souls were in agony and who longed for redemptive change so that human beings could relate in community on the basis of their common humanity before God. Thus, the Bible is preeminently well suited to offer balm to cultures and groups whose souls are in agony while they strain to discern the righteous way of sustaining and benefiting from constructive social change and transformation.

One new voice that deserves to be widely heard is that of Curtiss Paul DeYoung as expressed in his refreshing and most timely book entitled *Coming Together: The Bible's Message in an Age of Diversity*. Here are the fruits of the scholarship and praxis of a European-American minister and social activist who has uniquely chosen to sit where many so-called minorities have had to sit. He thereby writes as one who knows what it is to be an alien in your native land and to some extent marginalized because of choosing to break from the pack and to look at the social chaos and injustice of those below who hurt. With this provocative book Curtiss DeYoung joins the ranks of persons like the late William Stringfellow, Jim Wallis, and other white American males who, rather than resisting constructive and needed social change, have mustered up the courage to witness on its behalf in open dialogue with the Bible.

DeYoung's *Coming Together* is a significant step forward in what has come to be called cultural hermeneutics of the Bible. In six substantive chapters buttressed with a fine introduction and epilogue, this volume presents much more than a mere collection of interpretations of the ancient biblical world, typical of many traditional biblical interpreters. Instead of such standard fare, DeYoung offers a daring attempt to glean insights from the biblical past as he relates them to contemporary aspirations of a diverse array of racial and ethnic Bible interpreters among God's people. This book shows that many of us are being heard and that our struggles with the Bible are having a telling effect. We have an ally and friend in Brother DeYoung—we who are Native American, African, Latina/o, Asian, and the socially sensitive European American as well. How instructive it is to find one such as DeYoung reminding us that the Bible is far from being a relic of the distant past, designed only for the maintenance of power and superiority of one group! In his literature review, analysis of specific biblical passages, and his provocative prescriptions for the church today, DeYoung has performed a great service for us all.

The African American eclectic scholar and social critic W.E.B.DuBois in his often quoted *The Souls of Black Folk* declared many decades ago that "the problem of the twentieth century would be the problem of the color line." Curtiss DeYoung's wide reading and disciplined writing help us to see that DuBois was essentially correct, but clarification and expansion of the color line is necessary. The "color line" turns out to involve what we may call a "culture line," with Eurocentrism on one side of the line (the realm of the honorific) and all other cultures on the other side of the line (the realm of the pejorative). Even the ways in which the Bible has been interpreted by the so-called mainline Bible scholars (overwhelmingly white males), we have seen the triumphalism of Western culture and a certain captivity of the Bible maintained through technical linguistic and historiographic tools applied to preserve narrow parameters for biblical interpretation.

The process of cultural hegemony evident in biblical interpretation throughout the better part of the present century finds its parallel in such official governmental policies as the American immigration and naturalization regulations of the present century. Recent studies have shown, for example, that within a sixty-year period in the present century, the United States government carefully controlled the basic composition of the population with strict, often clandestine, immigration policies. This resulted in allowing only 174,000 persons of African origin into the country during the period in comparison with five million Latinas/os, eight million Asians, and forty-two million Europeans. Similar official rules have been consistently applied in selecting textbooks for American education at all levels, for determining films in Hollywood or what is to be presented on television, and for publishing versions of the Bible and allied Christian educational materials. In short, "the land of the free" has largely sacralized a process of socialization that champions everything European and conversely tends to stereotype and otherwise demonize most non-European cultural realities. Adding insult to injury, the so-called American mainstream has tended vigorously to deny that any such phenomena have taken place.

Obviously, new visions and prophetic perspectives are sorely needed in America and the world if the vitality of the Bible's agenda for social transformation is to receive a proper hearing. Some of my own research and writing has moved in this direction, as has the work of extramural colleagues like Justo González, Ivone Gebara, Sun Ai Park, R.S. Sugirtharajah, and Anne Nasimiyu-Wasike among others whom Curtiss DeYoung cites in this work, a true labor of love. In *Coming Together*, therefore, we have strong signs that a new day is truly dawning, despite the resistance and cynicism of many in society today. Let the reader be advised: this is not a book written from detached lofty places! No, this book emerges out of the heart and social praxis of a minister who has sought aggressively to bring together diverse racial and ethnic groups so that they may better understand one another and form coalitions of helping solidarity informed by new readings of the Bible itself. I am proud of my former student at the Howard University School of Divinity who has remained so faithful to a mission and sense of Christian witness that he has produced this marvelous window of new biblical opportunities that enables us to return again and again to the Bible rejoicing!

Cain Hope Felder
Professor, New Testament Language and Literature
Howard University School of Divinity
Chairman, The Biblical Institute for Social Change, Inc.

Acknowledgments

Coming Together: The Bible's Message in an Age of Diversity is the culmination of a pilgrimage that has been impacted by the insights of many individuals, the enlightenment that comes from varied experiences, the illumination of intellectual pursuit, and the mystery of God's grace and wisdom.

My journey was inaugurated by two parents who understood at a visceral level the oneness of humanity. They raised me in the Church of God (Anderson, Indiana), a church movement that taught that unity was at the core of the gospel of Jesus Christ. I am grateful to Arnold and Marylin DeYoung for their influence on my life and for their ongoing love and support.

Numerous others have tutored me on this pilgrimage, including the faculty I sat under at Howard University School of Divinity; the ministers of the National Association of the Church of God; the students I have taught at Bethel College; and the faith community of Milwaukee, Wisconsin. The following congregations have also been my teachers: Third Street Church of God in Washington, D.C.; Congregational Church of God in New York City; Park Avenue United Methodist Church in Minneapolis; First Church of God in Minneapolis; and Willow Street Church of God in Long Beach. I deeply appreciate the board of directors and the network of relationships that compose the TURN Leadership Foundation. These individuals have nurtured me on life's trek in countless ways.

I want to express my sincere gratitude to the persons who

took time to comment on portions of my manuscript: Robin Bell, Nicholas Cooper-Lewter, Marilyn Figueroa, William Huff, James Earl Massey, Aldean Miles, and Robert Odom. I also offer a heartfelt thank-you to Cain Hope Felder for taking time from his busy schedule to write this book's foreword as well as thoroughly read and comment on the manuscript. My own research builds on the foundation of his many important and significant contributions to our understanding of the Bible.

I want to offer special appreciation to my wife, Karen, whom I love and adore. She read and commented on the complete manuscript and, with my children, gave me "a season of grace" to spend extra hours completing the book.

Finally, I want to thank Dr. Harold Rast and the fine staff at Judson Press for their support in this endeavor.

This book is penned for the glory of God!

Introduction

The Bible's Message in an Age of Diversity

The purpose of this book is to provide Christians in particular and people of faith in general with a primer that addresses racial, ethnic, and cultural diversity from a biblical perspective. This is critical at this juncture in history because our world is experiencing dramatic transformations. The population shifts taking place around the world—due to migration patterns, large numbers of refugees, the demise of communism, and other factors—are causing "diversity" to emerge as the most crucial issue needing attention as we approach and enter the twenty-first century. As the face of the world changes, the effective dominance of Europe and Euro-America is being questioned afresh. In 1950, 25 percent of the world's population lived in Europe and North America. By 1989 it had decreased to 12 percent. It is projected that by the year 2000 it will be a mere 6 percent.[1]

This kind of rapid demographic metamorphosis is nowhere more apparent than in the United States. In the 1980s, sixteen states experienced a decline in their white population while forty-one states saw double-digit-percentage increases in their people-of-color populations.[2] The 1990 U.S. Census Bureau reported that over 25 percent of the population was people of color. It projected that by the year 2030 people of color will be one-third of the population and, by the mid-twenty-first century, people of color will outnumber whites in the United States of America.

The growing diversity in our world represents more than just racial or cultural differences. The gap between rich and poor continues to widen. Men and women are struggling to make sense out of changing gender roles. Our world is experiencing a broad range of religious expressions, philosophical outlooks, educational attainments, and the like. As a result of changing demographics and enhanced communication systems, the people of our world are increasingly interacting with each other. The United States, along with many other countries, has become a microcosm of heterogeneous perspectives from around the world. For many, these extensive changes have brought escalated tensions and heightened fears.

Persons of faith and goodwill can no longer remain silent. Like never before, we must address the concerns and issues related to the growing diversity in our world. Given this task, a key question arises: "What is the role of the Bible in an age of diversity?" Cornel West states that "we must look to new frameworks and languages to understand our multilayered crisis and overcome our deep malaise."[3] For people of faith, this means that the rich mosaic of cultural perspectives in our world needs to be considered when interpreting the Bible. If faith is to have any relevance as we approach and enter the next millennium, accepting this challenge can be most rewarding. In this age of diversity, we have the opportunity to breathe new life back into the message of God found in the Bible and revitalize its potency for our world. We need to be set free from narrow and sometimes oppressive ways of interpreting the Scriptures and be challenged to embrace a multicultural approach. All people need to hear their own stories in the Bible, and an appreciation for the outlooks of others and a knowledge of their stories are likewise critical for our understanding of God. I believe that faith in the twenty-first century depends on our ability to embrace the multicultural message of the Bible. That message, in short, calls us to come together as the people of God, despite our differences.

Coming Together addresses diversity from a biblical perspective. It attempts to be thoroughly multicultural in its outlook and presentation while giving a broad overview of the interrelated subjects that must be included in this discussion. The findings presented are biblically based and incorporate the research, insights, and perspectives of female and male scholars who are African, Native American, Latina/o, African American, Asian, European, as well as from many other contexts.[4] These many cultural viewpoints on the Bible are brought together and synthesized in some very unique ways. At times, the ideas presented are constructed by an intertwining of cultural standpoints. This powerfully demonstrates that that which is "human" can cross any cultural divide.

The first three chapters look at some foundational understandings for addressing diversity from a biblical perspective. In chapter one, the wide cultural mosaic of the Bible itself is explored in a comprehensive fashion. We take a look at the fundamental oneness of humanity (and the oneness found in Christ) and the cultural variety of this one human family. An acceptance of our shared humanness and our unique cultural identities is a necessary prerequisite for understanding the Bible in an age of diversity. Specific attention is given to discovering how people today in various settings, who have often felt left out of God's salvation story, can see how their story intersects with the biblical story of old. The focus of chapter two is to examine critically the racial and cultural background and social location of Jesus of Nazareth and his universal presence as the risen Christ. Any discussion of biblical faith for Christians rests on the central issue of how we understand Jesus Christ. We will also analyze the effects of a "white Europeanized Jesus" and explore the various ways the universal Christ is presented in cultures today. A sampling of approaches used by people of color when interpreting the Bible is illustrated in chapter three. We also look at how these diverse understandings can intersect with one another, including how the stories and insights from within cultures can be helpful for presenting biblical truths. We can use the wide-ranging understandings found in our world to provide a more inclusive biblical interpretation.

Whereas the first three chapters present a foundation for dialogue regarding biblical interpretation at the cultural roundtable, the final three chapters suggest activist approaches needed for creating a world that is in closer alignment with this understanding. In chapter four, we examine liberation as a central message of the Bible and the cry of a majority of the world's population. The worldwide significance of the biblical theme of freedom and empowerment is highlighted as vitally important to the mission of the community of God. The biblical agenda for addressing injustice is studied in the fifth chapter. This chapter examines the Bible's focus on the relationship between peace and justice and explores some biblically based strategies for addressing three forms of injustice—racism, sexism, and classism. The final chapter discusses biblical images of community and then offers some approaches for developing community in a world that is becoming increasingly fragmented. It also offers key insights for moving toward true reconciliation.

The credentials of authors I quote, as they relate to culture and expertise, are left out of the main text of the book (except when relevant to the discussion). This is done for two reasons. One is a matter of style; it gives the text a better flow. The other concerns cultural sensitivity and philosophy. In many cultures, ideas belong to the community. The qualifications of the person rendering the opinion are not as important as the idea itself.[5] Extensive footnoting and an appendix that attempts to acknowledge the cultural identities of the persons quoted are included for those who are interested.

These chapters are not for the timid or close-minded Christian. At several points, this book challenges the various systems of oppression and power that exist in our world. Also, many of the traditional methods of biblical interpretation are critiqued. This should not be perceived as an attack on individual persons or particular cultural groups. It is meant to challenge systems of injustice and understandings based on the status quo. Thus our study is enriched by sources that represent a very wide multiplicity of theological opinions. One of the tasks of theologians is to probe the vast regions of mystery in our faith. They are like the space explorers on the television series "Star Trek" who "go where no one has gone before." While I certainly do not endorse every position held by the sources used, I am not afraid of their inquiry. I trust that the reader will also not be so intimidated. If our faith is not worthy of scrutiny, it is not worthy to be called faith. This book includes some of the explorations of biblical scholars from around the world and hopefully stretches some limits on its own accord. *Coming Together: The Bible's Message in an Age of Diversity* poses questions, searches for answers, challenges some assumptions, and invites you to join in the dialogue.

Chapter One

One Human Family, Many Cultural Expressions

Cultural diversity has become a subject of lively debate. The challenges for people with different cultural perspectives living, working, and worshiping together are being discussed in university classrooms and on street corners—often with tensions, fear, and misunderstanding. Conversations are also taking place in churches, Christian colleges, and seminaries, and both ministers and laypersons are taking part. Even here, however, light is not always evident.

Does the Bible have anything to offer this ongoing dialogue concerning cultural diversity? The Israelites often found themselves trying to make sense out of their ethnocentrism and the resulting tendencies to feel superior and uniquely special. The early church proclaimed the gospel in a world that struggled with diversity in culture (Jew and Gentile), gender (male and female), and social class (slave and free). In the midst of these challenges, the biblical authors recorded how followers of God not only coped but also made surprising contributions to showing the importance of diversity.

The Bible addresses issues of diversity, but not by starting with the differences in the human family. Rather, it begins with the oneness of humanity. The opening chapters of Genesis proclaim, in essence, "in the beginning—one race—the human race."[1] In Genesis 1 God said, "'Let us make humankind in our image, and according to our likeness . . .' So God created humankind in his image, in the image of God he

1

created them; male and female he created them" (vv. 26-27).
The Bible announces that through one couple, Adam and Eve,
all of humanity flows. All men and women are created in the
image of God. This theme of the oneness of the human family
is found throughout the Bible. It was the bedrock of Jesus'
ministry as he called humanity to a re-Creation experience.
The apostle Paul echoed this theme when he told the philosophers in Athens that "from one ancestor [God] made all
nations to inhabit the whole earth . . ." (Acts 17:26).

While the Bible begins with the unity of humanity, it
clearly demonstrates that God values the diversity that
emerged within the human family. God honors by inclusion
people who represent the wide range of cultural expressions
that continue to develop in this one human family. This rich
mosaic of people is acknowledged and celebrated by the
biblical authors. The Bible is a confessional and historic
document written primarily from the perspective of the ancient Hebrews of Israel and the Diaspora, and Christians in
the region of Palestine. Yet the Hebrew Scriptures and the
New Testament also present the universal message of God's
salvation. Therefore, by necessity, a variety of people from
outside the particular cultural focus of those writing the story
were included. If we emulate the biblical authors, then our
starting point for discussion is our oneness rather than our
differences. Faced with fears that push us to separateness,
our common ancestry must challenge us to recognize those
who seem different from us as sisters and brothers. Even if
we want to forget our relatedness, the God revealed in the
Bible does not.

Written after the time described in the text, the first eleven
chapters of Genesis are not just ancient commentaries on
crimes and punishments. They are also devoted to explaining
the origins of humanity and how this one family came to be
so culturally diverse. The author began by identifying the
location of Eden where the first family lived:

> A river flows out of Eden to water the garden, and from
> there it divides and becomes four branches. The name of

the first is Pishon; it is the one that flows around the whole land of Havilah, where there is gold; and the gold of that land is good; bdellium and onyx stone are there. The name of the second river is Gihon; it is the one that flows around the whole land of Cush. The name of the third river is Tigris, which flows east of Assyria. And the fourth river is the Euphrates (Genesis 2:10-14).

The writer of Genesis named four rivers to describe the location of the home of the first humans. The Pishon and Gihon have been identified as the rivers known today as the Blue Nile and White Nile in the eastern portion of the continent of Africa.[2] The Gihon is clearly in Africa because it was said to circle Cush, the ancient black African nation often identified in the Bible as Ethiopia, located south of Egypt (currently the Sudan).[3] The Pishon was listed as flowing around Havilah. In Genesis 10:7, Havilah was identified as a descendant of Cush, therefore placing it geographically near Cush.[4] So the western boundaries of Eden were found on the African continent. The second two rivers mentioned in Genesis 2 are the Tigris and Euphrates. They are in the western part of the continent of Asia (currently Iraq). So the eastern boundaries of Eden are in Asia. Palestine is located in what would have been the center of Eden.

When the Hebrews heard the story of Creation and the location of Eden, they understood that the home of the first family encompassed the world they knew—from Africa to Asia. All the diversity of humanity that they had encountered came from one original homeland and from one original family. It is interesting to note that when God made a covenant with Abraham, the land that his descendants would live in would be "from the river of Egypt to the great river, the river Euphrates" (Genesis 15:18). The river of Egypt was the Nile. Therefore the boundaries were nearly the same as those of Eden—Africa to Asia.

The fundamental oneness of this diverse human family was once again reasserted by the writer of Genesis after Noah and his family left the ark following the flood: "The sons of

Noah who went out of the ark were Shem, Ham, and Japheth.
. . . These three were the sons of Noah; and from these the
whole earth was peopled" (Genesis 9:18-19). All of the nations
and cultures known to the Hebrews found their source in the
family of Noah, and ultimately in the family of Adam and
Eve. In Genesis 10, the writers provide a table of nations
descending from Noah's sons to further demonstrate this
fact. The story of the Tower of Babel (Genesis 11:1-9) was
included by the author at the end of the prologue in Genesis
as an explanation for how this one family, at the time of
writing, had taken on such wide diversity in culture, ethnicity, and language.

The first eleven chapters of Genesis helped the Hebrews
understand themselves as one group among the many people
who came from this original human family created in the
image of God. The universality of God's concern for the
human family is restated throughout the Scriptures. The
psalmist wrote, "Glorious things are spoken of you, O city of
God. . . . Among those who know me I mention Rahab and
Babylon; Philistia too, and Tyre, with Ethiopia—'This one
was born there,' they say" (Psalm 87:3-4).

Using the language of faith, God's love was stated as
inclusive of the world known to the Hebrews, from the continent of Africa (Rahab, which was Egypt, and Ethiopia) to the
continent of Asia (Babylon). We see this same spirit of inclusiveness repeated in the writings of the prophet Isaiah: "On
that day Israel will be the third with Egypt and Assyria, a
blessing in the midst of the earth, whom the LORD of hosts
has blessed, saying, 'Blessed be Egypt my people, and Assyria
the work of my hands, and Israel my heritage'" (Isaiah
19:24-25).

Here the prophet is reminding Israel that God's love is not
restricted to them but includes all people, from Africa (Egypt)
to Asia (Assyria). Isaiah has God using terms of affection for
all three nations: "my people," "the work of my hands," "my
heritage."

This theme of God's universality is also evident in the New

Testament. At Jesus' birth his family was visited by Magi from Asia (the East) [Matthew 2:1-12] and sought safety in Africa (Egypt) [Matthew 2:13-21]. In his teaching, Jesus acknowledged God's love for all people. In one parable he proclaimed: "Then people will come from east and west, from north and south, and will eat in the kingdom of God" (Luke 13:29; see also Matthew 8:11). At the crucifixion, Jesus again found support from Africa in Simon of Cyrene (Matthew 27:32; Mark 15:21; Luke 23:26) and faith from Europe, a part of the world not well known to the early Hebrews, in the Roman centurion (Mark 15:39). After the resurrection, Jesus challenged his followers to "go therefore and make disciples of all nations" (Matthew 28:19; see also Mark 16:15; Acts 1:8). Jesus presented "inclusiveness as a matter of divine compulsion."[5]

The story reached a climax at Pentecost when people from nations in Africa, Asia, Europe, and Palestine received the gift of the Holy Spirit after hearing the Good News spoken to them in their native language and dialect:

> Parthians, Medes, Elamites, and residents of Mesopotamia, Judea and Cappadocia, Pontus and Asia, Phrygia and Pamphylia, Egypt and the parts of Libya belonging to Cyrene, and visitors from Rome, both Jews and proselytes, Cretans and Arabs—in our own languages we hear them speaking about God's deeds of power (Acts 2:9-11).

Just as the Babel story in Genesis sought to give an explanation for diversity, Pentecost clarified God's desire for oneness. The post-Resurrection experience of inclusiveness at Pentecost, in a sense, reversed Babel. God's love for humanity was so great that each person heard the Good News in her or his own dialect. Pentecost was not primarily about speaking in unknown tongues. If it were, congregations that embrace speaking in tongues would be models of unity. Unfortunately, at times, they are as racially and culturally segregated as the church at large. Pentecost was primarily about gaining a clearer picture, in the midst the world's Babel-like confusion, of the fundamental oneness of humanity. This message of the oneness of humanity and God's universal love for all people finds its fitting conclusion in the book of Revelation. The author of the Revelation writes about a vision of "a great multitude that no one could count, from every nation, from all tribes and peoples and languages" worshiping God (Revelation 7:9).

Seeing Today's Diversity in Yesterday's Text

Unfortunately, the oneness of the human family and the universality of God's love have been distorted in postbiblical times. Instead of living as one human family with many cultural expressions, we have divided ourselves by many classifications. By way of example, the modern invention that we call "racism" created a system of racial hierarchy that undergirded the superiority of one "race" of people, white Caucasian Europeans, for the purpose of cultural and economic domination.[6] (The designations used have been so imprecise that people continue to debate about how many races actually exist and who should be included in each race.)

One result of this artificial racial hierarchy has been the portrayal of the majority of people in the Bible as members of the white Caucasian race. The view, held by too many, that Caucasian people are normative and people of other races and cultures are merely interesting curiosities or worse led to the belief that the important people in the Bible had to be white. Some writers have considered nearly all of the biblical people to be white.[7] Certain biblical interpreters, in an attempt to keep the Hebrews white, regarded the people of North Africa and biblical Ethiopia as Caucasian during the time of the Genesis accounts.[8] The lack of knowledge regarding the biblical authors' inclusion of people from a wide variety of cultures and with a wide range of skin colors was the result of white European dominance of biblical translation and interpretation together with only a slow, halting effort on the part of much of the church to confront and eradicate racism.

Interpretation based on preconceived notions of white

racial superiority is further illustrated by how few scholars have been able to even consider the possibility of Eden extending into Africa.[9] It has been suggested that the Pishon River referred to the Ganges River in India.[10] This would locate Eden exclusively in Asia and keep the first family far away from Africa. This notion of a white Hebrew race has been taken to such extremes that it has been suggested by many that Noah's sons were the ancestral originals of three races: Shem (Caucasian/white European), Ham (Negroid/black African), and Japheth (Mongoloid/Asian). It is amazing how few serious scholars question how Noah and his wife could give birth to children of three different races.[11]

The most we can suggest is that Ham, Shem, and Japheth (and their offspring), having descended from the one human family that emerged from Eden, initially settled in Asia, Africa, and Palestine. In Genesis 10 we are given an approximate geographic placement of these brothers' families. The children of Japheth were found in Palestine, Asia Minor, and perhaps Europe. The descendants of Ham lived in Africa (Egypt, Put [Libya], and Cush [biblical Ethiopia]), Palestine (Canaan), and probably Arabia. The offspring of Shem settled in West Asia and Palestine. These "cousins" lived as neighbors, often intermingling and intermarrying (as we shall see). The transposing of modern racial categories onto the sons of Noah is untenable.

We must see beyond the biases of past and present interpretations in order to uncover the truth. *In today's context of racial and ethnic fragmentation, it is essential to rediscover the wide cultural diversity of biblical peoples if we are ever to find our way back to the oneness of the human family.* The sentiments of Cain Hope Felder speak to this task:

> We need more than ever before to unite on a multiculturalist search for truth in which the strengths and contributions of all people finally receive their due. Biblically, we need to bring "new eyes" to ancient texts. If there is to be hope for tomorrow, these "new eyes" need to appear . . . in African American . . . Asian, Hispanic, Native American

and European American contexts . . . We need to open Scripture and see not just Greeks and Romans but Asians, Africans, and others.[12]

Discovering one's people in the biblical story can be empowering. This is particularly true for persons whose identity has been battered by societal prejudices. After repeatedly being told that persons of your race or culture are cursed by God or are somehow created as less than the dominant group, it revives your soul and renews your spirit to learn that people of your race and culture can be found in the biblical salvation story and were not afterthoughts or mistakes of God. What follows is a focus on the stories and contributions of people in the Bible who are representative of the cultural categories used today. Persons of African, Asian, and European descent in the Bible will be highlighted. Latinas/os, Native Americans, and people with multicultural and multiracial heritages will also discover how their stories can interact with the biblical story. The process of identifying the people of the Bible by the racial or cultural designations used today is often imprecise, and the following attempt should be considered a suggested approach for interpretation.

The Biblical Hebrews

We begin with a discussion of the racial type of the biblical Hebrews. The Hebrews did not have any concept of being a "race" other than the human race. What made them distinct was not their race but their religion. The Bible was content to leave it at that. Had our modern world been content to do the same, a focus on the racial background of the Hebrews would not have relevance. But the recasting of the Hebrews as a white Scandinavian-looking people requires that the issue be pursued. Too many generations have used the white pictures of biblical characters in their Bibles to make certain assumptions about the racial type of the biblical Hebrews and the superiority of the white race. Cain Hope Felder has put forth the contention that the Hebrews were an Afro-Asiatic people. He writes, "Scholars today generally recognize that the biblical Hebrews most likely emerged as an amalga-mation of races, rather than from any pure racial stock. When they departed from Egypt they may well have been Afroasiatics."[13] Felder further argues that, since Palestine extends from Africa and connects with Asia, it was at the center of the constant migration of people back and forth between these two continents. Therefore the people of Pales-tine, and perhaps other surrounding areas, were "essentially Afro-Asiatic peoples."[14]

This certainly makes sense if one simply observes the history of the Hebrew people. We have already established that Eden began in Africa and extended into Asia (an Afro-Asiatic homeland). Abraham and Sarah, the parent figures of the Hebrew people, were born and raised in Ur (Asia) [Genesis 11:31] and traveled into Egypt (Africa) [Genesis 12:10] before settling in Palestine. There are many refer-ences to Hebrews taking refuge in Egypt, and of course the Hebrews lived there for over four hundred years. In Exodus 12:38, the writer describes the Hebrews leaving Egypt as a "mixed crowd."[15] This implies that the Hebrews who left Egypt were a much more diverse people than the folks who entered with Jacob. Later, the Hebrew people were taken captive and moved into Asian lands such as Babylonia. Cer-tainly the culture of the Hebrews was impacted by both Africa and Asia.

With Abraham and Sarah coming from the region around the Tigris and Euphrates, the Asian-ness of the Hebrew people seems clear. Also, Palestine has been called "West Asia." The African-ness of the Hebrews has been difficult for many in the modern world to accept, and the fact that Palestine was also referred to as "Northeast Africa" is rarely noted.[16] Before the Suez Canal was constructed, Palestine was a part of the African land mass. It can also easily be demonstrated that African blood flowed through the veins of Hebrew people. A few high-profile examples will corroborate this fact.

Intermarriage to people of other races and cultures was

not uncommon among the Hebrews. Some of the most honored leaders among the Hebrew people were married to
Africans. In addition to Sarah, Abraham was married to
Hagar, an Egyptian (Genesis 16:3). Their union bore a son,
Ishmael. Hagar and Ishmael were eventually sent away from
the Hebrews. But from the time of Jacob on, when there was
intermarriage, the spouses and the children were integrated
into the family, with the children simply becoming Hebrew.[17]
Joseph married Asenath, an Egyptian woman, during his
time as a ruler in Egypt (Genesis 41:45). Their two sons,
Ephraim and Manasseh, were blessed by Jacob and became
tribes of the nation of Israel (Genesis 41:50-52; 48). All the
members of these Israelite tribes had African genes. Moses
married a woman from Cush (Numbers 12:1), and Solomon
married the daughter of an Egyptian pharaoh (1 Kings 3:1).
If we include the Canaanites among African peoples (because
they are from the Hamitic line), there are many more offspring of African descent. Among these are two unions that
are significant: Judah and his Canaanite daughter-in-law
Tamar had twins, Perez and Zerah (Genesis 38), and King
David and Bathsheba, had a son, Solomon, who became the
next king of Israel (2 Samuel 11–12). Bathsheba's first
husband was Uriah the Hittite, implying that Bathsheba
was also a Hittite. The Hittites were descendants of the
Canaanites.

Another clue to the fact that the Hebrews had an African
heritage was the fact that they were often thought to be
Egyptians. This would tell us that the physical appearance
of the Hebrews was very similar to that of their African
neighbors. Three notable cases of this ethnic confusion are
Joseph (Genesis 42:8), Moses (Exodus 2:19), and the apostle
Paul (Acts 21:38). Moses and Joseph were probably dressed
as Egyptians when they were misidentified, although it was
Joseph's own brothers who did not recognize him as a Hebrew. In Paul's case, he was debating fellow Israelites when
a Roman military officer confused him with an Egyptian
rebel.

It seems very reasonable to assume that the ancient Hebrews, as well as the Jews of the New Testament, were an
Afro-Asiatic people who would today be considered people of
color. Cain Hope Felder goes so far as to say of the early
Hebrews: "The conclusion is inescapable: by modern Western
standards, the earliest biblical people would have to be
classified as 'Blacks.' They had a definite measure of African
blood—and clearly resembled many individuals who would
today be identified as African Americans."[18]

Africans

With the first geographic references mentioned in the
Bible being found on the continent of Africa, we have demonstrated an African presence in the Bible that began in Eden
and infused the racial identity of the Hebrews. Yet even
without an understanding of the Hebrews as an Afro-Asiatic
people, the African presence in the Bible is significant both
numerically and spiritually.[19] African people and countries
are mentioned over eight hundred times in the Hebrew Bible
and over fifty times in the New Testament.[20] Yet the significance of Africa and African people in the Bible has been
denied by many in modern history because of the economic
benefit of slavery, colonialism, segregation, apartheid, and
racism. Even many Africans living on the continent have lost
a sense of Africa's importance in the biblical story. Ugandan
theologian John M. Waliggo, describing the effect of Western
Christianity on Africa, writes:

> When Christianity came to Africa towards the end of the
> fifteenth century, its theology soon sanctioned Africa's re-
> jection by giving support to the enslavement of Africans.
> This created a situation which was progressively to sanc-
> tion rejection of Africans in many other instances.
> After almost one thousand years of isolation, when
> Western missionaries came in contact with Christian
> Ethiopia in the early sixteenth century, they utterly re-
> jected its Christianity as heretical and listed hundreds of
> errors in it. This closed the door for cooperation between
> the Ethiopian church and Western Christianity. When the

European Christian Nonconformists were persecuted at home, they trekked to South Africa during the seventeenth century, and on arrival they rejected the blacks, the owners of the land, as the condemned children of Ham.

The nineteenth-century theology of the missionary movement rejected any value in the African traditional religions, despised many people's cultural values, and would not use them as a basis for Christian evangelization. . . . a committed African theologian examines the biblical message to discover whether it also rejects Africa and Africans or whether it can liberate them.[21]

It is hard to understand how the Bible, the faith history of a people whose land was "culturally and geographically, primarily an extension of the African land mass,"[22] could be used against African people. This is even more confusing when one considers that "African values and customs are often closer to the Semitic values that pervade the Scriptures and the story of Jesus than the European Christian values that have been imposed upon them."[23] The cornerstone of this pseudobiblical polemic against people of African descent has been the "curse of Cain" and the "curse of Ham."[24] The so-called curse of Cain comes from Genesis 4:15, "And the Lord put a mark on Cain, so that no one who came upon him would kill him." This mark has been interpreted by some as black skin. There is nothing in the text that would lead to such an interpretation. In fact, the mark was meant as a sign of protection, not a curse. Even if it was a curse, it would no longer be in effect at the time Genesis was written because all of Cain's descendants would have died in the flood of Genesis 7. If the mark was indeed black skin, this would not explain the existence of black-skinned people after the flood. Of course, black skin would not be a mark that set Cain apart because the original humans were dark-skinned. Therefore, black skin would not be a curse; rather it would be a blessing.

The so-called curse of Ham is a fabrication because Genesis 9:25-27 actually records that Canaan was cursed. The curse of Canaan was probably used by the ancient Israelites to support their conquest of Palestine, the land of the Canaanites. It is interesting that while it was Ham who offended his father, Noah, it was Canaan who was singled out for the curse. Ham's other sons, Egypt, Put, and Cush, are not mentioned or even implied in the curse. The so-called curse of Ham is a much later adaptation of the text for use in developing a rationale for enslaving and exploiting the children of Ham in Africa. As a result of this curse mentality, Egypt (and Put [Libya]) has often been "Caucasianized" or assumed to have a culture influenced by Europe, and ancient Cush has been disregarded or demeaned. Of course Egypt has always been in Africa, and Cush was one of the most powerful nations of the ancient world. Cush has been ignored because it was "an African empire, and a black African one at that."[25]

Cush, presently the Sudan, was called "Aethiopia" by the Greeks and Romans and was translated in the King James Version and some other Bibles as "Ethiopia." Cush was also known as "Nubia." According to historian David Roberts, "Nubian civilization lasted far longer than either classical Greece or Rome."[26] The height of Nubian culture was 3800 B.C. to A.D. 600. At times in history, Cush controlled Egypt. Among the pharaohs of Egypt are Nubians. One of these Cushite pharaohs, King Tirhakah is mentioned in the Bible (2 Kings 19:9). There is no doubt that the nation of Cush/Ethiopia was highly regarded by the biblical authors. The prophet Isaiah described it this way:

Ah, land of whirring wings
    beyond the rivers of Ethiopia,
sending ambassadors by the Nile
    in vessels of papyrus on the waters!
Go, you swift messengers,
    to a nation tall and smooth,
to a people feared near and far,
    a nation mighty and conquering,
    whose land the rivers divide.
                    (Isaiah 18:1-2)

Knowing that Cush was a powerful and mighty nation in
the ancient world leads to a clearer understanding of many
biblical texts. One example is the conflict between Moses and
his siblings, Miriam and Aaron, in Numbers 12:1-10. In the
first verse the author writes: "Miriam and Aaron spoke
against Moses because of the Cushite woman whom he had
married (for he had indeed married a Cushite woman)." This
text has often been cited as an example of race bias in the
Bible.[27] That is, Miriam and Aaron did not approve of Moses
marrying a black-skinned African woman. This perception is
strengthened if one views the heroes of the Bible, such as
Moses, as white or light-skinned. While the woman from
Cush may have been of a darker hue than her husband
Moses, it is important to remember that Moses and his
siblings, Miriam and Aaron, were Afro-Asiatics; they too were
dark-skinned persons.

Keeping in mind the exalted status of Cush, a better
interpretation of this text would be that Miriam and Aaron
were complaining about Moses marrying someone of a higher
social status.[28] Rather than an issue of race bias, this was an
issue of classism. Since Moses had been raised as a son of
Pharaoh, he would not have perceived a class difference
between himself and the Cushite woman. Miriam and Aaron,
having been raised in slavery, were questioning Moses' right
to "marry up." God responded to Aaron and Miriam's class
prejudice by striking Miriam with leprosy. This caused her
to turn "white as snow," in contrast to the Cushite woman's
darker skin, and provided an opportunity for Miriam to
experience life as a leper, a person on the lowest rung of
Israel's social ladder. (The author of Numbers provides no
explanation for why Aaron was not also struck with leprosy.)

In addition to the many references to nations of Africa in
the Hebrew Bible, there are individuals who played significant roles in biblical history. One of the books of the Hebrew
Bible, Zephaniah, was most likely written by an African. The
book of Zephaniah begins by introducing the prophet as
"Zephaniah son of Cushi" (1:1). Cushi usually refers to one

from Cush.[29] In 2 Samuel 18 we are told about one of King David's elite soldiers, a Cushite, who was given the responsibility of bringing the news to David that his son, Absalom, had been killed in battle. Solomon was visited by the queen of Sheba (1 Kings 10:1-10,13; 2 Chronicles 9:1-9,12). She was the queen of a Nubian empire that extended from Nubia over into southern Arabia.[30] It is possible that the Song of Solomon was written for Solomon's Egyptian wife. In Jeremiah 38 and 39, Ebed-melech the Ethiopian saved the life of the prophet Jeremiah.

African people continue to play a significant role in the New Testament. We can observe the role of Africa and Africans in the life of Jesus. In Matthew 2:13-22 we are told that Jesus' family fled to Egypt to save his life. The gospel writer interpreted this to be a fulfillment of the prophet Hosea's prophecy that "out of Egypt I called my son" (Hosea 11:1). Thanks to the people of Africa, the infant Jesus was saved from the murderous intentions of Herod. When it did come time for Jesus to die, an African, Simon of Cyrene, had the honor of providing support for Jesus by carrying his cross (Matthew 27:32; Mark 15:21; Luke 23:26). Jesus also illustrated one of his recorded sermons by referring to an African. He said that the queen of Sheba ("queen of the South") will rise up at the judgment and condemn the wickedness of first-century religiosity in Israel (Matthew 12:42; Luke 11:31).

The early church included people from Africa. This is first stated at Pentecost. Listed among the people who heard the disciples speaking in their native language and dialect were persons from "Egypt and the parts of Libya belonging to Cyrene" (Acts 2:10). We are told in Acts 8:26-39 of the first recorded Gentile convert after Pentecost, an Ethiopian finance minister traveling down the Gaza road back to Africa and his Nubian queen, Candace. Believers from Cyrene helped start the great missionary church at Antioch (Acts 11:20), and African prophets and teachers were a part of the leadership team in the church at Antioch: "Now in the church at Antioch there were prophets and teachers: Barnabas, Simeon who was called Niger, Lucius of Cyrene, Manaen a member of the court of Herod the ruler, and Saul" (Acts 13:1).

Lucius was from Cyrene in Libya, and Simeon was called "black." Some think that perhaps Simeon was the same Simon who carried Jesus' cross.

Another great leader in the early church was the African-born evangelist Apollos, from Alexandria in Egypt. His ministry was quite effective in Corinth (Acts 18:24-28; 1 Corinthians 1:12; 3:4-6,22; 4:6). He was noted for his great preaching ability. Some scholars believe that the book of Hebrews could have been written by Apollos.[31] This would explain the sermonic style of Hebrews 11:1–12:3. Its rhythmic and repetitive cadence using the phrase "by faith . . ." is even reminiscent of that heard from many preachers of African descent in America.

The presence of Africans in the Bible is an important reminder that God's concern for persons of African descent did not begin with the colonizer's missionaries in Africa or the slave master's preacher in the United States and the Caribbean. Africans, Caribbean Islanders, African Americans, others of African descent, and the rest of the human family can read about African foremothers and forefathers in the Bible and celebrate a heritage that reaches back to the very beginning in Eden and continues through the Hebrew Bible, the New Testament, and to the present.

Asians

While the first geographic reference in the Bible is to Africa, it is closely followed by a reference to two rivers found on the continent of Asia. As in the case of Africa, even if one does not accept the Asian-ness of the Hebrews, there are numerous references to the people and countries of Asia. In the Bible, the writers mention people and nations on the continent of Asia from Asia Minor (present day Turkey) to India. The ancient Asian empires of Assyria, Babylonia, and Persia play a significant role in the Hebrew Bible. We find

Noah's ark coming to rest on the Asian mountain called Mount Ararat (Genesis 8:4). As mentioned earlier, Abraham and Sarah, the parents of the Hebrew nation, came from the city of Ur in the heart of the Fertile Crescent, near where the Tigris and Euphrates meet and empty into the Persian Gulf (Genesis 11:31). They found a wife for their son, Isaac, among their relatives in Asia (Genesis 24:4). Isaac and Rebekah had the same idea when the time came to find a wife for their son, Jacob (Genesis 28:2). So Jacob was sent back to visit Asia, where he found two wives, Rachel and Leah.

Several kings of Asian empires intersected with the God of the Hebrews in the Bible. The book of Ezra tells of an Asian king whom the Lord used. "In order that the word of the LORD . . . might be accomplished, the LORD stirred up the spirit of King Cyrus of Persia . . ." (Ezra 1:1). Three Asian kings acknowledged the power of God because of mighty acts done in their presence. King Nebuchadnezzar saw Shadrach, Meshach, and Abednego survive a fiery furnace (Daniel 3). King Belshazzar saw what appeared to be the fingers of a human hand write a message to him on the palace wall about his impending death (Daniel 5). King Darius saw Daniel still alive after being thrown into a den of hungry lions (Daniel 6).

There were a number of Jews who acknowledged God while serving in the governments of great Asian kings. Most notable was Esther, who was married to King Ahasuerus of Persia. She was the queen of an empire that stretched from India to Nubia. Others who served in Asian governments were Nehemiah, Daniel, Shadrach, Meshach, and Abednego. The book of Jonah describes how the prophet Jonah was sent by God to preach in the heart of Asia at Nineveh, the capital of Assyria. In response to Jonah's bigotry against Asians, God expressed concern for Asia, saying, "And should I not be concerned about Nineveh, that great city, in which there are more than a hundred and twenty thousand persons . . ." (Jonah 4:11). The king of Nineveh turned to God as a result of Jonah's reluctant preaching.

There is also an extensive Asian presence in the New

Testament. It began with a visit to the home of the infant Jesus by some Magi from the East, most likely from Persia (Matthew 2:1-12). In the same sermon in which Jesus mentioned the queen of Sheba, he referred to the faith of the people of Nineveh (Matthew 12:41; Luke 11:30,32). The ministry of the early church, as recorded in the New Testament, focused a lot of attention on the continent of Asia. Among the people from the continent of Asia at Pentecost who heard the gospel in their own language and dialect were "Parthians, Medes, Elamites, and residents of Mesopotamia, . . . Cappadocia, Pontus and Asia, Phrygia and Pamphylia" (Acts 2:9-10). The Parthians, Medes, and Elamites resided east of the Tigris and Euphrates.

Large portions of Acts are devoted to descriptions of the apostles' ministry in Asia (Acts 13:13-52; 14:1-28; 16:1-8; 18:19-28; 19:1-41; 20:6-38). Paul's ministry to the Gentiles had its first real success in Asia (Acts 13:46-49). As a result, the apostles at the Jerusalem church called for a council in Jerusalem to address this influx of Gentiles into the church in Asia (Acts 15). Perhaps the apostle Paul's commitment to minister in Asia was nurtured by the fact that he was born in the city of Tarsus in Asia Minor (Acts 22:3). Paul expanded his ministry in Asia through letters he sent to Christians living there. These letters are preserved in the biblical books of Ephesians, Galatians, Colossians, and Philemon. The province of Asia, which was the farthest-west section of Asia Minor, is mentioned often in the Bible (Acts 20:4; 1 Corinthians 16:19; 1 Peter 1:1). In Acts 19:10 it says that "all the residents of Asia, both Jews and Greeks, heard the word of the Lord." The first three chapters of Revelation include letters to seven churches in the province of Asia: Ephesus, Smyrna, Pergamum, Thyatira, Sardis, Philadelphia, and Laodicea.

Regarding the outreach into Asia by the early Christians, R. S. Sugirtharajah writes that "early on, there was a strong eastward thrust of the Jesus movement through Persia and Afghanistan."[32] He adds that this effort even reached into

South India and China. Long before European missionaries visited Asia, there were Asians at the forefront of the movement of God in this world. God's concern for Asia, which began in Eden and continued with Abraham and Sarah in Ur, can be found throughout the Hebrew Bible and the New Testament. That concern is still alive today.

Europeans

There are limited references to Europe in the Hebrew Bible. The Scripture refers to people from Caphtor, that is, the Island of Crete. Cherethites, considered to be Cretans, served in King David's army.[33] Their leader, Benaiah son of Jehoiada, was a member of David's inner circle of leadership (2 Samuel 8:18). The Philistines were also originally from Caphtor. Although Caphtor/Crete is considered to be a part of Europe today, it was originally settled by descendants of Ham, according to the Bible (Genesis 10:14). In the prophetic literature, there is some mention of countries on the continent Europe. The book of Daniel mentions Greece several times (Daniel 8:21, 10:20; 11:2), and Daniel 11:3 refers to the rise of a "warrior king," most likely Alexander the Great.[34] In Jonah 1:3 the prophet Jonah tries to flee to Tarshish,[35] a city probably located in southern Spain.[36]

People and places from Europe play a more significant role in the New Testament. During Jesus' ministry, a Roman centurion asked Jesus to heal his servant (Matthew 8:5-13; Luke 7:2-10). Of this European Jesus said, "I tell you, not even in Israel have I found such faith" (Luke 7:9). Jesus was also sought out by some Greeks who were in Jerusalem for the Passover festival. They said to Philip, "We wish to see Jesus" (John 12:20-21). As Jesus died on the cross, a Roman centurion remarked, "Truly this man was God's Son!" (Mark 15:39).

For the early church, Europe became a focus for ministry. At Pentecost there were "visitors from Rome" and "Cretans" who heard the Good News in their own language and dialect (Acts 2:10-11). Nicolaus, one of the seven deacons appointed in Jerusalem, was a Greek convert to Judaism before becom-

ing a follower of Jesus Christ (Acts 6:5). In Acts 10, we find
the story of Cornelius, a centurion of the Italian Cohort, who
converted to the Christian faith. In this account, Peter struggled with his ethnocentrism when he was faced with reaching
out to Europeans and other non-Jews. He finally began to
comprehend God's universalism and said, "I truly understand that God shows no partiality, but in every nation
anyone who fears him and does what is right is acceptable to
him" (Acts 10:34-35).

The books of Luke and Acts were both addressed to Theo-
philus. He was probably a Roman official who was either a
believer in Jesus or was very interested in the gospel. The
apostle Paul's friend Luke, traditionally thought of as the
author of Luke and Acts, was not born a Jew (Colossians
4:10-14). There is scholarly query as to whether he might
have been the same person as Lucius of Cyrene and therefore
an African, or from Philippi (considering the author of Acts'
noticeable affection for the city) and therefore a European.
Whoever he was, Luke was not a Jew by birth or conversion.[37]

The outreach to Europe began in earnest when the apostle
Paul had a vision of a man in Macedonia beckoning him to
come and help (Acts 16:9-10). Extensive portions of Acts
describe the ministry in Europe (Acts 16:11-40; 17:1-34;
18:1-17; 20:1-6; 27:1-44; 28:1-31). The first convert in Paul's
ministry in Europe was a businesswoman named Lydia (Acts
16:14-15,40). There were also the Philippian jailer (Acts
16:23-34), Jason (17:5-9), Dionysius the Areopagite (17:34),
and others. In the last reference to Paul in Acts, he is
continuing his ministry in Europe while under house arrest
for two years in Rome (Acts 28:30-31). Among his many
letters were those written to European churches in Rome,
Corinth, Philippi, and Thessalonica. One of Paul's faithful
colaborers was a Greek named Titus (Galatians 2:3); a
Pauline letter bears his name. While there are few references
to Europe in the Hebrew Bible, God's concern for persons of
European descent is clear. Jesus ministered to Roman cen-
turions, the early church put a prime focus on outreach in

Europe, and the apostle Paul was last heard preaching the Good News in Rome, the center of European influence.

Hispanics—Latinas and Latinos

The Bible speaks of the apostle Paul's plans to minister in Spain (Romans 15:24,28). This can be understood as a biblical reference to God's inclusion of Hispanics in the story of salvation.[38] According to early church leader Clement of Rome, in a letter to the church at Corinth about A.D. 96, Paul did make it to Spain.[39] Another reference to Spain includes, as mentioned earlier, Tarshish, which was thought to be in southern Spain. In Acts 18:12-17 is a reference to Gallio, the proconsul of Achaia. He was born L. Annaeus Novatus in Spain, adopted by a Roman named L. Junius Gallio, and renamed Lucius Junius Gallio. While serving as the proconsul in Greece, Gallio was very supportive of Paul and the Christians.[40] These few references to Spain and people from Spain can be considered biblical precursors of the divine intention to include Spanish-speaking people around the world in the community of God.

Because Spain is a country in Europe that oppressed the indigenous people of America, references to Spain may not feel particularly representative for many Spanish-speaking people living in the Americas. The arrival of Columbus and other Europeans in the Americas introduced a new race and culture of people—Latinas/os. Justo González describes the birth of this new race as "an act of violence of cosmic proportions in which our Spanish forefathers raped our Indian foremothers."[41] Many Latinas/os are a mixture of European, African, and Native American heritage, with the blood of three continents flowing through their veins. This new race of people could be called "la raza cósmica" or the "cosmic race."[42] The history of Latinas/os often parallels the history of the biblical Hebrews, who became a multiracial people through enslavement, colonization, and captivity and in the process created a new racial and cultural identity. Orlando Costas described a somewhat different situation for Hispanics in the United States when he wrote:

> Hispanic Americans are the offspring of a double process
> of *mestizaje* (from *mestizo,* "hybrid," a racial and cultural
> mixture). This process has encompassed the triple encoun-
> ter between European (Iberian), Native American, and
> African peoples . . . [and] the encounter between the
> Anglo-American civilization and the civilization of Latin
> America.[43]

Virgilio Elizondo believes that the Galilean Jews of the
New Testament are the biblical people closest to this double
mestizaje experience. Throughout its history, Galilee experienced domination by many nations, including Assyria, Babylonia, Persia, Macedonia, Egypt, and Syria. By the first
century, Galilee was home to people originating from each of
these nations and cultures, as well as Jews.[44] To the "pure"
Jews of Jerusalem, the Galilean Jews were impure culturally
and probably racially as well. Elizondo compares the experience of the Galileans to that of Mexican Americans living in
the United States when he writes:

> The image of the Galileans to the Jerusalem Jews is
> comparable to the image of the Mexican-Americans to the
> Mexicans of Mexico. On the other hand, the image of the
> Galileans to the Greco-Romans is comparable to the image
> of the Mexican-American to the Anglo population of the
> United States. They were part of and despised by both.[45]

Fernando F. Segovia summarizes Elizondo's contention by
saying, "As a *mestizo* people, Mexican Americans represent
a Galilee of the contemporary world, a modern example of a
marginalized and oppressed people."[46]

By using the Galilean experience as a point of departure,
Hispanics in the United States have a powerful vehicle for
hearing their story in the Bible. The ministry of Jesus and
his disciples takes on a whole new significance. Jesus was
raised in Nazareth of Galilee (Matthew 2:22-23; Mark 1:9;
Luke 2:39-40,51), and his ministry headquarters were in
Capernaum of Galilee (Mark 2:1). He was known as "Jesus
the Galilean" or "Jesus of Nazareth." The core of Jesus'

followers were from Galilee, including the Twelve, the women who followed him (such as Mary and Martha), Lazarus, and others. Their Galilean accent caused them to stand out when they were in Jerusalem. Peter could not hide his accent when he denied knowing Jesus, and some bystanders commented, "Certainly you are also one of them, for your accent betrays you" (Matthew 26:73).

Galileans, like Peter and John, were at the forefront of spreading the gospel. At Pentecost, those gathered recognized the Galilean accent of the disciples who were preaching: "Are not all these who are speaking Galileans?" (Acts 2:7). James, the brother of John, was an early Galilean martyr (Acts 12:1-2). Galilee was at the center of a movement that would ultimately change the world because God took on flesh and experienced humanity as a Galilean.[47] As we stated in reference to Africans and Asians, God's concern for Hispanics did not begin with modern-day missionaries but was included in the Bible through Paul's plans to minister in Spain. Latinas/os can hear their story today through the history of the *mestizo* Hebrew people and in the Galilean experience of Jesus and his disciples.

Native Americans

There are no direct references to Native Americans in the Bible since the Americas were not known to the authors of the Bible. Cain Hope Felder has suggested that if Native Americans were a result of intermarriage between African and Asian migrants to the Americas in ancient times, then they are modern-day Afro-Asiatics.[48] Robert Allen Warrior believes that "the obvious characters in the story for Native Americans to identify with are the Canaanites, the people who already lived in the promised land."[49] Warrior's suggestion does open up some creative methods of interpretation.

Certainly the experience of Native Americans and other indigenous people around the world can be compared to that of the Canaanites. The Canaanites were the indigenous people of Palestine. Included among the Canaanite people were the Hittites, Hivites, Perizzites, Girgasites, Amorites, Arkites, Sinites, Arvadites, Zemarites, Hamathites, and Jebusites. For much of biblical history, the Hebrews dominated the Canaanites in their own land. This was not true in the beginning of their relationship, however. When Abraham and Sarah moved into the land of the Canaanites, they lived in peace with the indigenous peoples. Abraham even gave a tithe to and received a blessing from a Canaanite holy man, Melchizedek (Genesis 14:18-20; see also Psalm 110:4; Hebrews 7:1-17), whom Genesis 14:18 identifies as a "priest of God Most High." When Sarah died and Abraham needed to find a burial plot for his wife, he went to the Hittites and acknowledged that he was "a stranger and alien" in their land and needed a burial plot (Genesis 23:4). They responded by inviting him to take the best place available. Ephron the Hittite was the person who helped Abraham arrange for Sarah's burial. The next few generations of Hebrews and Canaanites continued to live in a peaceful coexistence. As was mentioned earlier, there was much intermarriage between the Canaanites and the Hebrews. So there was a definite trace of Canaanite blood in the veins of the Hebrews.

When the Hebrews returned to Palestine after their enslavement in Egypt, they came as conquerors of the land of Canaan. Perhaps the most celebrated person of Canaanite heritage in the Bible was a prostitute named Rahab (Joshua 2:1-21; 6:23-25). She helped the Israelites by hiding two spies sent by Joshua. Rahab made a deal with the spies to save her family in return for her kindness. When the walls of Jericho fell, Rahab and her family were the only ones in the city spared. After the conquest, she and her family lived with the Hebrews. Rahab was probably considered a traitor by the Canaanites because she hid Israelite spies who were on a mission that was key to the conquest of Canaan, but she was among Israel's heroes of the faith (Hebrews 11:31; see also James 2:25).

Two other Canaanites mentioned in the Hebrew Bible are Uriah the Hittite and his wife, Bathsheba (2 Samuel 11–

12:25). By this time in history, most of the Canaanites who had survived the conquest of Israel had assimilated into Israelite society. Uriah was a soldier in the army of King David. While Uriah was at battle, his king, David, ordered Bathsheba into the king's bedroom. Bathsheba discovered she was pregnant as a result of this rape. So David recalled Uriah from the battlefield, hoping he would lay with his wife and thereby believe he was the father. But as a faithful member of King David's army, he could not enjoy such a pleasure while his fellow soldiers were at battle. So King David had Uriah intentionally transferred to the front lines to be killed and then took Bathsheba to be his own wife.

The experiences of Rahab, Uriah, and Bathsheba are not unlike the Native American experience. Rahab was accepted into Israelite society as a hero because she betrayed her own people. Uriah and Bathsheba had assimilated into the dominant Israelite society and yet were treated shabbily—Bathsheba was raped and Uriah was killed. In the midst of this Israelite disregard for the indigenous people of Palestine, God redeemed the Canaanite heritage. Solomon, the most powerful of Israel's kings, was the son of Bathsheba and therefore half Canaanite (2 Samuel 12:24-25). The most significant redemption was that both Rahab and Bathsheba (also Tamar) were ancestors of Jesus (Matthew 1:3,5-6). God in human flesh had the blood of indigenous people running through his veins.

The indigenous people of Palestine also appear in the New Testament. Some believe that one of Jesus' twelve disciples, Simon, might have been a Canaanite.[50] He is listed as Simon the Cananaean in Matthew 10:4 and Mark 3:18. Two of the Gospels record an episode of a Canaanite woman interacting with Jesus:

> Just then a Canaanite woman from the region came out and started shouting, "Have mercy on me, Lord, Son of David; my daughter is tormented by a demon." But he did not answer her at all. And his disciples came and urged him, saying, "Send her away, for she keeps shouting after

us." He answered, "I was sent only to the lost sheep of the house of Israel." But she came and knelt before him, saying, "Lord, help me." He answered, "It is not fair to take the children's food and throw it to the dogs." She said, "Yes, Lord, yet even the dogs eat the crumbs that fall from their masters' table." Then Jesus answered her, "Woman, great is your faith! Let it be done for you as you wish." And her daughter was healed instantly (Matthew 15:22-28; see also Mark 7:24-30).

The interaction between Jesus and this Canaanite woman is significant for indigenous people seeking to relate to Jesus. The woman is presented in the text as a mother who is greatly concerned for her daughter. She is identified as a Canaanite, perhaps one of the few remaining descendants of this proud people who had experienced genocide, assimilation, and domination at the hands of Israel. When she comes to Jesus for help, she is rebuffed with the same ethnocentrism that Canaanites had often experienced from the children of Israel. It is shocking to see Jesus ignore her and compare her to a dog. Was Jesus, in his humanity, revealing his ethnocentrism and prejudice? This is certainly possible, considering his upbringing in Jewish society. Or was Jesus illustrating prejudice for his disciples, who wanted Jesus to send her away? The reasons Jesus responded the way he did can be debated. But what is most inspiring about this text is the strength and wisdom of this Canaanite mother. She refused to accept a narrow view of God's love. She demanded to be included by gently challenging Jesus' exclusive ethnic focus regarding who should receive his ministry. Jesus was so moved by her unyielding faith that he invited her to participate in the blessing of God, and her daughter was healed.

Native Americans can hear their story in the Bible as modern-day Afro-Asiatics or in the experience of the indigenous Canaanite people. Melchizedek, Ephron, Rahab, Uriah, Bathsheba, and the Canaanite woman, like the indigenous people of today, represent varied responses to different times, yet all are honored by God because of the Canaanite blood that flows throughout the veins of the Savior.

Multiracial and Multicultural

With a growing number of people identifying themselves as biracial, interracial, multiracial, or multicultural, it is important to acknowledge the presence in the Bible of multiracial people. We have already demonstrated that the biblical Hebrews were multiracial and multicultural. That is why the Hebrews have been identified as Afro-Asiatics, a racially and culturally blended people. While the Hebrew Bible regulated marriages outside of the faith, it expressed little concern about marriages outside of their ethnic group. The list of multicultural unions in the Hebrew Bible includes Abraham and Hagar, Moses and his Cushite wife, Judah and Tamar, Joseph and Asenath, Salmon and Rahab, Ruth and Boaz, David and Bathsheba, Solomon and Pharaoh's daughter, and Esther and Ahasuerus. Their offspring included Ishmael, Perez, Zerah, Ephraim, Manasseh, Boaz, Obed, and Solomon.

The best known multiracial and multicultural person in the New Testament was Timothy. His father was Greek and his mother was Jewish (Acts 16:1-4). Timothy must have experienced some cultural prejudice due to his interracial heritage. He was circumcised as an adult so he could be accepted culturally among the Jews as a minister. It was well known that his father was a Greek. Interracial, biracial, multiracial, and multicultural folks can find themselves in the Bible as reflected in the lives of the Hebrew people and in followers of Christ like Timothy. In fact, the Hebrew Bible is the story of a multiracial and multicultural people seeking to follow God. The New Testament is the story of a culturally segregated people (Jew and Gentile) coming together through the Spirit of Christ.

Oneness in Christ

Much more could be written regarding the cultural diversity of the people in the Scriptures. Without doubt the Bible includes people representative of the worldwide human family. While some in the early church struggled when addressing the oneness of Jews and Gentiles, most believed that unity in the midst of cultural diversity was God-ordained and could be realized through the Spirit of Christ. The apostle Paul summed up this message of oneness powerfully when he wrote: "There is no longer Jew or Greek, there is no longer slave or free, there is no longer male or female, for all of you are one in Christ Jesus" (Galatians 3:28; see also Romans 10:12; 1 Corinthians 12:13; Ephesians 2:11-16; Colossians 3:11).

This acceptance of the fundamental oneness of humanity, as reaffirmed in Christ, caused situations like the following to go unnoticed or unmentioned by the biblical writers: The three most significant leaders in the life of the Corinthian church in Europe were Peter of Galilee, Paul of Asia, and Apollos of Africa; Timothy was a biracial and bicultural person of Greek and Jewish descent born in Asia; Lydia, the first convert in Europe, was from the province of Asia—an Asian businesswoman working in Europe. Even when there was an intentional mention of racial and cultural diversity, it was done with little fanfare. One example is in Acts 13:1 regarding the leaders of the church at Antioch: "Now in the church at Antioch there were prophets and teachers: Barnabas, Simeon who was called Niger, Lucius of Cyrene, Manaen a member of the court of Herod the ruler, and Saul." There was no elaborate statement made about this being an experiment in cross-cultural ministry. It was the norm and not the exception.

"One human family, many cultural expressions" is a biblical truth that needs to be reclaimed and proclaimed in this age of diversity. The Bible is a multicultural document. The Hebrew Bible proclaims God's universal love for humanity from the very beginning. This message of oneness keeps emerging even in the midst of Israel's ethnocentrism. The New Testament declares a faith initiated by Jesus that was truly multicultural at its core. As Virgilio Elizondo says:

> The early spread of Christianity, especially in view of the multiple crossings of religious, cultural, and political boundaries—"polarizations"—that it entailed, was nothing

less than miraculous. . . . The new way was for everyone; no one was excluded because of race, color, nationality, class, or culture. What mattered was one's openness to belief in Jesus.[51]

Questions for Discussion

1. Identify the various ways your community is becoming more diverse. Has this created any "concerns"? What are they? In what ways are they being addressed?

2. In what ways does the Bible's emphasis on the oneness of humanity challenge your thinking? Why does it appear that our world is so far removed from the biblical ideal of the oneness of humanity? What are some of the causes for this fragmentation?

3. Why is it meaningful to see today's cultural diversity in the Bible? What is the value of people hearing their own story in the Scriptures?

4. Is it important to demonstrate that the Hebrews were an Afro-Asiatic people rather than a white European people, as pictured in many Bibles? Why?

5. What new information or insights did you gain as you read about the presence of Africans, Asians, and Europeans in the Bible? Has this changed your perspective on any of the familiar stories of the Scriptures? Do you have a different view of Africans, Asians, or Europeans because of their inclusion, in significant ways, in the Bible?

6. Thinking of the Galilean experience as comparable to that of Hispanics, reconsider the Gospels in light of the cultural barriers that Jesus and his disciples faced in their ministry. In what ways did Jesus overcome the limitations placed on him as a Galilean by society? How did Jesus use his culture to undergird and strengthen his efforts? What are the unique ways in which the Galilean context of the Gospels speaks to Latinas/os and others today?

7. What are some of the ways that the experience of Native Americans parallels that of the biblical Canaanites? Can Native Americans find an invitation to faith in God's relationship with the indigenous people of Palestine?

8. Considering the number of multicultural relationships in the Bible, in your opinion what is God's view of interracial marriage and multiracial children? Why?

9. In light of what you have read in this chapter, define the following terms: *cross-cultural ministry, church, human family, diversity, children of God.*

10. How has chapter one changed your understanding of who the people in the Bible were and what the message of God is? How are you going to share this with others?

Chapter Two

Jesus Christ: Culturally Human, Inclusively Divine

The message of the Bible is truly multicultural. It reveals to us a God who reaches out in love to all people. Yet even with this knowledge, we may still have a mental image of God that contradicts this divine universality. Although we may believe that God is spirit, we often visualize God as being from a particular culture or race. Sometimes this mental image of the Almighty corresponds to our own race and culture. For some, visualizing God as from their culture and race strengthens their ability to relate to God in the vertical dimension through prayer. But an exclusive image of the Divine weakens the possibility of experiencing God in the horizontal dimension through one's relationships with others. A monocultural image of God develops from a faulty understanding of the biblical teaching that humans are created in the image of God. A theological reversal occurs that reasons, "If I am created in the image of God, then God must look like me." Instead of being created in the image of God, many have tended to create God in their own image.

This reversal becomes even more problematic when the group that is in power creates God in its own cultural and racial image and then imposes that image of God on others. It could be argued that the United States was founded on the premise that God was a white male. When the United States Constitution was written with the words "we the people," the "we" referred to white men. Only white men could vote; no women or people of color were included in that "we." By accepting the idea that God was male and white, women and people of color were not only left out but were treated with contempt because they were not created in the image of God. It was considered permissible to degrade and harass women and dehumanize and humiliate people of color because God was perceived as being a white male. Women and people who were not "white" functioned in society in a role that relegated them to a less than human status.

The genocide of America's indigenous people and the enslavement of Africans were based on the contention that Native Americans and Africans were not really human in the fullest sense of the word. African slaves were even designated as three-fifths of a human being in the United States Constitution. Someone who was not fully human could be brutalized without engendering guilt. Society gave whites permission to torture, rape, and kill people of color because, according to the constitution, they were only three-fifths human. They were not created in the image of the white male God.

It may be hard for whites today to hear about this history. Yet denial precludes true reconciliation. Unfortunately, while the more blatant forms of expression may have been reduced, this thought process can be found in the deeper realms of our consciousness. The image of a white male God still affects attitudes as well as the ability to interact with people who appear different from us. A distorted image of God not only affects the person who is being marginalized by the image; it also impacts the person who "benefits" from the image. Feeling "superior" or "chosen" because of one's whiteness or maleness causes a spiritual and psychological isolation from the rest of the family of God. An exclusive image of God can destroy lives.

Not everyone has accepted the image of God as a white male. Books such as *What Color Is Your God?*[1] and *God Is Red*[2] have challenged this perception by requiring us to reconsider the question of our image of God. One way to address this concern about the whiteness of the image of God is to accept the perspective of Albert Cleage, who in the 1970s said:

> If God created man in his own image, then we must look at man to see what God looks like. There are black men, there are yellow men, there are red men and there are a few, a mighty few, white men in the world. If God created man in his own image, then God must be some combination of this black, red, yellow and white . . . In America, one drop of black blood makes you a black. So by American law, God is black.[3]

Cleage's statement, perhaps shocking to some, moves us in the right direction. If all of humanity is created in the image of God, then God's image includes all races and cultures, both genders, and so on. If we were to ask what color or what culture God is, our answer must be that God is multicolored or multicultural. God's signature, the rainbow, symbolizes the biblical teaching that God's image embraces all of humanity.

Yet the image of a white God and the idea that Christianity is a religion for white people remains pervasive in many corners of this world. This can be directly linked to the fact that for hundreds of years the dominant image of Jesus—around the world—has been a white, Caucasian-featured person. The most effective way of projecting an image of God is through the use of images of Jesus in art and more recently in the media. William Mosley writes, "Art, then, functions as a kind of 'visual preaching,' frequently with the express purpose giving concrete form to abstract or theological notions."[4] What image or picture do we visualize in our minds of the historical Jesus? Perhaps we have a mental image of one of the previous centuries' many famous paintings of Jesus portraying him as a white European. A discussion of the race and culture of the historical Jesus is important because images of Jesus ultimately affect our view of God and, therefore, our perception of who is created in the image of God.

The Racial and Cultural Identity of
Jesus of Nazareth

For many Christians, the race and culture of the historical person Jesus of Nazareth seems to be of limited importance. Their primary focus is the act of Jesus Christ dying for our sins. For this reason, it is important for them to prove that Jesus existed, but the details of his human existence of over thirty years are not essential.[5] There has been a resurgence of interest and research in the life of Jesus as an historical person, however. Yet most of the research done by European and white American scholars regarding the historical Jesus, both in the past and in the present, has expressed no interest in the racial features or skin color of Jesus of Nazareth.[6] Meanwhile, a parallel search for the historical Jesus conducted by scholars of color does address the racial and cultural identity of Jesus of Nazareth. Although the image of a white Jesus dominates our world, it is not universally accepted as accurate. There are Asian scholars who speak of Jesus as from Asia, and African-American scholars have written of a Jesus who is racially black.

We can all agree that Jesus of Nazareth, while living on this earth as a human being, had a particular racial and cultural look. The Jesus of history was culturally exclusive in his human existence. Since Jesus has been cast in a white image, it is important to discover if this is an accurate portrayal of the race and culture of the historical Jesus. We must consider whether Jesus would share the Afro-Asiatic heritage of the Hebrew people as detailed in the previous chapter. This problem could easily be solved if we had a portrait of Jesus dating back to the time that he spent on earth or to a time when there were still people alive who had seen Jesus in the flesh. Of course we have no such paintings or even written descriptions of the physical appearance of Jesus in his human form dating back to the first century.

The only physical description of Jesus in the New Testament is found in the vision of John on the Isle of Patmos, as recorded in the book of Revelation. In the vision, John describes a resurrected and glorified Christ using symbolic language. Considering the possibility that the author had seen Jesus in the flesh, or was a disciple of someone who saw Jesus in the flesh, certain aspects of the description could be based on historical fact. Jesus Christ is described this way:

> His head and his hair were white as white wool, white as snow; his eyes were like a flame of fire, his feet were like burnished bronze, refined as in a furnace, and his voice was like the sound of many waters (Revelation 1:14-15).

The vision describes a person with coarse white hair and reddish brown (burnished bronze) skin. The glorified Christ, as described by John, certainly did not appear in the vision as a white European.[7]

In the second chapter of the Gospel of Matthew, the writer records an event in the life of Jesus that sheds some light on the physical appearance of Jesus and his family. Joseph, Mary, and the infant Jesus fled Palestine into Egypt to escape the death threats of Herod. The purpose for traveling to the continent of Africa was to hide from Herod's soldiers. For Jesus and his family to blend in with African people, their appearance must have been quite similar to that of the people living in Egypt at that time. Jesus and his family would not have easily hidden in Africa if they were white-skinned with Caucasian features.[8]

As we pointed out in the previous chapter, it is important to consider the geographic location of Palestine, where Jesus was born. Some Asian scholars contend that "Jesus came from Asia, or to be precise, west Asia."[9] As was mentioned in chapter one, Palestine has also been called "Northeast Africa." Along with most other Jews of Palestinian Hebrew ancestry, Jesus no doubt had a distinct Asian-ness and African-ness about his culture and probably his physical features. In addition to Jesus being African by virtue of the location of Palestine, he also had Hamitic (African) ancestors. Three women from the line of Ham were included in his genealogy: Tamar, Rahab, and Bathsheba (Matthew 1:1-16).[10] Although this information comes from the genealogy of

Joseph (Jesus' earthly adoptive father), Jesus' mother was also a descendant of David and would have shared Tamar and Rahab as ancestors, if not also Bathsheba.[11] When the angel Gabriel was explaining to Mary how she as a virgin was going to become pregnant, he referred to David as an "ancestor" of Jesus (Luke 1:32). This of course could only be true if Mary was of the line of David, since the angel was explaining to her how she would be the only human parent. Throughout the Gospels, Jesus is presented as a son of David.

We can only reconfirm our earlier contention that Jesus, like other Jews in Palestine who had descended from the Hebrew people, was Afro-Asiatic. In the United States the historical Jesus would presently be called a person of color and probably considered an African American because of his African heritage.[12] Historically, persons living in the United States having any trace of African blood have been classified as "negroes."[13] To say that Jesus was racially black simply means that the historical Jesus had African blood flowing through his veins and would easily fit in among the wide range of skin colors and hues found in the African American community today.

How Did Jesus Become a White European?

Given that Jesus was an Afro-Asiatic Jew, how did his image become white? The process that painted Jesus white is a critical issue. Why was the image of the historic Jesus of Nazareth, born in Palestine to a people at the crossroads of Asia and Africa, transformed into a geographically distant one? The earliest representations of Jesus do not even include human characteristics. They were symbols, such as a fish or a lamb.[14] The first images of Jesus in human form were of a young "good shepherd," often with a Roman look. These first appeared in the third century in the Roman catacombs.[15] Eventually adult representations of Jesus began to appear. The earlier ones pictured Jesus with "an Oriental cast" and "a brown complexion."[16]

Soon European artists were attempting to develop an

image of Jesus Christ that was culturally appropriate for their setting. It began with the Byzantine artists in the fourth century who created a white image of Jesus with a beard and his hair parted down the middle. This likeness became the standard.[17] Also in the fourth century, a letter circulated claiming to be written in the first century by Publius Lentulus, a friend of Pilate. The letter, later determined to be a fourth-century forgery, described Jesus as follows:

> His hair is the colour of wine [probably meaning yellow] and golden at the root—straight and without lustre—but from the level of the ears curling and glossy, and divided down the centre after the fashion of the Nazarenes [Nazarites]. . . . His beard is full, of the same colour as His hair, and forked in form: His eyes blue extremely brilliant.[18]

Europe, like other regions, developed culturally appropriate representations of Christ for communicating the gospel. But why did Europe's culturally appropriate Christ become cast in stone as the dominant image of the historical Jesus? It would seem that Jesus was permanently cast in a white image to support European colonial expansion and the capture and enslavement of black Africans. A white Jesus served the purpose of being God's stamp of approval on the actions of white people. Such an image was also useful for demonstrating that white people were superior to people of color by virtue of the whiteness of Jesus. The propagation of white images of Jesus continues even into our own time through media portrayals in movies and television, as well as in the pictures of nearly every Bible produced for use around the world.

A culturally appropriate image of Jesus for evangelizing Europeans was co-opted by the ruling class to serve its desire for power and economic gain. The white Jesus is a product of Europe that was exported to the rest of the world to facilitate the domination of people of color. The white image of Jesus has been a powerful tool for undergirding European colonialism, enslavement of Africans, genocide of indigenous peoples, and white racial superiority. If there had not been this desire for domination, Jesus Christ would have been presented in racially and culturally appropriate ways in other cultures. Missionaries from Europe would have discarded the Western images of Jesus upon arrival in Africa, the Americas, Asia, and the islands of the great oceans. With the help of the indigenous people, new images of Jesus Christ would have been shaped that spoke powerfully to the people encountered.

The Effects of a White Jesus

The effects of a Western white Jesus on people of color have been far-reaching. As stated above, a white Jesus prevented images that were culturally appropriate from appearing. In contexts outside of Europe, the whiteness of the image made Jesus seem like a foreigner or a stranger. The Christ of all nations was not easily recognized. In describing the image of Jesus that was presented in Latin America by Spanish colonizers, J. A. Mackay spoke of this Jesus as an impostor. The real Jesus Christ "sojourned westward, went to prison in Spain, while another who took his name embarked with the Spanish crusaders for the New World."[19]

The extreme foolishness of using white and Western images of Jesus can be further illustrated by the comments of R. S. Sugirtharajah, who writes that "when Jesus made his belated second visit to the eastern part of Asia, he did not come as a Galilean sage . . . he came as an alien in his own home territory."[20] The image of the historical Jesus would have been culturally appropriate for Asia, but the Asian-ness of Jesus had been stripped away so successfully that he appeared as a stranger even in Asia. When Jesus comes as a stranger or an alien, we lose the significance of the incarnate Jesus who came as Emmanuel, "God with us."

Nowhere has the "strangeness" of a white Jesus been more dramatic than in Mexico and much of Latin America. The effect was the emergence of the image of Mary as the dominant symbol of faith and, in a sense, a replacement for Jesus. In 1531, the Virgin (Mary) of Guadalupe appeared near

Mexico City "to an Indian convert named Juan Diego. And she appeared as a young, brown-skinned Aztec woman who spoke Nahuatl, the language of the conquered Aztecs."[21] Because they had been unable to accept the white Jesus brought by the conquerors, when Mary appeared as a brown-skinned Aztec, religious revival broke loose with "a spontaneous explosion of pilgrimages, festivals, and conversions to the religion of the Virgin."[22] Aaron Gallegos writes that "until Our Lady of Guadalupe appeared in 1531, there were very few *Mexicas* who converted to Christianity, as opposed to the eight million who did so in the next seven years."[23] A culturally inappropriate white image of Jesus produced an image of Mary as *"la Morenita* ('the brown Lady')."[24]

Virgilio Elizondo believes that this image of a Mary who was indigenous to Mexico synthesized Spanish Catholicism and the face of the indigenous people "into a single, coherent symbol-image."[25] He further states:

> The cultural clash of sixteenth-century Spain and Mexico was resolved and reconciled in the brown Lady of Guadalupe. In her the new *mestizo* people finds its meaning, its uniqueness, its unity. Guadalupe is the key to understanding the Christianity of the New World, the self-image of Mexicans, of Mexican-Americans, and of all Latin Americans.[26]

Elizondo makes the case that the most powerful image for Christian faith in Latin America is Mary rather than Jesus. The brown Mary became the doorway to faith in God because Jesus was presented in the white image of the oppressors.

A white Jesus has not only seemed foreign; he has often been perceived as the enemy by people who encounter the message of Christianity. Sometimes this Caucasian image of Jesus has been used to signify that God was on the side of those who were conquering or enslaving people of color. "When Western Christians brought Jesus to Asia, many also brought with them opium and guns," writes Chung Hyun Kyung. "They taught Asians the love of Jesus while they gave Asians the slow death of opium or the fast death of a bullet."[27]

If the Jesus of the oppressor appears to be endorsing your domination or your death, he hardly seems like a savior that will offer you any help.

The impact of the portrayal of Jesus as one who sides with the oppressor was intensified because he looked like the enemy. The fact that this Jesus' white skin contrasted with the darker skin of those who were being oppressed has had a dramatic effect. Many of the young African-American activists of the 1960s and 1970s "loathed the Christ who supported the ravage of Africa, fostered the bondage of Black people, stood silently by during the rapes of Black women, and shamed Black people 'by his pigmentation so obviously not [their] own.'"[28] The white Jesus became identified with the white racist. The biblical Jesus of love was transformed into the enemy and despised by those who experienced the brutality of their oppressors. William Mosley comments on this effect, saying that "for a Black person to love the White version of God is to hate self (Black self) because in Western color symbolism white and black connote polar opposites."[29]

For many, when Jesus appeared in contexts outside of Europe, he seemed to be a captive of the West. This made it difficult for people to understand Jesus as separate from those who brought him from Europe. The Gospels were interpreted using a Western bias that caused Christian faith and Western culture to appear to be synonymous. This remains a difficult legacy for Christians outside of Western contexts as they try to interpret the message of Jesus for their setting. "For the Christian of the churches of Africa it is a question of need, first, to deliver Christ from Christianity—that is, from institutions, practices, theological currents . . . which always render him unrecognizable in other cultures," writes Efoé Julien Pénoukou. "Even today, many African Christians continue to think that the West has delivered Christ to them bound hand and foot."[30]

Not only has a white image of Jesus made Christianity seem like a captive of the West; it has subtly given the impression that European and Euro-American ways of thinking and acting are normative for Christianity. Kosuke Koyama writes:

> Languages, such as Spanish, French, English and German, are center languages in this Christian enterprise [and] these "center-theologies" (of the "blond Jesus") [are irrelevant] to the world outside of the West, and most likely to the West itself. Even today most of the world's Christians, including their theologians, believe that somehow Jesus Christ is more present in America than in Bangladesh, and therefore, America is the center and Bangladesh is a periphery. By thus thinking, they unwittingly entertain the idea that . . . America is the standard for all.[31]

This means that any attempt to understand the message of Jesus Christ outside of the realm of Western thought is somehow not normative and therefore inferior or an exception to the rule. It must be conformed to what is normative.

The effects of regarding Western Christianity as the normative and superior form of the Christian faith in the world are numerous. An understanding of Christian faith that originates outside of the West is considered to be second class (if it is considered Christianity at all). Obviously this demeans any other form of Christianity, including the ancient rites of the Eastern Orthodox Church, Egyptian Coptic Church, and others. Since the white Western Jesus is often unappealing in non-Western settings, evangelism is made difficult, if not impossible. Even those who do embrace a culturally foreign approach to Christian faith may eventually reject Christianity if they are not able to integrate their sense of culture with their understanding of the Divine.

The white image of Jesus has also reduced the Christian faith's ability to proclaim a message of liberation. The Jesus who preached good news to the poor and freedom for the oppressed had to be altered in order for systems of exploitation to be put in place. While it is difficult to change the words of the Bible, one can easily modify and manipulate the interpretation of Scripture to the benefit of those in power. This can be illustrated by looking at the Christian religion of slaveholders in the United States. One former slave recounts the actions of the minister at her church:

> Why the man that baptized me had a colored woman tied up in his yard to whip when he got home, that very Sunday and her mother belonged to that same church. We had to sit and hear him preach . . . . And he had her tied up and whipped. That was our preacher![32]

Slaveholders developed a form of Christianity that allowed for "the justification of slavery," for "Christians to be slaves," and for Christianity to be compatible "with the extreme cruelty of slavery."[33]

The Christian religion of the slaveholder focused on a belief in the Incarnation, that God was made flesh in Jesus Christ. It was by believing that God came in Christ that one gained salvation. There was little emphasis on the historical Jesus, but rather on God's act in Jesus Christ. Christianity became a religion of right belief. You could own slaves as long as you had the right belief. Once you were converted to the right belief you did not have to worry—you were free to be as brutal to your slaves as you felt necessary.[34] The primary action-orientation of this form of Christianity was "evangelism," which was understood to be introducing people to a right belief about Christ. Many were convinced that Africans were allowed into slavery because God wanted them to be saved. Slavery, therefore, allowed Africans the opportunity to gain the right knowledge and belief. In fact, some believed that slavery was the only way Africans could know Jesus Christ as their Savior.[35]

The effect of this emphasis on the Christianity of white people in the United States has been traumatic. In order to allow for slavery and justify the slave master's desire for domination, Christianity was stripped of its liberating power. The Jesus who preached freedom and liberation was replaced with a Christ who served as a symbol of right belief (which included the white man's divine right to own African slaves). Furthermore, slaveholders forced their slaves to worship this white Jesus who looked like a slave master. According to Nicholas Cooper-Lewter:

> Theology and slavery were merged . . . The effect was tragic for master and slave. Slaveholders came to think of themselves as omniscient and omnipotent, like gods who ruled over the slaves the way God ruled over humankind. . . . A white God, a white savior and a white master functioned as one. The white trinity was the property of the white culture.[36]

The tragic contradiction in this formulation of Christian faith was that the slaveholder enslaved and beat people who looked much like the Afro-Asiatic Jesus of history. Every time the slave master beat, raped, or killed African slaves, he or she was symbolically beating, raping, and killing Jesus. The slaveholder had, in essence, enslaved the Savior of humankind. One can hear the voice of Jesus echoing through time, "Truly I tell you, just as you did it to one of the least of these who are members of my family, you did it to me" (Matthew 25:40).

Another effect of the religion of the slaveholder was that two forms of Christianity developed side by side: the slave master developed a faith based on right belief and the incarnation of God in Christ, while the slaves developed a faith that emphasized the message of liberation in the Bible, with Jesus as the liberator par excellence. The slaveholder had a white Christ and the slaves had a black Christ. "According to slaveholding Christianity, knowledge of God's act in Jesus was sufficient for salvation," writes Kelly Brown Douglas. "According to slave Christianity, however, salvation was not linked necessarily to God's act of becoming incarnate in Jesus, but to what Jesus did in history on behalf of the downtrodden." She further states, "Salvation is tied to liberating activity, not to knowledge. In order for Christians to receive salvation, they must engage in liberating acts, not enslaving acts."[37]

These conflicting interpretations of Christian faith and the role of Jesus Christ still affect the relationship between African Americans and whites in the United States. They are a stumbling block to any hope for racial reconciliation. Many dialogues on reconciliation reach an impasse when discussing what is most important for Christian faith—evangelism or social justice, right belief or liberating action. This disagreement finds its source in these two faith traditions (although today you can find African Americans who have accepted only the tradition of right belief and whites who have embraced only liberation). The faith tradition that one has inherited or embraced usually determines one's view on racial reconciliation. Those who emphasize right belief will judge the success of racial reconciliation by the number of people who publicly proclaim a "new" belief about issues of race. This is often demonstrated by public statements of repentance for the sin of racism. Those who embrace liberation will judge success by a change in action, that is, that individuals are really behaving differently in their private and professional lives and are challenging the systems that keep racism in place.

This dichotomy of faith has developed in many places where the dominant group has attempted to shape and control the understanding of faith in Jesus Christ and stripped it of its emphasis on liberation. Like the children's story about the emperor who thought he was wearing a fine new suit of clothes but was in reality naked, the oppressors parade around with an incomplete form of faith they call Christianity. When the emperor paraded in front of his subjects in his exquisite "clothes," it took a child to say that the emperor was wearing no clothes. The Spirit of God is never without a witness. Often an underground movement keeps the biblical message of liberation alive. (We will discuss liberation at greater length in chapter four.)

The ill effects of a white Jesus have been many on both people of color and whites. The development of culturally appropriate images of Jesus was significantly stifled in Africa, Asia, the Americas, and the islands of the great oceans. So the Jesus that was presented in these settings appeared as a stranger, a foreigner, an enemy, an oppressor, a captive of the West, and the like. The white image of Jesus has encouraged the emergence of a brown Mary as a symbol of Christian faith, made the ways of Europe and Euro-America seem normative, resulted in ineffective evangelism, led to the rejection of Christianity by many, reduced the Christian faith's ability to liberate, caused the development of multiple forms of Christianity, inhibited true reconciliation across racial and cultural lines, and much more. The wholesale propagation of the white image of Jesus has been a tragedy of monumental proportions in our world. Many generations have lived and died without knowledge of the truth about Jesus (and in some cases, without truly knowing Jesus). This must change as we approach a new millennium.

The Importance of an Afro-Asiatic Jesus

To counter the effects of the white Jesus, it is important to proclaim that the Jesus of the Bible, who lived in Nazareth, was an Afro-Asiatic Jew. This is a case where if "you know the truth . . . the truth will make you free" (John 8:32). "Indeed, for Blacks to walk across the bridge from a Jesus of white symbolic distortions to Jesus as He was and is," writes William Mosley, "Black imagery must necessarily be employed."[38] People of color need to visually see that Jesus was not white. Although the messages of the colonizer, the slaveholder, and the white supremacist were lies, the image of a white Jesus is deeply imbedded in the psyche.

An Afro-Asiatic image increases Jesus' relevancy for people in Africa, Asia, the Americas, and the islands of the great oceans. Jesus will no longer be perceived as a stranger, a foreigner, an enemy, an oppressor, a captive of the West, or in any other way that is threatening or unapproachable. Many have lifted up the white Jesus as proof that Christianity is a "white man's religion." This has been an effective tool for the proselytizing efforts of other religions. The Nation of Islam is an example of a religion that is filled with ex-Christians who have joined to find the "true religion for black people." An Afro-Asiatic Jesus returns Jesus to his rightful place as the founder of a faith that has its roots in Africa and Asia. Jesus came as a Savior for all nations representing the God who created all peoples. More effective approaches to worldwide evangelism can be developed with an Afro-Asiatic Jesus.

True reconciliation across racial and cultural lines becomes a stronger possibility with an Afro-Asiatic Jesus. Just the designation "Afro-Asiatic" makes a multiracial, multicultural statement about our faith. People of color may be more trusting of an image of Jesus that is relevant and more authentic. The white image of Jesus carries with it the excess baggage of the history of racial and cultural prejudice. Also, white people may need a Jesus of color to be set free from racism. If white people are able to visualize the Jesus of the Bible as Afro-Asiatic, brown or black, perhaps this will facilitate the removal of the blinders of prejudiced attitudes. Something profound will happen to the soul of white people if they can pray to, express love for, and proclaim as Lord an Afro-Asiatic Jesus. This could lead to a heartfelt understanding of people of color as sisters and brothers in the human family (and in the family of God) who are not from some "distant" or "other" family. Whites who intellectually assent to an Afro-Asiatic Jesus cannot then experientially accept society's racial hierarchy. Renewed perceptions of Jesus must lead to transformed realities in the world in which we live.

Proclaiming an Afro-Asiatic Jesus is more than just reclaiming a truer visual image of the historical Jesus. We must not just "paint the statues brown and keep the Western cultural prejudices intact."[39] Embracing an Afro-Asiatic image of Jesus also means addressing the cultural baggage that came with the white image. A white image of Jesus was used to propagate the thought that the ways of Europe and Euro-America were normative and superior to other cultural perspectives. An Afro-Asiatic Jesus can help undo this damaging thought process. Thinking of Jesus as a person of color declares that cultures that are not Euro-centered are equally valid and valuable.

Of course we must not replace a white Jesus with an Afro-Asiatic Jesus simply because it is marketable. One of the interesting phenomena around the emergence of the "black Jesus" in the United States has been how extensively it has been marketed. There are even Hallmark greeting cards that now have a picture of a black Jesus on them. One would like to think that this is due to a commitment to historical accuracy rather than because there is a profit to be made. The same market forces that used a white Jesus for economic gain can just as easily manipulate people with a Jesus of color for financial profit.

Where Is Jesus to Be Found Today?

An acceptance of the conclusion that Jesus of Nazareth was Afro-Asiatic is vitally important for the future of the Christian faith around the world. Yet Jesus as the Christ must not be confined to the context of a human being who lived and breathed at the gateway to Africa and Asia in the first century. The image of Christ must be free to take on new cultural appropriations in order to be Good News in all cultures. As the early disciples spread the message about the life, death, and resurrection of Jesus, they found new ways to speak of the Christ when they entered cultures that were not influenced by Judaism. This was critical if the faith of Jesus was to expand beyond the confines of Palestine and be understood in other geographical, cultural, and historical contexts. In the prologue of the Gospel of John (1:1-18), the author uses the term *logos* as a word picture for Jesus Christ. This rhetorical image helped Greek readers understand the implications of who Jesus was.[40]

We can discover visual images and word pictures that describe Jesus Christ for our time. As Steve Charleston writes, "In the Pauline sense, I can assert that while as a man Jesus was a Jew, as the risen Christ, he is a Navajo. Or a Kiowa. Or a Choctaw. Or any other tribe."[41] Today's images of Jesus Christ need to be relevant and speak to our world in an age of diversity. They must be "bold enough to incorporate

life-enhancing and affirming elements from within the culture."[42] Cultural perspectives on Jesus Christ can become
Christian "somewhat as a latecomer to the dining room takes
a vacant seat—the one reserved for this late arrival. As new
cultures encounter Christ, various 'vacant seats' in Christianity will be taken."[43]

The "white-Caucasian-European-Western" Jesus is an image that has prevailed around the world for centuries. This
traditional image of Jesus is now being challenged by new
images in the "search for a new face of Christ."[44] While Jesus
tended to be culturally exclusive as an historic person, Jesus
as the divine, resurrected Christ is supposed to be inclusive.
Culturally authentic images of Jesus Christ speak powerfully to the inclusive nature of God. In many cases, the image
of Jesus Christ that emerges in various cultural settings not
only speaks to the need for a culturally appropriate Christ but
also addresses the devastating results of long-term injustice.

We will now briefly look at five diverse images of Jesus
Christ. These have been selected because they are rooted in
the culture of their origin, but they also speak to the broader
issues facing our world in this age of diversity. They attempt
to make Jesus Christ relevant for our time by highlighting
an aspect of Jesus' ministry or a particular cultural need. The
following five images of Jesus Christ are not examined in
their fullness, nor are they necessarily the most popular
image of Christ within that particular culture. The images
to be examined are the Gold-Crowned Jesus; the Galilean
Jibaro Jesus; Jesus the One Crowned with Thorns; Jesus the
Great Healer; and the Jim-Crowed Jesus. They have been
intentionally placed in this sequence because each image
logically leads to the next. While each image speaks to a
different theme, together they present a broad picture of how
people around the world are embracing Jesus Christ.

The Gold-Crowned Jesus

R. S. Sugirtharajah says that the key question "is not what
the historical Jesus looked like but what he means for Asia

today."[45] Korean poet Kim Chi Ha has attempted to answer the question of Jesus' relevancy to Asia in a play called *The Gold-Crowned Jesus.*[46] The play opens with the display of a cement statue of Jesus Christ wearing a gold crown on his head. The play revolves around a number of conversations that take place near the Christ statue. A company president, a police officer, and a priest discuss their common belief that "success" demonstrates God's blessing. A beggar, a leper, a prostitute, and a sympathetic nun are heard dialoging about their desperate circumstances. In both of these cases, the concrete Jesus is silent.

The gold crown on the head of Jesus is meant to signify his allegiance with the rich and powerful elite. Because they are unable to accept this understanding of Jesus, throughout the play the beggar and the leper question where the real Jesus is. The query comes out of their need for Jesus. C. S. Song comments:

> When a beggar turns to the question, it is not his head or his faith that turns to it. It is the stomach, his empty stomach! . . . When a leper asks the question, his immediate concern is not the defense of the faith and correct doctrine. What is at stake is his humanity—his humanity eaten away by the horrible disease and himself excluded from human community.[47]

Despite their intense longings to discover a Jesus who will respond to their cries, the Jesus statue remains silent.

As the play continues, the leper notices the gold crown on the head of Jesus and, considering the possibility of a life free from poverty, removes the gold crown. It is at this point that the concrete Jesus comes to life and says:

> I have been closed up in this stone for a long, long time, . . . entombed in this dark, lonely, suffocating prison. I have longed to talk with you, the kind and poor people like yourself, and share your sufferings. I can't begin to tell you how long I have waited for this day, . . . this day when I would be freed from my prison, this day of liberation when I would live and burn again as a flame inside you, inside the very depths of your misery.[48]

The rich and powerful people are surprised to discover Jesus conversing with the beggar, the leper, and other marginalized people. Shocked by what they see, they grab the gold crown from the leper. Then the priest places it back on the head of Jesus. Instantly Jesus becomes a silent cement figure again and remains this way through the end of the play.

The "Gold-Crowned Jesus" is an image that presents Jesus as a captive of the powerful elite. The church, in league with powerful economic interests, has often promoted an image of a Jesus who sides with the status quo. "The golden crown on his head is the ideology of the established Church, which was forced on Jesus in order to make him support the Church institution," writes Byung Mu Ahn.[49] The missionaries of colonial Europe brought a Jesus who was set in concrete and unable to adapt to the cultural realities. Yet as C. S. Song states, "The ready-made Jesus encased in a statue, enshrined in a cathedral, endorsed by church traditions and doctrines, is not the real Jesus."[50] The play seeks to demonstrate that the real Jesus can live only when set free from the concrete captivity.

The play also makes the point that it is the *Minjung* (Korean poor) who set Jesus free from the concrete. In the same way that the woman who touched the hem of Jesus' garment (Mark 5:25-34; Luke 8:43-48) released the power of his healing, "the cries of the Minjung . . . took off the crown of Jesus." Byung Mu Ahn declares, "So we, for the first time, came to hear his voice and see his tears. That is to say, we experienced that Jesus, confined in the cement, could only be liberated by the Minjung."[51] The biblical understanding of Jesus as Good News to the poor is held captive in many cultures and nations and must be set free. Jesus is released from concrete dogma when he is linked up with the life of the vast numbers of people in this world who are desperate for hope.[52]

The Galilean *Jibaro* Jesus

After Jesus is set free by the *Minjung,* he joins the poor in solidarity as a Galilean *jibaro* (a Puerto Rican peasant). According to Orlando Costas, Latinas and Latinos in the United States can think of Jesus "as the promised son of God who became a Galilean *jibaro* and lived the Hispanic experience of poverty and ignorance, of being 'slighted for his . . . manner of speech,' of rejection, loneliness, exile, suffering, and death—all of these leading 'to the Almighty Father, in the unity of the Holy Spirit.'"[53] The "Galilean *Jibaro* Jesus" lives the experience of people who are marginalized by poverty and prejudice. Jesus was raised as a Jew in Galilee. As a Galilean, he was "a borderland reject."[54] He lived in a culturally diverse setting and was disenfranchised by both colonial Rome and religious Jerusalem.

The experience of feeling cut off from one's culture of origin and unaccepted by the dominant culture is one that many people today can relate to. Our world is teeming with people who have become refugees, immigrants, or displaced persons, as well as others who are caught in a cultural limbo. They often do not feel fully accepted in either culture. Also they find themselves pulled in opposite directions by old loyalties and new demands as they face uncertain cultural understandings. As a Galilean *jibaro,* Jesus understood this predicament. As a person from Galilee, Jesus lived in the midst of the struggle between two worlds: Rome and Jerusalem. Each world placed expectations on him, and often he was an outcast in both worlds.

Jesus chose to be in solidarity with the masses of people, the *jibaros.* This solidarity, which began at his birth, creates a sense of trust for a majority of the world's population who live in similar circumstances today. Justo González writes:

> We are comforted when we read the genealogy of Jesus, and find there, not only a Gentile like ourselves, but also incest, and what amounts to David's rape of Bathsheba. The Gospel writer did not hide the skeletons in Jesus' closet, but listed them, so that we may know that the

Savior has really come to be one of us—not just one of the high and mighty, the aristocratic with impeccable blood lines, but one of us.[55]

Jesus demonstrated his solidarity with the *jibaros* of his day by "being born one of them, learning from them, going to their homes, and eating with them."[56] Once the gold crown is removed, setting Jesus free from the concrete image, he becomes a Galilean *jibaro* and lives with the people as one of them. Virgilio Elizondo declares, "It is in the face and person of Jesus the poor Galilean that the face of God is manifested."[57]

Jesus the One Crowned with Thorns

The Burakumin people of Japan have added an emphasis on liberation to the images of the "Gold-Crowned Jesus" and the "Galilean *Jibaro* Jesus." The Burakumin—the indigenous people of the island of Japan—have been treated poorly by the larger society. Out of their experience they have come to identify Jesus as "the one crowned with thorns."[58] They view Jesus as both a cosufferer and a liberator. As Kuribayashi Teruo states:

The crown of thorns has become a symbol of the solidarity of God with the marginalized, the oppressed, and the exploited. It has come to signify the person of Jesus, who makes the groaning of the despised his own cry for liberation. The symbol reveals that God is also suffering with them, while promising their freedom from that oppression.[59]

The crown of thorns was meant to humiliate Jesus as a criminal (Matthew 27:27-31). It was a mockery of the claim made by the people a few days earlier when they proclaimed Jesus as the King of the Jews. Jesus was further humiliated when Pilate displayed him in front of the crowds in Jerusalem wearing the crown of thorns and asked the people to vote on whether or not he should die (John 19:5-6). The crown of thorns was placed on his head to signify that Jesus was powerless at the hands of the Roman authorities. Yet through the Resurrection, the crown of thorns became a symbol of Jesus overcoming suffering.[60] The crown of thorns says that "weeping may linger for the night, but joy comes with the morning" (Psalm 30:5). The Burakumin look to "Jesus the One Crowned with Thorns" to remind themselves that morning will come even as they struggle through the night of suffering.

It is interesting to note that the Burakumin were not church attenders when they embraced "Jesus as the One Crowned with Thorns." In a country where Christians make up a small percentage of the population, "they simply took the Bible and read in it their daily experience."[61] Through their study of the Bible, they "came to relate their own experience to the biblical symbol of Jesus' passion."[62] All around the world people have started reading the Bible for themselves. Rigoberta Menchú calls the Bible the "main weapon" for empowering the indigenous people in Guatemala to struggle for freedom.[63] The Bible has become a critical tool for empowerment. "If Jesus is to have any meaning for Asian peoples, he must take off the gold crown as Kim alludes to in the play. He must regain a simple crown of thorns and join the oppressed in their suffering and joy," writes Teruo. "If Jesus is a savior merely for the powerful, he has nothing to do with the wretched in Asia."[64] "Jesus the One Crowned with Thorns" intimately understands the pain of oppressed people, yet at the same time leads the way in the hope for liberation.

Jesus the Great Healer

An understanding of Jesus as a liberator who lives in solidarity with people who are hurting naturally leads to the conclusion that his healing role must not be overlooked. In many cultures in Africa, the role of the healer is a highly significant one. Anselme T. Sanon states, "To see the face of Christ, to recognize his African face, is to find an African name for him."[65] One of the names Jesus is called in various parts of Africa is "the Great Healer." This should come as no surprise because "in his programmatic discourse, borrowed from the prophet Isaiah, Jesus presents himself primarily as a healer."[66] In Luke 4:18-19, Jesus proclaimed his agenda for ministry:

> The Spirit of the Lord is upon me, because he has anointed me to bring good news to the poor. He has sent me to proclaim release to the captives and recovery of sight to the blind, to let the oppressed go free, to proclaim the year of the Lord's favor.

According to Anne Nasimiyu-Wasike, Jesus' ministry "inaugurated the restoration of individuals and societies to wholeness."[67]

With the great amount of suffering occurring in several countries on the continent of Africa, it makes sense that Jesus needs to come as "the Great Healer." Yet as Cécé Kolié writes, "To proclaim Jesus as the Great Healer calls for a great deal of explaining to the millions who starve in the Sahel, to victims of injustice and corruption, and to the polyparasitic afflicted of the tropical and equatorial forests."[68] In the midst of terrible tragedy, one often questions how God could let this happen. The proclamation of Jesus as "the Great Healer" could almost be seen as a cruel joke. The message of healing must be declared in the larger context of society. Those who are suffering physically and psychologically are not the only ones in need of healing. Those in power who perpetuate suffering also need to be healed from their greed, ambition, and callousness. Kolié writes that "Jesus' therapy is articulated upon acts and deeds calculated to alter social relationships. Jesus is aware that it is never on the physical level alone that one is deaf or blind, and that consequently neither can healing or salvation remain on that level."[69] "Jesus the Great Healer" addresses the ills of social systems that produce suffering and ultimately heals the souls of suffering humanity.

Once set free from the concrete and living in solidarity with the masses, Jesus emerges as a liberator who is a healer, a therapeutic force. Kolié sums up the message: "'We proclaim a crucified Messiah, a scandal to the Jews, madness to the Greeks'—and sickness to the Africans. For the person of black Africa . . . the presence of someone ill in the family is a scandal."[70] "Jesus the Great Healer" provides a holistic therapy that addresses the need for physical, psychological, and spiritual healing at both the individual and institutional level. Both the powerless and the powerful are invited to come to "Jesus the Great Healer" and receive a life-transforming touch.

The Jim-Crowed Jesus

A need for a healing touch from Jesus in the United States was born in the dehumanization of slavery. While the white Christ was wearing the gold crown of superiority, the black Christ was wearing the crown of thorns of chattel slavery. This crown of thorns helped Jesus Christ develop an intimate relationship with the slaves and therapeutically empowered them to struggle for their freedom. The black Christ embodied the contradiction between true Christianity and the cruelty of slavery. The black Jesus—friend, fellow sufferer, confidant, and liberator—convinced the slaves that because of the Resurrection, suffering was not the last word—freedom was.[71]

Slavery was replaced with the Jim Crow system of legal segregation in the South and cultural and social segregation in the North. Anyone having at least one drop of African blood was considered "black" under this system. Although legal segregation has been outlawed in the United States, cultural and social segregation remain intact and the "one drop rule" is still the determining factor. Out of this context James Cone boldly proclaimed in the 1970s:

> If Jesus Christ is to have any meaning for us, he must leave the security of the suburbs by joining blacks in their condition. What need have we for a white Jesus when we are not white but black? . . . No matter how seriously we take the carpenter from Nazareth, there is still the existential necessity to relate his person to black persons,

asking, "What is his relevance to the black community today?"[72]

As was demonstrated earlier in this chapter, Jesus had a least one drop of African (Hamitic) blood running through his veins. What would this mean for Jesus if he walked the streets of the United States today? Would a Jesus with black African ancestry, facing Jim Crow attitudes, be considered "cursed"? Nicholas Cooper-Lewter has responded to these questions by speaking of "the Jim-Crowed Jesus."[73] He has applied to Jesus the social customs and "rules" of segregation as they were in their legal form and as they continue to function culturally throughout the United States today. Cooper-Lewter has concluded that:

> He was not a "good" Negro, one who knew his place and stayed in it. He did not agree to treat every white person as his superior. He did not accept the idea that love should never be expected to be the love of equals for each other where white people and people of color were concerned. He did not accept the idea that he could never assert or intimate that a white person might be lying. He did not accept the idea that he could never impute dishonorable intentions to a white person. He did [not] accept the idea that he could never lay claim to, or overtly demonstrate, superior knowledge or intelligence. And he did not give up his ministry because the penalties for not following proper etiquette were severe, often death.[74]

Nicholas Cooper-Lewter points out that Jesus would not comply with the rules of the Jim Crow system of segregation stating how a person of African descent is to behave in society. Jesus grew up in a society that had many rules governing his actions. One of the things that irritated the Pharisees the most was how often Jesus broke the rules. He often crossed the boundaries of social acceptance by talking to women in public; associating with Samaritans; eating with lepers, tax collectors, and other "sinners"; and the like. Jesus often confounded the political and religious leaders with his behavior. He would eat, work, and heal on the sabbath. Jesus refused to submit to those in power, such as Caiaphas, Herod, and Pilate, and this led to his execution.

Jesus would be "Jim-Crowed" by the system of segregation in place today, yet he would refuse to become a victim. He would stand strong and defy the system. "The Jim-Crowed Jesus" does not allow his life to be determined by the distorted "rules" of societies. He stands up to exploitation and leads others to do the same. He is "the Almighty's answer to the perverted use of scripture"[75] because he refuses to be victimized or held captive by any modern-day misinterpretation of the Bible. "The Jim-Crowed Jesus" is a Jesus who has been set free from the concrete understandings of church tradition and now stands in solidarity with the marginalized of this world, heals the wounds of victimization, and transforms unjust systems.

A White Jesus for Today: Jesus the Truth Teller

The five images of Jesus discussed above are examples of how, during the last half of the twentieth century, Christian faith around the world has exploded with new visual and rhetorical images of Jesus Christ. Some of these images are based on the recovery of information about the historical Jesus, while others are attempts to address current issues in a cultural setting. Meanwhile, the white Jesus of the colonizers, slaveholders, and racial supremacists continues to prevent culturally appropriate images of Jesus for white people from emerging. Many people of color in our world are creatively seeking fresh reflections of Jesus, while white people remain captive to a defective image of Jesus. Although white people need to accept that Jesus of Nazareth was Afro-Asiatic, Jesus as the Christ can appear in culturally appropriate images to address their current issues.

I would like to suggest that such a culturally appropriate image would allow Jesus to come to white people as a truth teller. Jesus had this relationship with his own people, the Jews. He told the truth to his people who were in power, as well as those out of power. He told a group of Jewish men that only the one without sin could begin the stoning of a woman caught in adultery. Then he told the woman to go and sin no more (John 8:3-11). Jesus was sometimes harsh in his honesty when challenging Jewish political and religious leaders. He called some among the scribes and Pharisees "whitewashed tombs," "snakes," and a "brood of vipers" and challenged their "hypocrisy" because they had neglected justice, mercy, and faith and had developed a religion based on their vanity, legalism, greed, and self-indulgence (Matthew 23:1-39). Jesus was truthful with other power brokers as well. He confronted a rich young ruler who was held captive by his wealth and told him he could be set free by selling all that he had and giving it to the poor among his people (Matthew 19:16-22; Mark 10:17-22; Luke 18:18-25). On another occasion, Jesus visited the home of Zacchaeus, a corrupt tax collector who was oppressing his own people. Whatever it was that Jesus said to him caused Zacchaeus to admit that he had defrauded his own people and commit to making restitution (Luke 19:1-10). The Jewish working class and poor also heard the truth from Jesus. He told them of their need for liberation from those among their own people who were keeping them down. He reminded them that they had dignity and must never accept a victim mentality. They could be victors with God's help. Jesus encouraged them to receive healing from the stress of life's struggles: "Come to me, all you that are weary and are carrying heavy burdens, and I will give you rest" (Matthew 11:28).

A white Jesus for today would be found living in solidarity with poor and working-class whites. He would offer them a faith that lifted their spirits and empowered them in their daily efforts to satisfy life's basic needs. This Jesus would also stay in the homes of middle-class whites and talk with them about their spiritual needs (as he did with Mary and Martha of Bethany in Luke 10:38-42). Jesus would warn of the trap of materialism and remind them that one's identity must be found in God, not possessions (or the desire for material things). At length, Jesus would listen to poor and middle-class white people as they voiced their concerns and fears regarding employment, adequate health care, education for their children, safe neighborhoods, and the like. These interests, Jesus would say, are the shared concerns of all people in the human family. He would tell them to not let their need to take care of their own family divide them from their other sisters and brothers in the human family. They should resist the temptation to blame or scapegoat people of color as white supremacist groups do. The real problem is a system that needs to be fixed.

This white Jesus would go to the offices and homes of rich and powerful white people and listen to them describe the stresses of their lives. He would then challenge them to use their wealth and influence to create a more just society. As Jesus said in the first century and would say today, "From everyone to whom much has been given, much will be required; and from the one to whom much has been entrusted, even more will be demanded" (Luke 12:48). In other words, while the responsibility is considerable, the opportunity to serve God is even more far-reaching. He would say to those with power that they should follow the example of the apostle Paul, who used the "power" of his Roman citizenship to gain access to Caesar and bring the gospel of Jesus to those at the highest levels in the system of power (Acts 22:25–28:31). Jesus would ask those with wealth to use their financial resources to underwrite ministries of compassion, reconciliation, and social justice, just as people of means supported the ministry of Jesus in the Bible (Luke 8:3; Matthew 27:57).

A white Jesus would not give speeches on cultural diversity or prepare research studies on people of color; instead, a truth-telling Christ would be honest about the history of systems based on theories of white superiority. He would describe how a group made up primarily of elite and powerful white males created a system of oppression that has brutalized people of color around the world and exploited the masses of white people who were (and are) manipulated daily with fraudulent mythologies. The system has been called by different names—colonialism, slavery, apartheid, segregation, genocide, racism—but regardless of what it is called, it has had the same effect. A white Jesus would honestly admit that the institutional forms of Christianity were often used to support this system, causing a spiritual illness that still affects the church today.[76]

A white Jesus would also celebrate the lives of those dedicated white Christians who have stood for justice and not bought the dominant lie. He would invite others to join in the struggle against unjust systems around the world and become "'friends' of the oppressed."[77] Jesus would invite these friends to "deny themselves and take up their cross daily and follow me" (Luke 9:23). This attitude would be necessary because, as Ada María Isasi-Díaz writes:

> In many ways the "friends" are often harshly victimized by society at large because they have been part of the oppressors and know how to thwart the control and domination which keeps the oppressors in power. Furthermore, "friends" can prick the conscience of the oppressors in ways the oppressed cannot, because the "friends" know the manipulations and the betrayals that the oppressors must make to stay in power.[78]

A white Jesus would remind white people that their modern relationship with people of color began as an economic one. Africans were enslaved as free labor for the purpose of building up the economic base of the United States and other "white" countries. Other people of color were used as cheap laborers. Now that the technological age has arrived, there is less need for "cheap" labor, and the white power structure does not know what to do with its former slaves and low-cost workers. Due to a fear of retribution, there are those who believe that police force and penal institutions are the only "real" solution for the current state of race relations.

A white Jesus would tell the truth about white-on-white violence. This is easily seen in civil wars, religious rivalries, World Wars I and II, and the "Cold War." Less apparent are the indignities experienced by middle-class, working-class, and poor whites who are victimized by the same powerful white elite as people of color. Chief executive officers at major corporations are making extravagant salaries and bonuses, but they use the excuse that their company is in financial trouble when terminating workers. This is creating an environment where many white people feel powerless. James Baldwin commented on the similarity between the treatment of people of color and that of "average" white people when he wrote:

> Slaveholders do not allow their slaves to compare notes: American slavery, until this hour, prevents any meaningful dialogue between the poor white and the black, in order to prevent the poor white from recognizing that he, too, is a slave. The contempt with which American leaders treat American blacks is very obvious; what is not so obvious is that they treat the bulk of the American people with the very same contempt.[79]

A truth-telling Jesus would tell white people that their "white" identity is a modern creation developed to support the domination of people of color. The historical Jesus was painted white to encourage this process. White identity is built on a foundation of what it is not, finding much of its strength in the thought "at least I am not black." Andrew Hacker writes:

> No white American, including those who insist that opportunities exist for persons of every race, would change places with even the most successful black American. All white Americans realize that their skin comprises an inestimable asset. It opens doors and facilitates freedom of movement. It serves as a shield from insult and harassment. Indeed, having been born white can be taken as a sign: your preferment is both ordained and deserved. Its value persists not because a white appearance automatically brings success and status, since there are no such guarantees. What it does ensure is that you will not be regarded as black, a security which is worth so much that no one who has it has ever given it away.[80]

White people are having an identity crisis. The melting pot in the United States stripped away European ethnicity and created an identity based on skin color rather than culture. Because of the history of racism, some white people are embarrassed to be white. Others try to deny this white identity by taking on another through immersing themselves in a different culture. A white Jesus would encourage white people, who are struggling to be free from the legacy of racism, to receive God's gift of liberation. Whites need to reclaim the biblical message of liberation. Whites are hurt by systems of oppression and racism. Jesus comes to liberate the minds and souls of white people. He would challenge them to let go of the concept of "whiteness"—not because of self-hatred but because it is a false identity originally developed for the purpose of excluding people of color (and may now also be marginalizing whites themselves). Jesus would invite white people simply to be a part of the human family. Yes, their skin color is described as "white" and their cultural roots are European, but their mind-set should no longer be "white"; it should be human.

An Inclusive Christ

Jesus entered history in the first century as a Jewish Afro-Asiatic male from Galilee. He came into the world at a time when ethnic tensions were simmering just below the surface and communities were isolated from each other. Jesus of Nazareth came with a prophetic word, calling for a just society based on individuals and institutions reconciling themselves with God and each other. In the course of history, the image of a white Western Jesus was used to dominate people of color around the world for economic gain. The effects on people of color and whites have been devastating. We must regain the post-Resurrection understanding of Jesus as the Christ who is free to be incarnated in all cultural settings in order to proclaim the Good News that leads to a relationship with an all-inclusive God!

Questions for Discussion

1. Close your eyes and try to imagine what God looks like. Do the same with Jesus Christ. Describe the images that come to your mind. What is the source of these images? What do they mean?

2. Define what it means to be created in the image of God. How widely is this definition accepted?

3. How do you feel about an Afro-Asiatic Jesus? Does this have any affect on your faith? Is it important to embrace Jesus as a person of color? Why?

4. Why has Jesus Christ been presented primarily in images that are white? How has this benefited some people?

5. Reflect on the negative effects of a white Jesus described in this chapter. Which ones have you observed? Cite examples. What additional effects would you suggest?

6. Have you noticed two (or more) forms of Christian faith such as described in the experience of slavery in the United States? What can be done to bring these understandings closer together? How do differing understandings of faith affect attempts at reconciliation?

7. What insights did you gain from the different cultural views of Christ? Which one seemed most relevant to your experience? Which one challenged you most? Were you uncomfortable with any of the ways Jesus Christ was presented? Why?

8. If Jesus were to come today as a truth teller, what would we need to hear?

9. In what ways should our presentation of the gospel of Jesus Christ be changed to address the needs of a multicultural society?

10. What in chapter two challenged you the most? Have any of your perspectives on Jesus Christ changed? How would you now describe Jesus Christ?

Chapter Three

The Enhancing Prism of Cultural Perspectives

Translating the message of Jesus Christ into various cultural settings is not new. Biblical interpretation has always been shaped by historical settings and cultural experiences. When the authors of Matthew, Mark, Luke, and John wrote the story of Jesus Christ, they selected the episodes from his life that would have the greatest meaning for their respective audiences. They emphasized certain aspects of the story that were most relevant to the cultural, historical, and social circumstances of the readers to whom they wrote. Also, the story's implications were so immense that the early church leaders acknowledged that one written account could not even come close to capturing its full essence. As we look at the biblical story of Jesus Christ from the four canonical perspectives of the Gospel writers, we gain a more complete understanding.[1]

If this was true for Matthew, Mark, Luke, and John, could it not be equally true today? The implications of the story of Jesus Christ are still so monumental that one individual perspective, one denominational view, one cultural interpretation cannot really come close to capturing its essence. As one opens oneself to hearing the Bible interpreted by people living in different social settings, with wide ranges of cultural experiences, one can thus gain a fuller understanding of the modern relevance of the ancient mysteries of God. Certain aspects of the biblical story invariably will have greater meaning in particular social, historical, and cultural settings. Yet for some, the idea of Christian faith being "shaped" by one's cultural setting may be offensive or threatening. Isn't the gospel unchanging? Yes, the truth of the gospel is unchanging, but the way it is communicated and understood is adaptable to cultural realities. Perhaps our resistance to examining the Bible from new perspectives springs from the fact that the "unchanging gospel" that we cling to so dearly is, in reality, the interpretation of our tradition, family, culture, denomination, or the dominant Western European and Euro-American cultures.

As suggested in the previous two chapters, the dominance of one approach to interpretation has greatly affected our understanding of faith. James Earl Massey describes this effect:

> Despite a common confession as Christians, members of communities that have experienced oppression or marginalization read the Bible from a different perspective, always wary of so-called objective approaches and interpretations that are insensitive to human need and problems resulting from exploitation of others. Communities that have a remembered history of injustices perpetrated against them by the dominant society do not find meaning, identity, or affirmation in "mainstream biblical interpretations" that overlook or disregard their social location.[2]

The prevailing emphasis on the dominant culture's perspective for interpretation of the Bible limits the possibilities of biblical faith flourishing in other cultural settings. The following concerns of two theologians from different continents, Asia and Native America, further demonstrate how obvious it is to many that biblical interpretation and translation have been dominated by European and Euro-American scholars:

> While the Christian faith is presented as universal, valid for all times and meant for all peoples, the content of its dogma, moral teachings, and pastoral orientations has largely related to the needs, concerns, and interests of the

Western peoples. It is as if Christianity, having converted Europe, had in turn been made European.[3]

It seems to me that much of the gospel has been interpreted throughout history by Europeans and Americans. Before long it is not the gospel that is being interpreted but an interpretation of the gospel. Some things become so commonplace that you can't think of understanding them differently.[4]

When one cultural interpretation dominates, it also restricts our ability to understand the multiple dimensions of truth contained in Scripture. Without the diverse perspectives of God's rainbow of humanity, we cannot grasp the true universalism of the biblical story. We may not be able to understand certain aspects of the biblical story because we lack the necessary points of reference. We may miss the nuances that someone else can see clearly because his or her life experience is more closely aligned with that of the story being examined. Perhaps a culture or society's "historical experience . . . can identify better with the content of the Bible."[5] We really do need diverse perspectives to gain wholistic understandings. Massey reminds us that "the Bible is the property of the entire church, and each reading community within the church has insights to share with an interest to enlarge the church's vision of God and God's work among and through us in the world."[6]

No matter which cultural perspective dominates interpretation, a monocultural approach for Bible study is not sufficient in an age of diversity. Unfortunately, too many of us are not studying the Bible from a multicultural perspective because we are involved in what Justo and Catherine González call "Lone-Ranger" Bible study. They describe this as follows:

The Lone Ranger himself did not roam the West alone. He had Tonto with him. . . . And in spite of this the white hero was called "lone," because his Indian companion, who repeatedly saved his life, simply didn't count. He did not count for two reasons: first, he was seen as a projection of his white leader; second, the Lone Ranger never listened to him. There is then a type of "Lone-Ranger" Bible study which, although not necessarily done in private, is done in the same sort of almost meaningless company which Tonto provided for the hero. This happens when our biblical interpretation fails to be challenged by others, either because they share our own perspective, or because, since they differ from us, we classify them as "Tontos" whose perspectives we need not take into account.[7]

Multicultural approaches to Bible study may not be considered normative because the perspectives and the people that are available to initiate such approaches have not been taken seriously. Perhaps "the others" have been expected to accept traditional interpretations in order to be considered orthodox. Or it is possible that non-Western cultural perspectives have been tokenized by labeling them as out of the so-called mainstream, only relevant for that particular cultural group (such as "a black thing" or "an Asian way") and of no value to anyone else. Certainly there is an ignorance on the part of many regarding the biblical interpretation that has been seriously pursued by persons outside the domain of Europe and the "mainstream" of North America. In fact, exciting and significant discoveries are being made out of the limelight of Western influence.

Considering the effects of the demographic changes taking place in our world, as mentioned in this book's introduction, *the future of Christian faith in our world, in fact, depends on multicultural approaches to biblical interpretation*. We can no longer continue to study the Bible as "Lone Rangers" and expect our efforts at outreach through evangelism, discipleship, empowerment, and social action to be effective. We must be able to appreciate, understand, and utilize multiple perspectives on the Bible. This is both challenging and exciting. The challenge is to see the biblical texts through new eyes. The excitement comes in what we will discover.

Impact of Culture on Rules of Interpretation

When seeking to understand the Bible from cultural perspectives other than our own, it is important to note that our cultural and social settings shape the rules or methods we use for interpretation.[8] What we bring to the text from our culture, economic status, race, denomination, theological assumptions, and faith experience are often taken for granted and not challenged or even acknowledged. When we begin to examine the Scripture from other social locations, we must learn to recognize our tacit, self-serving rules of interpretation and set them aside, at least temporarily, so that we can become familiar with the approaches used by others. In order to gain a greater appreciation for how culture impacts the rules of interpretation, we will study two examples: the perspective of Latin American women (Latinas) for interpretation as defined by Elsa Tamez[9] and some rules for interpretation in an Asian context as suggested by Stanley Samartha.[10]

For Tamez, rereading the Bible from the perspective of Latin American women is necessary because of the way the Bible has been used to limit the opportunities of Latinas. She writes: "In truth, the problem would not be serious if everybody considered the Bible for what it is: a testimony of a Judeo-Christian people with a particular culture, for whom holy revelation works always in favor of those who have least."[11] A Latina perspective is critical for Hispanic women to hear their story in the Bible. Reading the Scriptures from the perspective of Latinas, according to Tamez, requires the interpreter to first gain distance from the text. This means reading the Bible as though one had never read it before. This is difficult because we often accept traditional interpretations of texts. Yet one must attempt to read without referencing these understandings. After removing the traditional understandings, one needs to come closer to the text by reading with the eyes of life experience. "This is the process of coming closer to daily life, which implies the experiences of pain, joy, hope, hunger, celebration, and struggle," states Tamez. "In Latin America the Bible is not read as an intellectual or academic exercise; it is read with the goal of giving meaning to our lives today."[12] This gives the interpretative task a sense of urgency and a need for relevance. The Bible is a source of discovering how, with God's help, we can live in a world that is filled with unpredictable moments.

Latinas read the Bible with the poor as a point of departure because this is where most find themselves. Elsa Tamez writes, "In a context of misery, malnutrition, repression, torture, Indian genocide, and war—in other words, in a context of death—there is no greater priority than framing and articulating the readings according to these situations."[13] A majority of the world's people find themselves in this context. This is particularly true for the women of the world. As the Bible is read from the perspective of the poor, it will also speak with greater power to this majority of the world's people. Of course, many of the authors of the biblical texts found themselves in the same context described by Tamez. Also, the entire Bible is read with the eyes of women, with a feminist consciousness. Yet this way of reading the Scriptures is not limited to women. Tamez believes that men can learn to read the Bible in a way that can perceive the viewpoint of women in the Bible and women today. Because the task of biblical interpretation has been traditionally reserved for men, most women have the ability to view the Bible from a male vantage point. Unless men attempt to read the Bible with the eyes of women, they will not have a balanced understanding of Scripture.

Similar approaches are used by women scholars in other cultures. Renita J. Weems describes such a process for reading the Bible from the perspective of African American women:

> How African American women read the Bible is a topic that has to do with not only uncovering whose voice they identify with in the Bible—female as opposed to male, the African as opposed to the non-African, the marginalized as opposed to the dominant. It has equally and more precisely to do with examining the values of those readers and the corroboration of those values by the text; it has to do with how the text arouses, manipulates, and harnesses African American women's deepest yearnings.[14]

Elsa Tamez believes that the deepest longings of Latin American women are touched as their reading of the Bible intersects with their experiences as women whose daily lives are familiar with struggle.

Like Tamez, Stanley J. Samartha is committed to discovering rules of biblical interpretation that make sense in his setting. He states:

> Every time a Biblical scholar in Europe sneezes, theologians in Asia should not catch a cold and manifest the symptoms all over the footnotes! To depend on rules of interpretation developed in countries alien to Asian life is a hindrance to the Church's growth in maturity. It reduces our credibility, diminishes our spirit, and distorts the universality of Jesus Christ to whom the scriptures bear witness.[15]

His challenge to Asian scholars is to examine the Scriptures in the original Semitic languages and produce fresh translations and interpretations. Most translation and interpretation of the Bible has been done by Western scholars. Asian scholars can bring forth from the original biblical languages understandings that reflect the nuances of an Asian cultural setting that was a significant part of biblical history. This process will take much time, but it is essential for authentic interpretation in diverse Asian settings.

Samartha suggests a few additional approaches that make interpretation more authentically Asian. The countries of Asia have much longer traditions of indigenous religions (Hinduism, Buddhism, Taoism, Confucianism) with their own well-loved scriptures. Therefore, biblical interpretation needs to be done in an atmosphere of respect for and willingness to dialogue with other religious traditions. It must be acknowledged that people in Asia have been sustained by these other religions for thousands of years. Tissa Balasuriya adds:

> As an Asian I cannot accept as divine and true any teaching which begins with the presupposition that all of my ancestors for innumerable generations are eternally

damned by God unless they had been baptized in or were related to one of the Christian institutional churches.[16]

The multiple faith traditions of the East create a very different interpretive challenge from that in the Judeo-Christian West. Because Christianity is a newcomer religion among some of the most ancient religions, Asian interpreters "try to take Jesus out of the study into the dusty streets of Asia and let him mingle with other seers and savior figures."[17]

This difference of approach required in the East can be further observed when speaking about the authority of the Bible. In the West, it is not unusual to hear a preacher exclaim, "The Bible says . . ." to underscore her or his point. It is considered essential that everything be biblically based. An emphasis on the "authority" of the Bible is not always helpful for biblical interpretation in Asia because of the many other competing "authoritative" scriptures. Samartha says that the Bible "must *become* authoritative to us in our life as we grapple with our problems today."[18] An understanding of a biblical text comes as one responds in faith to the God to whom the biblical text points. Kwok Pui Lan supports Samartha's contention:

> For most Chinese, the truth claim of the Bible cannot be based on its being the supposed revealed Word of God, for 99 percent of the people do not believe in this faith state-ment. They can only judge the meaningfulness of the biblical tradition by looking at how it is acted out in the Christian community.[19]

In other words, the Bible has authority in direct proportion to how Christians live the faith proclaimed in its pages.

Even in a brief look at the presuppositions affecting inter-pretation in these two settings, we have learned much that will be of assistance in developing a broader and more diverse view of how the Bible can be understood. Elsa Tamez's description of the perspective of Latin American women challenges us to let go of our existing assumptions about the Bible so that we can gain fresh insights, allow the biblical texts to intersect with life's daily experiences, use the poor as a point of departure, and read the Bible with the eyes of women. Stanley Samartha suggests that in the Asian context we must remember that other religions have a long history of sustaining people in the midst of their struggles and that therefore it is more important for biblical authority to be lived than proclaimed. The value of their insights is not limited only to their own contexts. In this day of increasing heterogeneity around the world, Latinas and Asians are often found living in places far from their countries of origin. The perspectives offered by Tamez, Samartha, and others enrich the ability to be in dialogue with new neighbors. Also, these insights have much to teach us in our study of the Scriptures, no matter what our cultural or socioeconomic setting.

The rules of biblical interpretation will differ, sometimes radically, from culture to culture.[20] Yet they are quite useful for discovering truth. In fact, the greater the number of perspectives we take into account on a scriptural passage or theological concept, the stronger our interpretation will probably be. Examining the various methods used for interpreting the Bible around the world will help us acquire the tools necessary for developing a framework for multicultural understandings of Scripture. By seeking out a diversity of viewpoints in the search for truth, the student of the Bible can avoid "Lone-Ranger" interpretations.

The Effect of Traditional Spirituality on Biblical Interpretation

The rules of interpretation that emerge within a particular culture greatly affect the insights that can be gained in Bible study. Sometimes these viewpoints come from traditional understandings of God and humanity within a culture and provide new perspectives on the Bible. We must respect and seek to understand indigenous forms of spirituality. The effect of the spirituality of a cultural context on the way the Bible is interpreted can be observed in the context of Native America. George Tinker contends that the Native American beliefs that God is revealed in place or space, the Creator is in relationship with the created, and the created are in relationship with each other affect biblical interpretation.[21]

Tinker states that the Native American understanding of God is that "God reveals God's self in creation, in space or place and not in time."[22] This idea that God is revealed in space or place is radically different from the Western linear concept of history. Western spirituality is about periods of time and historic events. Traditional Native American as well as Asian and African spirituality are concerned with sacred experiences and holy places. It is a faith that is lived in community. Tinker explains that "personal transformation is *not* the goal of Native ethic religion; one feels called not to transcend one's natural humanity, but to live it, and live it in the context of a particular community and that community's particular geography."[23] This emphasis on the spirituality of "place" explains why many Native Americans are traumatized when they are forced to leave the land their families have lived on for centuries or watch as their burial places are desecrated. For Native peoples, "at the core of their self-understanding [is] the sense of having been created in kinship with the land."[24] These are the lands where they and their forefathers and foremothers met God.

According to Tinker, the effect on biblical interpretation of this way of thinking can be observed in Jesus' teaching on the kingdom of God. The first question asked by the Western approach to Scripture is *when*. The first question asked by the Native American approach to the Bible is *where*. The question of *when* is answered in Jesus' statement that "the time is fulfilled, and the kingdom of God has come near; repent, and believe in the good news" (Mark 1:15). The question of *where* is answered in Jesus' statement that "the kingdom of God is not coming with things that can be observed; nor will they say, 'Look, here it is!' or 'There it is!' For, in fact, the kingdom of God is among you" (Luke 17:20-21).[25] Which question we ask determines which passage is emphasized in our faith understanding. A multicultural approach would ask both questions and thereby gain a fuller understanding of the kingdom of God. As we have just seen, Jesus answered both questions.

The traditional understanding of God as Creator affects one's perspective on God's relationship with the created. Tinker writes, "Each Native American tribal community in North America had a relationship with God as Creator that was healthy and responsible long before they knew of or confessed the gospel of Jesus Christ."[26] He further states that "this relationship began with the recognition of the Other as Creator, the creative force behind all things that exist, and long predated the coming of the missionaries."[27] According to Tinker, then, Jesus' call to repentance (metanoia) in Mark 1:15 is a call to return to one's relationship with God the Creator rather than a call to change one's mind. To repent is "to return to the ideal relationship between Creator and created."[28]

Not only are we to be in relationship with the Creator, according to Tinker, we are to be in relationship with others in God's creation. The Lakota and Dakota peoples of North America pray, mitakuye oyasin ("for all my relatives").[29] Relatives include all of creation. Homer Noley writes, "Among Native American concepts, humankind is seen as a part of the continuum of spiritual existence which involves all of Creation."[30] This is represented in many Native American tribes by a circle. "The Native American concern for starting theology with Creation is a need to acknowledge the goodness and inherent worth of all of God's creatures," George Tinker explains. "We experience evil or sin as a disruption in that delicate balance, which negates the intrinsic worth of any of our relatives."[31]

The preexisting understanding of a Creator God revealed in space or place in Native American spirituality and culture allowed for fresh insights in biblical interpretation when Native Americans encountered the Bible. We must not disregard the unique perspectives found in the spirituality of various cultures, especially when one discerns common themes in many traditional spiritualities. Often particular cultural emphases will bring to light truths in Scripture otherwise unseen. These unique cultural perspectives are not only of value for persons from the particular culture; they offer new approaches and insights for all who seek biblical truth. The wholesale adaptation of cultural spirituality into Christian faith or the merging of faiths is not being encouraged here. Rather the cultural and spiritual categories that exist in settings such as Native America can help us develop tools for multicultural biblical exploration.

Infusion of Biblical Faith into Culture

As in the case of Native American spirituality, traditional spiritual understandings in a culture offer unique perspectives for biblical interpretation. Culture and the Bible may also interact in response to social circumstances. When Africans were brought to the Americas as slaves, their culture and religion, in ways similar to Native Americans, were systematically stripped away as a part of a process of transforming African people into work animals. Africans had a rich spirituality before slavery. Many of the people brought from Africa to the Americas as slaves observed Islam or traditional African indigenous religions. It should also be noted that Christianity (and before that, Judaism) was in Africa from the first century, as we saw in chapter one. So some of the enslaved and tortured African people certainly could have been Christians.[32]

While many, if not most, of the enslaved African people rejected the form of Christianity presented by the slaveholders,[33] an "invisible church" of the slaves, later evolving into the African American church tradition, emerged as a new form of faith. This fresh paradigm retained many elements from the African cultural and religious heritage and then was infused with themes and texts from the Bible that spoke to their social conditions. According to James Earl Massey, this was necessary:

> Victimized by a slavery system, "Christianized" by a skewed reading of Scripture by the Southern church, and

dominated, even after emancipation, by a racist majority culture, African Americans were faced with the necessity of constructing a world view and world of their own, a world in which their selfhood, meaning, pride, solidarity, and advancement could be nurtured.[34]

Nicholas Cooper-Lewter and Henry Mitchell, writing about the infusion of biblical faith into African culture, state that "people who grow up in the traditional Black community are spontaneously equipped with a system of core beliefs. . . . They are the bedrock attitudes that govern all deliberate behavior and relationships and also all spontaneous responses to crises."[35] This system of core beliefs "has innocently and informally, even unintentionally, built its 'summa theologica' from Bible verses both close to earlier (African and Old Testament) wisdom and known to help cheer and heal souls under siege."[36] (See Figure 1, page 78.)

Many African people enslaved in America, often unable to read English Bibles, memorized verses that spoke words of hope and liberation to their life experience. In this setting, where there had been a methodical attempt to strip people of their culture (and humanity) through physical, emotional, and spiritual terrorism, these Bible verses and related biblical themes helped shape the culture of many Africans in America and enabled generations to survive the horrors of slavery, segregation, racism, poverty, and other attempts at dehumanization. These Bible verses soon became core beliefs that were reinforced by a strong oral tradition of Bible stories that told of people in settings similar to those of the enslaved Africans in America who struggled for liberation (including the Exodus, Old Testament characters, and Jesus).

This spiritual method of survival for Africans who were captured and enslaved in a strange land remains a potent faith for people today. Nicholas Cooper-Lewter, concerned that some of the descendants of enslaved Africans may have lost the power of these core beliefs, writes:

The slaves who became African Americans used to know the necessity of counteracting the niggerizing effects of living in a hostile environment. That is why they would slip away at night to praise a God of change and protest a life of bondage.[37]

Hebrew culture, like African American Christianity, was also an infusion of biblical faith and culture. The Decalogue (Ten Commandments) and the Exodus experience defined Hebrew culture; for the Hebrews, faith and culture were

---

Figure 1: Ten Core Beliefs of "Soul Theology"*

The providence of God
"And we know that God works in everything for good."
(Romans 8:28)

The justice of God
"For whatsoever a man soweth, that shall he also reap."
(Galatians 6:7)

The majesty and omnipotence of God
"Hallelujah: for the Lord God omnipotent reigneth!"
(Revelation 19:6)

The omniscience of God
"Your Father knoweth what things ye have need of,
before ye ask." (Matthew 6:8)

The goodness of God and creation
"And God saw every thing that He had made, and, behold, it
was very good." (Genesis 1:31)

The grace of God
"For by grace ye are saved [and acceptable] through faith."
(Ephesians 2:8)

The equality of persons
"There is neither Jew nor Greek, there is neither bond nor
free, there is neither male nor female; for ye are all one in
Christ Jesus." (Galatians 3:28)

The uniqueness of persons: identity
"Stir up the gift of God which is in thee." (2 Timothy 1:6)

The family of God and humanity
"Have we not all one Father?" (Malachi 2:10)

The perseverance of persons
"And let us not be weary in well doing: for in due season
we shall reap, if we faint not." (Galatians 6:9)

*From *Soul Theology: The Heart of American Black Culture*
by Nicholas Cooper-Lewter and Henry H. Mitchell.

often difficult to distinguish. The integration of faith and culture has the potential for good and for harm. If the faith remains a source of healing, liberation, and empowerment, then the culture is healthy. But if the faith becomes dysfunctional, legalistic, and stifling, then the culture will be sick and oppressive.

Integrating Diverse Perspectives for Interpretation

While the search for various rules of interpretation and perspectives gained by indigenous spirituality and social circumstances in cultures can be exhilarating, it may also be overwhelming. The challenge is to integrate these various viewpoints in a way that breathes life into the biblical texts and yet avoids creating token interpretations or politically correct cultural curiosities. Education expert James A. Banks has developed a model for creating a multicultural educational curriculum called "the transformation approach for integrating of ethnic content."[38] This method "changes the basic assumptions of the curriculum and enables students to view concepts, issues, themes, and problems from several ethnic perspectives and points of view."[39]

Banks' model is very effective in facilitating the study of historical events from a variety of perspectives. An event is examined from the outlook of everyone involved. This is done so that history is told not only by those in power who typically write histories but also by the powerless and the conquered. Often history books do not acknowledge the "histories." For example, an event such as the Vietnam War could be studied from the vantage point of South Vietnam, North Vietnam, the United States, China, the Soviet Union, Laos, Cambodia, Thailand, Europe, the United Nations, the Hmong people, the elite Vietnamese, the poor Vietnamese, soldiers, civilians, U.S. war protesters, prisoners of war, family members of soldiers who were killed, and so on. By examining the Vietnam War from different perspectives, one gains a better sense of the true history (or histories) of that event.

In using the "transformation approach" to study events in the Bible, we would try to look at the Exodus event from the perspective of not only the Hebrews but also the Egyptians and the Canaanites. Jesus' death and resurrection would include, in addition to the views of the twelve disciples, those of Mary Magdalene, Mary the mother of Jesus, Pilate, Herod, the Jewish leaders, the masses who followed Jesus, and others. Each of these events could also be examined from the viewpoint of contemporary peoples. Sometimes it helps to consider, for example, how the Exodus or the death and resurrection of Jesus are understood today by Native Americans, Asians, African Americans, Latinas/os, American Whites, Jews, Arabs, Pacific Islanders, Europeans, Russians, and others. While pragmatic considerations may tell us that this is not always feasible, neither should we take the easy way out of "Lone-Ranger" Bible study. Serious biblical interpretation requires that we view the text through multiple lenses.

Banks' transformation model can also be used to examine a passage of Scripture from several cultural perspectives to gain a more complete understanding. Using the four examples detailed above, let us illustrate this process by examining a very familiar, and often memorized, Bible verse—John 3:16. This verse, in the King James Version, says, "For God so loved the world, that he gave his only begotten Son, that whosoever believeth in him should not perish, but have everlasting life." This passage has traditionally been interpreted as a promise of salvation for people who place their faith in Jesus Christ. (See Figure 2, page 81.)

The traditional interpretation of this verse is enhanced by Native American spirituality, which adds that God's love was for a place, "the world," and it is eternal, not bound by time and history. It also says that Jesus came as an expression of God's love for all of creation, not only humans. Therefore we should love and care for all of God's creation. The perspective coming from traditional African American Christianity informs us that this verse confirms that God and creation are good. So even if people tell us we are worthless and it seems that God does not care, Jesus' coming informs us that we are loved by a good God. It also affirms that while there is a life beyond this one, God sent Jesus as an expression of God's love and sustaining power for life on this earth. The experience of Latin American women, when applied to this text, tells us that God's love for us is greater than that of a mother at the birth of her first child. Latinas also remind us that the world that Jesus came into is the real world of suffering and of joy. It is a world where most people are poor and need to hear about this God of love who is interested in overcoming death with life. The Asian context reminds us that God's love has always been extended to all people in the world, including those of other religious faiths. It would also proclaim that, just like God became flesh in Jesus to demonstrate love, so we must take the love message of the Bible and clothe it in flesh.

This familiar verse all at once takes on broader and richer meanings because of the addition of other voices to the dialogue. As we have discovered, when cultural perspectives

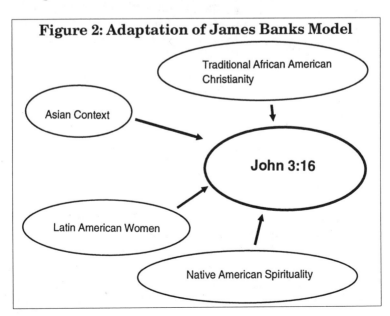

Figure 2: Adaptation of James Banks Model

Traditional African American Christianity

Asian Context

John 3:16

Latin American Women

Native American Spirituality

intersect with the text, biblical interpretation comes alive. A multicultural framework for interpretation, such as the Banks model, provides us with full and fresh understandings of the truth contained in the Bible. Of course, even multicultural approaches must be subject to critique. Also, there will be times when a focused approach is needed for communities that face daily realities that pertain uniquely to their context. While this is necessary, we must not lose sight of the fact that multiple cultural viewpoints offer engaging insights and expose seldom-observed nuances in the Scriptures that enrich all of us.

Using Elements of Culture for Communicating Biblical Truths

Not only is an understanding of culture helpful for interpretation; it is essential for communicating the truths of the Bible. Whether we are accepting Jesus' challenge to reach out to "the least of these" (Matthew 25:31-46), to "go into all the world and proclaim the good news to the whole creation" (Mark 16:15), to "make disciples of all nations" (Matthew 28:19), or to be witnesses "to the ends of the earth" (Acts 1:8), a knowledge of various cultural perspectives is necessary. This can be achieved by using what Kwok Pui Lan calls "dialogical imagination,"[40] where the effort is to take the biblical text and a people's history and culture and "bring the two in dialogue with one another."[41] The message of the Bible is best communicated when cultural understandings and traditions are employed. A "dialogical imagination" is required to choose the most effective images, stories, and concepts from a culture for bringing the Bible to life.

Jesus often used elements of the culture of those to whom he was ministering when communicating the gospel. He found that agricultural images were effective for teaching people in farming communities and aquatic images worked well for communicating to people in seashore villages. Perhaps the best example of a time when Jesus engaged in "dialogical imagination" was when he encountered a woman from Samaria (John 4:4-42). He used his understanding of Samaritan culture and religious beliefs to communicate his message.[42] An understanding of Samaritan life was critical for Jesus' ministry to be effective because of the intense animosity between the Jews and the Samaritans during the first century. When the Israelites were taken into captivity, left behind in the region of Samaria were poor and working-class Hebrews who intermingled with their captors. When the captives returned to Palestine, they sought an advantage through the claim that the Hebrews living in Samaria had intermarried with the colonizers. Not unlike oppressed peoples in other eras, the people of Samaria had their own story. They claimed that they were the descendants of the patriarch Joseph and his African wife, whose offspring had become the half-tribes of Ephraim and Manasseh. A rivalry between the returning captives (Jews) and the working-class Hebrews (Samaritans) developed.[43]

By the first century, this hatred between the Jews and the Samaritans was extremely intense. Sometime during the early years of the first century, Samaritan revolutionaries scattered human bones in the sanctuary of the Temple in Jerusalem during the Passover Feast as an act of protest and rebellion.[44] So extreme was the prejudice against Samaritans that one rabbi of the time wrote, "He that eats the bread of the Samaritans is like one that eats the flesh of swine." It was also a common belief that Samaritan women began their menstrual cycle at birth. Therefore the ritual purity of Samaritans was always suspect and the kosher-conscious Jew avoided contact.[45]

Into this environment of mistrust and segregation, Jesus arrived in Samaria well prepared for his encounter with this woman. Jesus must have studied the faith and culture of the Samaritans before making the journey because he knew that the Samaritans were seeking a Messiah (the *Taheb)* who would restore belief and reveal truth.[46] When Jesus told the woman that he knew she had previously been married five times and the man with whom she was now living was not her husband, he was not just saying something about her; he was disclosing something about himself. By revealing the truth about the woman, Jesus unveiled the truth about his mission. He was informing her that he was the Revealer, the *Taheb,* the Messiah. She immediately changed the direction of the conversation and began to talk about faith.

Jesus' understanding and use of Samaritan cultural beliefs enabled him to communicate the gospel to this woman from Samaria. The Samaritan woman confirmed this when she said to the people in her village, "Come, see a man who told me all that I ever did. Can this be the Christ?" (John 4:29, RSV). The woman took the message of Jesus, couched in her cultural framework, back to her village and became the first evangelist of the Christian era. Had Jesus attempted to use phrases and images from his Jewish setting, he would probably not have had much success, particularly considering the relationship between the Samaritans and the Jews. The communication of the gospel in more recent times has been hindered because the concepts from the cultures where Christian faith was shared were not used. Also the relationship that existed between the groups of peoples, one dominating the other, has been an impediment. This has too often been the case when missionaries from Europe and the United States have gone to countries and cultures that have a negative view of them due to past or present political and economic domination.

The apostles of Jesus also needed to communicate the gospel in a wide variety of cultural settings. The book of Acts is filled with examples. The apostle Paul's use of "dialogical imagination" can be examined because of the Bible's extensive reporting on his travels and inclusion of many of his letters. Paul spent most of his life in ministry in an environment very different from the Jewish setting of Jesus and most of the disciples. He was effective among the Gentiles because he was "at home in the dreams and hungers, psychological and political, the mysteries and mythologies, of the Hellenistic world."[47] A good example of Paul's ministry in other cultures is found in his visit to Athens (Acts 17:16-34). This episode illustrates Paul's approach to preaching in a setting outside of his Jewish cultural milieu.

Athens was the home of a well-known university, the cultural seat of Europe, and the "world's intellectual mecca."[48] Paul, upon his arrival in Athens, began preaching in the Jewish synagogue, as was his usual strategy for ministry. But he took a new approach by also speaking in the marketplace. Some scholars surmise that this was the same marketplace where Socrates debated.[49] Paul's preaching in the marketplace earned him an invitation to speak before the Stoic and Epicurean philosophers of Athens. Paul started his message by noting that the people of Athens were very religious. He referred to an altar to the "unknown god" (Acts 17:23) that he had seen upon his arrival in the city and quoted from Greek poets (17:28). Paul, speaking to these philosophers, used their arguments and beliefs to challenge them to search further for the truth.[50] Paul believed that if they would take their search for truth further, it would lead them to the God who raised Jesus from the dead. Paul, like Jesus with the woman from Samaria, used elements of the culture that would strengthen his ability to communicate the gospel message. By using concepts and illustrations that were well known in the setting where he was preaching, Paul was able to help ease the difficulty in sharing the message of a God that could be known.

The ministry of Paul to the Gentiles becomes even more intriguing from our perspective today if we notice that Paul, an Asian-born, Afro-Asiatic Jew[51] who looked like an Egyptian (Acts 21:38), used European culture to bring the gospel to Europe. Using the terminology of the 1990s, Paul, a person of color, brought the message of Jesus Christ to the white world. Even if we examine Paul's ministry only in its historical context, it is interesting to note that he, a member of a colonized Jewish ethnic minority, took the message of Jesus to the Roman Empire through the use of concepts familiar to the Greeks and Romans.

A Cultural Old Testament?

Within many cultures, if not every culture, there are religious practices or traditional stories that are useful for presenting the Christian gospel. Perhaps these traditions have been placed there and nurtured by God, down through the centuries, in preparation for the time when the gospel of Jesus Christ would be presented.[52] Steve Charleston builds a case for an "Old Testament of Native America."[53] Regarding spirituality of Native American people, Charleston writes:

> They have their own original covenant relationship with the Creator and their own original understanding of God prior to the birth of Christ. It is a Tradition that has evolved over centuries. It tells of the active, living, revealing presence of God in relation to Native People through generations of Native life and experience. It asserts that God was not an absentee landlord for North America. God was here, on this continent among this people, in covenant, in relation, in life. Like Israel itself, Native America proclaims that God is a God of all times and of all places and of all peoples.[54]

George Tinker warns that when the Hebrew Bible is imposed on Native Americans, it has two "dysfunctional" effects:

> First, it functions to proscribe (explicitly or implicitly) the validity of Native American traditions. Second, it inherently prescribes replacing one's own history with someone else's history as a prerequisite for conversion.[55]

Steve Charleston contends that the biblical interpreter who is from a setting with a traditional form of spirituality in the culture needs to include the Hebrew Bible while working with that traditional spirituality and the New Testament in developing understandings of God.[56] The Hebrew Bible is important for understanding the history and spirituality of the people into which Jesus of Nazareth was born. Of course, at the center of the faith is Jesus Christ. This helps maintain the orthodoxy of the results. "There was much in the memory of Israel that Jesus confirmed; there was also a great deal that he sought to correct. The same applies to the Old Testament memory of Native America. There is much that the Christ confirms and much that stands corrected," states Charleston.[57]

Ancient cultural traditions, the "old testament" of these cultures, can pave the way for the New Testament gospel of Jesus Christ. While it may be difficult for some, Charleston asserts that "as Christians, we're going to have to make some elbow room at the table for other 'old testaments.' Not only from Native America, but from Africa, Asia, and Latin America as well."[58] These "cultural keys for evangelism,"[59] when discovered, greatly facilitate the proclamation of the gospel. The following stories from two different cultural settings, worlds apart, demonstrate the ways in which cultural traditions can be used for creating an understanding of biblical truths.

Aboriginal—Australia

It would be easy to forget about the historical realities and indigenous cultures "down under" in Australia. The aboriginal historical and cultural experience has been strikingly similar to that of indigenous peoples in the Americas. Many of the aboriginal Christian leaders have found their traditional spirituality to be helpful in understanding biblical themes. Djiniyini Gondarra, an Australian aboriginal theologian and pastor, tells the ancient religious story of Djankawu, a great spirit and the father-mother figure for aboriginal people:

> They say that in the dreamtimes Djankawu lived in the flesh with our people. He shared with them the sacred knowledge of ceremonies, songs, dances, and the sacred stories about how things began to form in the universe and in the Earth. He gave the tribes names, a kinship system, and taught them many things. He revealed himself to men as one of them. To the women she revealed herself as a mother figure.[60]

The story of Djankawu demonstrates that the aboriginal people of Australia already understand the concept of incarnation in their traditional spirituality. While the idea of Jesus Christ as God coming to earth in the flesh has been a stumbling block for the gospel in many settings, it is a cultural key in the aboriginal context. Deacon Boniface, a Catholic leader and Australian aboriginal, states, "When I read the gospels, I read them as an aboriginal. There are many things in the gospel that make me happy to be an aboriginal, because I think we have a good start. We find it easy to see in Christ the great dreaming figure . . ."[61]

Ojibwe—Native America

The second story comes from the research of Doug LaFriniere, an Ojibwe Christian minister and historian of Native American Christianity. He has done extensive study on indigenous Native American Christian leadership and their use of traditional stories in evangelism. In his research, LaFriniere discovered the Ojibwe "Legend of the Vine," a story told by the elders to initiates to describe the reason for Medicine religion. He tells it this way:

> There was a vine in Ojibwe land that grew all the way to heaven. Spirits would descend and ascend daily on the vine to come and see how the Ojibwe people were doing. Every day they were happy, full of joy, had much peace, there was much game, there was no sickness, and there were no long sleeps. They were a happy people. But the Creator had told them that they should never climb this vine, for if they climbed the vine something terrible and tragic would happen to them. So they never climbed the vine.
>
> One young fellow, who became very well acquainted with one of the spirits who came to visit, asked if he could climb the vine. The spirit said he could climb the vine and see what heaven was like. So the young man climbed the vine.
>
> The grandmother of the young man became distraught and missed him. One morning she decided that she too would climb the vine, except that she did not have permis-

sion from anyone to climb the vine. She got her house in order and decided to climb the vine.

As she was climbing the vine, the people were looking around for her and looked up and saw her climbing the vine. The people cried out, "Old lady, old lady, come down. Don't climb the vine. The Creator has told us that some tragedy will befall us if we climb the vine." She continued climbing the vine until she reached the star that the vine was wrapped around. When she stepped out onto the star the vine broke and down she and the vine came. The people gathered around her and became angry with her. They called her derogatory names and kicked dirt on her. From that day forward the peace and joy went out of the hearts of the Ojibwe people. Famine overtook them, the game left, and the people were distressed.

One day some spirits came to the Ojibwe people and asked, "Is there anything we can do to help you?" The people said, "Yes, please reconnect the vine so that we can have a relationship again with our Creator." The spirits said, "We cannot reconnect the vine. The vine can never be reconnected again. You will have to suffer."[62]

When Doug LaFriniere presents the gospel in Ojibwe settings, he tells his listeners that the Creator God has reconnected the vine through Jesus Christ. He uses as his text John 15:1, where Jesus said, "I am the true vine." By employing this story from the "old testament" of the Ojibwe people, LaFriniere utilizes the culture, like Jesus did with the Samaritan woman, to proclaim the message.

With the increased interaction of the cultures in our world, we stand on the threshold of exciting new insights in our search for truth. Despite the challenge of comprehending the truth contained in the Bible from a variety of cultural perspectives, and the further difficulty of integrating these diverse understandings, we must begin to take steps, even though they may be small, in this direction. New avenues of biblical understanding await us as we become more fluent in the values and traditions of other cultures. Rather than isolating ourselves because of a fear of change, a need for domination, or a self-centered ethnocentrism, we can rejoice in the thought that our understanding of God becomes clearer each time we learn from the contributions of our sisters and brothers in the human family.

Questions for Discussion

1. How has our understanding of the Bible been affected by our culture and life circumstances? Describe how your own personal perspective has been affected.

2. Are any of the rules for interpretation suggested by Elsa Tamez and Stanley Samartha relevant to your life and understanding of faith? In what ways?

3. Give some examples of how Native American spirituality affects biblical interpretation.

4. Have you ever needed a "Soul Theology" when faced with difficult circumstances? Share some illustrations.

5. How can Christians be united when different rules of biblical interpretation are being applied? What are your suggestions for developing shared understandings?

6. Using the James Banks model, select a Bible passage or theological concept and look at it from as many perspectives as possible. What new insights have you gained?

7. Identify and critique the ways that Jesus and the apostles used culture in sharing the Good News.

8. How do you feel about using elements of culture for communicating biblical truths? Who determines which stories and values to use?

9. Is the concept of a "cultural old testament" an appropriate way for people to approach faith? Why or why not?

10. What in chapter three will be most helpful for you as you read the Bible and share your faith with others?

Chapter Four

The Source of Liberation and Empowerment

Our faith is richer because of the varied cultural perspectives of people from around the world. These outlooks have offered us new insights on truth while enhancing the multiculturalism of the Bible itself. Yet, deeply imbedded in these convictions, from widely differing cultural settings, has been a cry for liberation. In the 1940s Howard Thurman wrote in his book, *Jesus and the Disinherited:* "The masses of [people] live with their backs constantly against the wall. They are the poor, the disinherited, the dispossessed." Then he asked, "What does our religion say to them?"[1] That question still haunts us. In this age of diversity—when a majority of the world's people are poor, feel oppressed, and experience prejudice based on nationality, race, culture, gender, skin color, social status, or religion—we must take up again a most urgent question, "Is faith in God liberating?" Clearly, many Third-World theologians have expressed the view that most of the people in our world do not have the time or the luxury to embrace a faith that does not help set them free in a comprehensive sense.

Those of us who believe in the God of Abraham, Sarah, Jacob, Moses, Jesus, Mary Magdalene, Peter, Apollos, Phoebe, Paul, and Priscilla must ask ourselves afresh if our biblical faith is truly liberating. Does the Bible offer Good News? Will this faith empower us personally to triumph over life's daily struggles? Can this faith lead to liberation and

justice at a societal and structural level? Is the Bible a source
of liberation and empowerment for people, cultures, and
societies? If we cannot answer these questions with a strong
and resounding yes, then the Bible, and our faith, has little
to offer our world in this age of diversity.

We have already had several occasions to show that the
Bible has been used as a tool for oppression. Colonial expansion, slavery, crusades, holocaust, segregation, sexism,
apartheid, classism, cultural genocide, racial prejudice, and
a host of other forms of injustice have been supported by a
selective use of Bible verses. "The gospel was not liberating
for Indian people but was a form of bondage," George Tinker
states. "It's not the gospel that's not liberating, though; it's
the proclamation of the gospel that puts Indians in bondage."[2] Many people throughout the world echo his sentiments. Conquest, domination, and mission have been
intertwined into a "theology of domination."[3] Misuse of the
Bible to endorse the domination of one group over another
has caused many to see the Bible as anything but a source of
liberation. Rather, too often, Christianity is viewed as the
religion of the rich and powerful and the Bible as the cornerstone undergirding systems of exploitation.

Yet concurrently, throughout history, people have been
empowered by a liberating biblical faith that instilled in
them the resolve to survive poverty, sexism, racism, and
many other injustices. Still today, people who feel that they
do not have a voice cry out in many different languages for a
faith that liberates. These cries for freedom are being expressed by Christians in as many ways as there are places of
oppression: Latin American liberation theology, black liberation theology, feminist theology, womanist theology, *minjung*
theology, Caribbean emancipation theology, American Indian
theology of place, *mujerista* theology, Asian liberation of
theology, aboriginal liberation theology, and on and on. In this
context of struggle, biblical interpretation becomes "both a
response to the call of the gospel and the cry of the people,
which are both really the same."[4]

Many, influenced by dominant cultures around the world, have attempted to undermine or de-Christianize these expressions of faith by oppressed peoples. Because of the use by some of a Marxist social analysis, it has even been implied that an emphasis on liberation in one's faith is communist-inspired. Orlando Costas gave a compelling response to this insinuation when he wrote, "It is an undeniable fact that liberation theology is the most formidable Christian response to the Marxist critique of religion. Indeed, it has been demonstrated that religion does not have to be an opium; it can be a force for positive revolutionary change."[5]

Liberation can be defined by using Elsa Tamez's description of a life that is liberated. It involves "an equitable distribution of possessions and power and, with it, the elimination of poverty; the presence of God; just government; humanization; peace; life; freedom; truth; joy."[6] In other words, a life where we stand before God and each other free to experience the fullness of all that God created us to be. All around the world, in various cultural settings, people are seeking a faith that will set them free from the external circumstances and the internal responses that keep them from experiencing life as God meant it to be. Whether it be from government repression or personal depression, people are crying out for liberation. Many are discovering in the Bible the source for experiencing liberation and empowerment in all realms of their lives—political, economic, social, and spiritual!

The Bible's Message of Liberation

Liberation is a central message in the biblical proclamation. More and more people are rediscovering this fact. They are coming to the conclusion that the message of liberation is significant in the Bible by examining the two foundational understandings of God in the Bible—the God "who led Israel out of Egypt and who raised Jesus Christ from the dead."[7] As we shall see, in the Exodus event and in the life, death, and resurrection of Jesus, it is demonstrated that the God of the

Bible is indeed, fundamentally, the God of freedom and empowerment.

The Exodus Event

Central to the faith understanding of the Hebrews was the Exodus event, when God led them out of the bondage of slavery in Egypt (Exodus 1–15). The author of Exodus told the story in great detail: the Hebrews suffered and cried out for help; Moses was called by God to take leadership in negotiating for the Hebrew's freedom; Pharaoh remained stubborn; God intervened in miraculous ways to liberate the Hebrews from slavery. Each generation retold the story, and it is recorded in various forms throughout the Hebrew Bible. The Exodus story became Israel's creed and was stated in capsulized form: "We were Pharaoh's slaves in Egypt, but the Lord brought us out of Egypt with a mighty hand" (Deuteronomy 6:21).

At the very core of the faith of the Hebrew people and their understanding of this God they followed was an act of liberation. Even God's name was revealed in the context of the liberation story of the Hebrew people. The name Yahweh, "I AM WHO I AM," was revealed to Moses as a confirmation that God was going to liberate the Hebrews from slavery (Exodus 3:13-15).[8] This revealed name of God and the circumstances of that revelation speak of One who is not only a God of the heavens but "is also the God of justice and compassion who is a very helpful presence in time of oppression and trouble."[9]

The Hebrew view of God was that the Lord desired freedom not slavery, liberation not oppression, hope not despair. This God would respond to cries for help and provide a way of escape. Elsa Tamez sums up this Exodus understanding of God (Yahweh) when she writes:

> Yahweh concretizes in Himself the justice and love that are experienced in the course of history. And since justice and love cannot become concrete realities except in a society where there is no oppression, Yahweh comes on the scene at every moment in solidarity with the oppressed,

for the purpose of assuring the concrete realization of love and removal of oppressors.[10]

The story of the Exodus was the foundational faith story of the Hebrews, who later became the ancient nation of Israel. It informed them of who they were and who this God was they followed. The Exodus story was "the clue to who God is and how he acts" and "the model for how his people should seek justice in society as the only appropriate response to the liberation they had experienced."[11] The retelling of the Exodus story later became a part of the liturgy of ancient Israel and took on the role of a national epic. This liturgy reached its climax every year in the Feast of the Passover.

The liberative spirit of the Exodus event found concrete form in the year of jubilee (Leviticus 25; see also Luke 4:16-20). It was to be a time when all debts were forgiven and everyone could have a fresh start. The author of Leviticus described the jubilee year as follows:

> You shall count off seven weeks of years, seven times seven years, so that the period of seven weeks of years gives forty-nine years. Then you shall have the trumpet sounded loud; on the tenth day of the seventh month—on the day of atonement—you shall have the trumpet sounded throughout all your land. And you shall hallow the fiftieth year and you shall proclaim liberty throughout the land to all its inhabitants. It shall be a jubilee for you: you shall return, every one of you, to your property and everyone of you to your family (Leviticus 25:8-10).

The twenty-fifth chapter of Leviticus ends with a reminder from God that the Hebrews "are my servants whom I brought out from the land of Egypt" (v. 55).

Although it seems that the jubilee year was never practiced as outlined, the intent was to make liberation a vital part of Israel's system of government. Freedom was to be more than rhetoric. It needed an action component. It needed to be integrated into the political system and the culture.[12] The jubilee informs us that not only is it God's will that we create a society where freedom is guaranteed but that it is humanly possible to do so. Unfortunately, the Israelites decided to relegate the Exodus experience to a theological statement without any practical applications. They wanted to worship the God of their liberation but not develop a society that followed the liberating principles of God.[13]

The proclamation of God as liberator, the God of the Exodus and the jubilee, found renewed vigor with many of the prophets in the Bible. Isaiah is a prime example when he writes:

> The Spirit of the Lord GOD is upon me, because the LORD has anointed me; he has sent me to bring good news to the oppressed, to bind up the brokenhearted, to proclaim liberty to the captives, and release to the prisoners; to proclaim the year of the LORD's favor, and the day of vengeance of our God; to comfort all who mourn (Isaiah 61:1-2).

Isaiah was speaking as a visionary at a time when the Israelites were seeking to rebuild their community.[14] He was reminding them that their hope for community was rooted in this God of liberation who was going to set them free and then call on them to set others free. Isaiah firmly believed in "God's commitment to justice and concern for the poor and suffering" and the need to empower the people to "confess their faith in God by showing that same commitment and concern."[15]

The God of the Hebrews was a God of liberation and empowerment. The act of God's self-revelation in the Exodus event demonstrated and later symbolized this truth. The jubilee year was placed in the law of the new nation as a constitutional guarantee that the Hebrew people would live according to this understanding of the God they worshiped and followed. When the Hebrews (or the ancient nation of Israel) did not follow the way of the God of the Exodus, the prophets challenged them to return to the foundation of their faith.

The Exodus continues to be a powerful story today for those seeking freedom from bondage. It is a reminder that God works in human history through people. Moses was sent by God to the Hebrew people to convince them that they needed to leave Egypt to be free. Although they were crying out "on account of their taskmasters" (Exodus 3:7), they had not organized an escape. Perhaps after generations of slavery, "the Hebrews had developed the mentality of slaves."[16] Cyris H. S. Moon believes that the Exodus story instructs us that God is not "the sole actor in the movement for liberation. Rather, humanity is invited to act as a partner with God." He adds that "if oppressed people are to obtain liberation, they must—with God's aid—confront the pharaohs of the world . . ."[17] The Exodus story and the jubilee laws have inspired people to believe that God desires their freedom and that a just society is possible. A belief in this God of liberation has motivated countless people to stand up to the pharaohs of their societies. Many have become the Moses of their time and place in history, saying, "Let my people go!"

Jesus As the Incarnation of the Jubilee

Jesus was raised in the tradition of the Exodus and the prophets. The ministry and message of Jesus extended "the experience of Exodus to the whole world. In Jesus, God is revealed as the liberator not only of Israel, but of all humankind."[18] His opening sermon text comes from the section of Isaiah 61 that sought to reinspire the spirit of the Exodus and the jubilee. The words of Jesus, in his inaugural sermon at Nazareth, spoke of his understanding that the Good News of God was liberation. He indicated that he was intent on implementing this in his ministry:

The Spirit of the Lord is upon me,
    because he has anointed me
        to bring good news to the poor.
He has sent me to proclaim
release to the captives
    and recovery of sight to the blind,
        to let the oppressed go free,
to proclaim the year of the Lord's favor. . . .

Today this scripture has been fulfilled in your hearing
(Luke 4:18-19,21).

By quoting Isaiah 61, Jesus declared in his inaugural
sermon at Nazareth that his ministry was seeking to reintroduce the spirit of the jubilee. The reign of God (that is, the
kingdom of God) that Jesus proclaimed throughout his ministry would dawn when the spirit of the jubilee was written
on people's hearts. This God of Jesus was a God of freedom
who desired that all people live a liberated life.

Jesus understood the need for liberation firsthand in his
human experience. God took on flesh in an environment of
oppression—Jesus was a Jew living under the domination of
colonial Rome. Because Jesus was not a Roman citizen, "if a
Roman soldier pushed Jesus into a ditch, he could not appeal
to Caesar; he would be just another Jew in the ditch."[19] Jesus
had to live daily in a setting that did not value or understand
his cultural background. In addition to the daily burden of
being a Jew in colonial Rome, Jesus was born under unusual
circumstances, and many considered his birth illegitimate.
Shortly after his birth, Jesus and his family fled to Egypt as
Palestinian refugees. He grew up in a working-class family
and during his ministry often slept outside with "nowhere to
lay his head" (Matthew 8:20). Jesus experienced the unre-
strained brutality of Pilate's law enforcement officers when
he was arrested and they "spit on him, and took the staff and
struck him on the head again and again" (Matthew 27:30,
NIV). Jesus' social experience was that of one who needed
liberation. The life of Jesus of Nazareth parallels that of
many people of color and others who experience life as cultural or racial outsiders today.

In the midst of these circumstances, Jesus reached out in
solidarity to others and demonstrated that the God he
preached about and prayed to was a liberator. Unlike the
Israelites, Jesus did not just proclaim a theological statement
on liberation; he lived it. When John the Baptist sent his
followers to discover if Jesus was the one they were looking
for, Jesus told the messengers:

Go and tell John what you have seen and heard: the blind receive their sight, the lame walk, the lepers are cleansed, the deaf hear, the dead are raised, the poor have good news brought to them (Luke 7:22; see also Matthew 11:4-5).

For Jesus, liberation was active. It was more than a concept. It was experienced in dramatic ways. It could be observed. People who were enslaved physically, emotionally, economically, spiritually, and politically were being set free by Jesus in the name of this God of the Exodus and the jubilee. Jesus was the incarnation, the fulfillment, of the jubilee (Luke 4:21).

Jesus sought out the people in society who seemed to "lack" something, people who were sick, poor, children, sinners, mentally disturbed, demon possessed, or the like.[20] In fact, it appears from reading the Gospels that Jesus felt compelled to reach out to the people with the greatest needs[21]—a rare ministry trait in his day and in our day. His ministry of liberation impacted those most in need of freedom. Jesus crossed the boundaries placed by society that defined with whom he should interact. The Gospels give us account after account of Jesus ministering to people society had determined to be outcasts. While the biblical writers did not always include their names, certainly Jesus knew them. The following are brief summaries of but a few examples from Jesus' daily work of liberating individuals who felt powerless:

There was a blind man named Bartimaeus whom everyone told to be quiet when he called out for help. Jesus gave Bartimaeus back his dignity and his sight (see Mark 10:46-52).

There was a woman who had been caught in adultery, and the religious leaders were ready to stone her to death. Jesus gave those men a short lecture on hypocrisy, and they all dropped their stones and left. Then he told the woman to go and live for God (see John 8:3-11).

There was a corrupt little tax collector named Zacchaeus whom no one liked. Jesus invited himself over to Zacchaeus' home for dinner, and Zacchaeus gave up thievery and chose charity (see Luke 19:1-10).

There was a woman named Mary Magdalene who was believed to be evil. Jesus delivered her spirit from that which possessed her, and she later became the first witness to Jesus' resurrection (see Luke 8:2; John 20:11-18).

There was a naked man called Legion who lived in the graveyard. Everyone was afraid of him. Jesus clothed him in his right mind and sent him home (see Mark 5:1-20).

There were countless others isolated by life's circumstances to whom Jesus intentionally reached out so that they might be set free. As Virginia Fabella writes, "He showed us that we cannot work toward our true humanity, our true liberation, unless we seek the true humanity, the true liberation, of all."[22] Each time Jesus crossed society's imposed boundaries and liberated a powerless individual, he demonstrated the larger need for social change in society. In describing the final judgment during his last message to his disciples before his death, Jesus said that as followers of God they could determine the authenticity of their faith by examining their actions on behalf of others:

> For I was hungry and you gave me food, I was thirsty and you gave me something to drink, I was a stranger and you welcomed me, I was naked and you gave me clothing, I was sick and you took care of me, I was in prison and you visited me. . . . Truly I tell you, just as you did it to one of the least of these who are members of my family, you did it to me . . . (Matthew 25:35-36,40).

If their faith was in this God of freedom, then they would exhibit a lifestyle of liberation.[23] Followers of Jesus are also called to incarnate the jubilee. Jesus' words in Matthew 25 demonstrate that the message of liberation from his first sermon (recorded in Luke 4) remained a consistent and central theme.[24]

For the Hebrews, the act of the Exodus from Egypt was a defining moment revealing the identity of the God whom they served. It was during the Passover celebration of the Exodus that the death and resurrection of Jesus became, for his followers, the moment that defined the identity of the God that Jesus had been telling them about. The Resurrection was the ultimate act of liberation and empowerment. It symbolized God's victory over death, sin, and oppression. The resurrection of Jesus demonstrated that God's power to liberate was stronger than any power of oppression, even crucifixion. The Resurrection validated Jesus' message that God is a liberator, and it served as "a symbol of the triumph of justice for the human community."[25]

In reference to the Exodus, Elsa Tamez stated that God's revelation comes in concrete ways. She reaffirmed this fact when writing about Jesus: "The Good News takes a very concrete form. The central message is this: the situation cannot continue as it is; impoverishment and exploitation are not God's will; but now there is hope, resurrection, life, change. The reign of God, which is the reign of justice, is at hand."[26] The Exodus, the jubilee, the prophets, the message and life of Jesus, and the Resurrection all point to the preeminent position that liberation and empowerment take in the Bible's description of God.

Liberating the Bible

If the central message of the Bible is that God is a God of liberation, then why is this understanding not more widespread? Why do we hear that Christianity is the "white man's religion"? Because the Bible has been used as a tool for oppressing people, for many the Bible itself may need to be liberated. After centuries of interpretation with a nearly exclusive Western European flavor and repeated misuse for political domination, the need for a liberation of biblical interpretation is apparent in many settings. Tissa Balasuriya believes that for Christian faith to reach its potential in an Asian context, it must be liberated from Western theological forms. He calls for a "liberation of theology in Asia." Theology, according to Balasuriya, needs to be liberated from being "culture-bound," "church-centered," "male clerical," "capitalistic," "lacking in socio-economic analysis," and "absent of an action-orientation."[27] While Balasuriya's analysis addresses the discipline of theology in an Asian milieu, it is also applicable to biblical interpretation in many cultural settings.

Biblical interpretation has certainly been "culture-bound." Balasuriya describes the effect in the Asian context: "The combination of the 'sacred' duty of civilizing, baptizing, and saving the pagans with the military, economic, political, and cultural domination by Europe over our countries has been disastrous for Christianity itself."[28] George Tinker, speaking of a similar effect in the Native American context, adds that missionaries often "confused their spiritual proclamation of the gospel of Jesus Christ with the imposition of new and strange cultural models for daily life . . . the distinction between the gospel and Euroamerican culture was far less clear."[29] The use of the Bible in creating oppressive structures and destroying cultures is a sad and tragic legacy for Christian faith. The message of the Bible needs to be liberated from the shackles of a mentality of monocultural superiority if it is to be heard clearly. This means that we must acknowledge that all biblical interpretation is influenced by culture and therefore open to challenge and refinement. When the Bible is cast in the mold of the dominant culture, those outside that sphere are asked either to assimilate (thereby denying their God-given uniqueness) or to reject the faith. Many missionary endeavors have failed because of this approach.

In addition to cultural imprisonment, our understanding of the Bible has also been "church-centered." Often any expressions of biblical interpretation outside the auspices of the organized church are disregarded. In fact, the kingdom of God is at times automatically identified with the organized church. Even the denominational division of Christianity, an example of European church-centered cultural and historical realities, has been imposed on the rest of the world as though it was the will of God.[30] Biblical interpretation has also been reserved as the work of the official representatives of the church, most often the elite adult "male clerical." Seldom have women, laypersons, or anyone outside of the centers of power played more than a token role in developing scriptural understandings. A faith that is interpreted from one cultural, denominational, and gender perspective by one elite group of people will not only be biased; it will not be life-giving to persons outside the circle of interpretation (and also to those interpreters who cut themselves off from the rest of God's people). If the Bible is not set free from church-centered interpretations conducted by elite male clerics, most of the world's population will not perceive the Bible as a source of liberation.

Much of biblical interpretation does have "capitalistic" influences, as Balasuriya contends, because most biblical scholars have "been within the framework of Western capitalism and benefiting from it."[31] Somehow biblical passages about economic sharing and redistribution, such as the jubilee in Leviticus 25 and the early church in Acts 2 and 4, are not discussed or are considered impractical idealisms. There are many people who are poor and oppressed under capitalist systems. Biblical faith becomes unattractive when they are led to believe that the economic system under which they are exploited is supported by the Bible. This is true of any economic or political system that is not equitable and uses the Bible to underpin its existence. A Bible that is used to support systems and practices that are inequitable and discriminatory will not be seen as a source of liberation.

This problem is further compounded by a "lack of a socioeconomic analysis" where "the social aspects of the kingdom of God, sin, conversion, and salvation are neglected" and "are considered merely human, humanitarian, horizontal, and natural as if they were not related to the spiritual, to God."[32] When the Bible is reduced to addressing only the personal concerns of individuals and does not serve as a critique of society, it loses its ability to offer a wholistic Good News. This leads to an "absence of action-orientation" that causes many to view the Bible as merely a guidebook for personal piety with little relevance to the issues in one's life and in the world.

A Bible that is presented as culturally foreign, biased toward the powerful, understood only by the elite, favoring the economic system of the dominant group, having nothing to say to one's social reality, and calling for no action is not liberating and certainly not attractive. The Bible itself must be liberated from these imposed viewpoints so that it can be free to be a source of empowerment and liberation. If the greatest need in this age of diversity is a faith that is liberating, then the Bible must be reinterpreted in ways that recapture its essence. Just as Jesus reclaimed the spirit of Exodus and jubilee in his day, we must reintroduce the gospel as the source of liberation for individuals and societies in our day.

Amazingly, some who have been oppressed through a distorted use of the Bible have still been able to see through to the truth. As Jacquelyn Grant observes:

> The God of the Old and New Testaments became real in the consciousness of oppressed Black women. Though they were politically impotent, they were able to appropriate certain themes of the Bible which spoke to their reality . . . An ex-slave woman revealed that when her experience negated certain oppressive interpretations of the Bible given by White preachers, she, through engaging the biblical message for herself, rejected them.[33]

This is our challenge. We must engage the biblical message in such a way that we can see through oppressive interpretations and rediscover the truth of liberation and empowerment. This is critical if the message of the Bible is to reach and impact our world both now and in the future.

Many biblical interpreters around the world, both in academic communities and in grassroots communities, are seeking to strip away layers of interpretation that have had a monocultural bent or an imperialistic application. Even whole Bibles have been transformed. *The Original African Heritage Study Bible*,[34] released in 1993, corrects earlier

versions of the Bible that portrayed people of color in dispar-
aging ways and celebrates the multiculturalism of the Bible.
Rather than attempting a new translation, the publisher
chose the King James Version. The reason given was that this
is the version used by a majority of people in African American churches. The editors have been able to offer new understandings and interpretations of the Scriptures by utilizing
the study Bible format. By choosing the King James Version,
one could say that the editors have liberated the slave master's Bible from its history of oppressive usage. Another Bible
that has taken on a more liberating flavor is the *Christian
Community Bible,*[35] published in 1988. It is also a study Bible,
but it provides a fresh translation from the Hebrew and
Greek. The *Christian Community Bible* was prepared in the
Philippines with a Third-World perspective using a community approach to interpretation. Its commentary highlights
the Bible's concerns for social justice.

When the "Liberated" Become the Oppressors

In addition to the struggle to correct faulty biblical interpretations, this attempt to portray the God of the Bible as a
liberator is challenged by some who are seeking liberation.
Robert Allen Warrior believes "that the story of the Exodus
is an inappropriate way for Native Americans to think about
liberation"[36] because God employed

> . . . the same power used against the enslaving Egyp-
> tians to defeat the indigenous inhabitants of Canaan.
> Yahweh the deliverer became Yahweh the conqueror. The
> obvious characters in the story for Native Americans to
> identify with are the Canaanites, the people who already
> lived in the promised land. As a member of the Osage
> Nation of American Indians who stands in solidarity with
> other tribal people around the world, I read the Exodus
> stories with Canaanite eyes.[37]

This challenge by Warrior is one that must be considered.
We cannot simply disregard the hard questions of new voices
in the dialogue on biblical interpretation. In an age of diver-

sity we must be willing to accept such challenges and examine new perspectives. In the case of Warrior's statement, it is also critical for exploring our assumption that the Bible can be a source of liberation given the diversity of peoples in our world.

The book of Joshua describes in great detail the move of the Hebrew people, now called the Israelites, into Palestine ("the Promised Land"). It is a story of the conquest of the indigenous peoples of Palestine, the Canaanites and others, at God's initiative and with God's blessing. In the portrayal of the procurement of "the Promised Land" and in other passages in the Hebrew Bible, God is presented as ordering and even delighting in the oppression or killing of whole societies. This has been described by some as necessary for God's plan of redemption.[38] It certainly is a portrayal of God that is in contrast with the God of the Exodus and the God of Jesus.

It is very important to remember that the faith of the Hebrews was a faith formed in the experience of the Exodus and that the God they worshiped was a God of liberation. This central understanding of God is essential for dealing with other episodes recorded in the Bible in which the Israelites claim that God was in favor of their oppressive acts. We must view the Israelites' declarations about God through the lens of the revelation of God in the Exodus event, the core of their faith understanding. A God who, by definition, sets people free does not turn around and become an oppressor. The Bible even makes reference to God's acts of liberation on behalf other nations: "Did I not bring Israel up from the land of Egypt, and the Philistines from Caphtor and the Arameans from Kir?" (Amos 9:7).

We must be willing to struggle with these inconsistencies and not be swayed from the essence of the Bible's proclamation that God is a liberator, even if, as the apostle Paul said to the believers at Galatia, "an angel from heaven should proclaim to you a gospel contrary to what we proclaimed to you" (Galatians 1:8). The conflict seems to lie with God's self-revelation through the Exodus event and an Israelite cultural interpretation of a God that endorsed everything Israel did. The Hebrew Bible served as both Holy Scripture and a people's history. The history writers in the Bible wrote with the purpose of placing Israel as the centerpiece of God's will for humanity. Many of the prophets (and later Jesus), on the other hand, were much more willing to see God as the God of all people in the world. As in Amos 9:7, God speaks of liberating the Philistines and the Arameans as well as Israel.

Throughout history many have used "God's will" to build support for objectives that have much more to do with power, control, and economic gain than the will of God. The biblical story of Israel's conquest of Canaan has provided a framework for such attempts at exploitation. Some have claimed to be the chosen people of God entering their promised land and have declared that the indigenous peoples were the Canaanites waiting to be conquered. The history of the United States, South Africa, and other countries resound with these themes. As stated above, the Bible itself must be liberated from such use. This is critical so that "people who seek to be shaped and molded by reading the text [Exodus] will differentiate between the liberating god and the god of conquest."[39]

What happened after the Exodus also provides "an example of what can happen when powerless people come to power."[40] How could the Hebrews, who had just been set free from oppression in Egypt, oppress the Canaanites? One of the greatest tragedies in history is when people who have been set free from oppression turn around and oppress someone else. Unfortunately, history is full of such examples. Some claim their freedom in the name of God and then in the name of God lord over another group of people. The "liberated" often use the Bible to support their oppressive actions. Such a claim of biblical authority has caused an indigenous Palestinian theologian, Naim Stifan Ateek, to ask: "How can the Old Testament be the Word of God in light of the Palestinian Christians' experience with its use to support Zionism?"[41]

For previously oppressed, now liberated, people to avoid becoming oppressors themselves, there must be a "revolution of images."[42] Too often, the newly liberated have learned well the ways of power that have been used against them. Rather than creating new ways for ordering relationships in society, such as the jubilee, the old ways are simply adapted and reshaped by the formerly oppressed. Soon they become the oppressors, another group of people cry out for liberation, and the cycle continues. Liberation must, as Amos Niven Wilder writes, "operate at a deeper level where the wrestling is with the loyalties, banners, and spells that rule a way of life and its institutions."[43] Liberation involves more than just changing one's social or economic circumstances. True liberation means being set free from the need for control and being empowered to create an equitable society. Without the personal healing of the souls of people who have been damaged by oppression, the liberation and empowerment of hurting people will lead to the next generation of oppressors. Oppressive ways are learned and passed on from one generation to the next. They are passed on in both the cultures of the powerful and the powerless (who want to be powerful). Liberation must be followed by healing before empowerment takes place. This is true for individuals, cultures, and societies.[44]

Such a therapeutic process of healing was in place for the Hebrew people. God sent a healer and a liberator in the person of Moses. Although born a Hebrew slave, Moses was raised in Pharaoh's household. He did not personally experience the damage to his psyche and his spirit that comes from the dehumanization of enslavement. Moses did not inherit the feeling of powerlessness inbred in the culture after nearly four hundred years of bondage. He had not been indoctrinated with the belief that he was by nature a slave and therefore less than human. Yet because he had significant contact with his Hebrew family and his spiritual roots, Moses did not accept uncritically the benefits of power he enjoyed as Pharaoh's adopted grandson. So when Moses was sent by God to lead the Hebrews to freedom after centuries of bondage, he carried neither the emotional nor the cultural scars of slavery (Exodus 1–4).

The subsequent forty years that the Hebrews wandered in the wilderness after the Exodus from slavery provided enough time to complete the healing process. In fact, nearly a whole generation of Hebrews died during this period, allowing for fresh leadership to emerge that had limited experience with the pain of slavery. They even had in place a plan for a new society based on the jubilee regulations. Unfortunately, it seems that the necessary healing did not take place during the forty years of roaming the wilderness. When Moses died, Joshua became the next leader. Joshua was one of the few remaining Hebrews still alive who had lived as a slave under Pharaoh. It was Joshua who led the Hebrews, now called the Israelites, into battle against the indigenous people of Palestine. Robert Allen Warrior does offer a note of hope for those following the God of the Bible when he writes:

> Perhaps, if they are true to their struggle, people will be able to achieve what Yahweh's chosen people in the past have not: a society of people delivered from oppression who are not so afraid of becoming victims again that they become oppressors themselves . . .[45]

The Power of Personal Liberation

Perhaps one of the reasons for so much injustice in our world is that people need to be set free on the personal level—emotionally, psychologically, and spiritually. Liberating the social and economic aspects of life is apparently not enough. An important question then becomes, in an age of diversity, is the Bible a source of personal liberation? Vine Deloria, Jr., directly challenges the power of biblical faith to liberate the personal when he writes about the difference between Native American tribal religions and Christianity:

> . . . there is no question which tradition is capable of speaking meaningfully to the diversity of peoples. A Sweat Lodge, a Vision Quest, or a Sing performed in a sacred

place with the proper medicine man provides more to its practitioners than a well-performed Mass, a well-turned sermon argument, or a well-organized retreat. Christian rituals simply have no experiential powers.[46]

Deloria would have us believe that biblical faith, particularly in its rituals, has little value for personal liberation or healing. What must be kept in mind is that faith in God, as presented in the Bible, does not focus on rituals as the prime source of experiential power. The emphasis in the Scriptures is on a direct relationship with a personal God. The Bible does speak of the experiential side of liberation, but in a relational mode rather than a ritualistic one. Many can witness to the experiential power of a personal relationship with God.

One such witness was Martin Luther King, Jr. He provides us with an example of an individual who was committed to social liberation yet needed and experienced moments of personal liberation as well. Late one night during the 1950s bus boycott in Montgomery, Alabama, a phone caller threatened King's life, saying, "Nigger, we are tired of you and your mess now. And if you aren't out of this town in three days, we're going to blow your brains out, and blow up your house." Unable to sleep, King went to the kitchen to drink some coffee and found himself overwhelmed by the pressures of leadership. King recounted his prayer that night: "Lord, I'm down here trying to do what's right. I think I'm right. I think the cause we represent is right. But Lord, I must confess that I'm weak now. I'm faltering. I'm losing my courage." Then, in the midst of his prayer, he felt as if he could hear an inner voice speaking to him: "Martin Luther, stand up for righteousness. Stand up for justice. Stand up for truth. And lo I will be with you, even until the end of the world." When later reflecting on this event of personal liberation and empowerment in a sermon, King said, "I heard the voice of Jesus saying still to fight on. He promised never to leave me, never to leave me alone." He said that the mystical experience had an immediate affect: "Almost at once my fears began to go. My uncertainty disappeared."[47]

This God that King preached about as the source of liberation for African Americans in racially segregated Montgomery,
Alabama, became a source of personal empowerment in a
time of real fear for King. The words of encouragement that
King heard in his mystical experience were from biblical
themes. "And, lo, I will be with you, even to the end of the
world," is from Matthew 28:20.[48] These words and themes
from King's biblically nurtured faith provided him with a
personally transforming experience.

Three days later an elderly woman, known to everyone as
Mother Pollard, rose to her feet after King finished preaching
and walked to the front of the church.[49]

> "Something is wrong with you," said Pollard. "You
> didn't talk strong tonight."
> "Oh, no, Mother Pollard," King replied. "Nothing is
> wrong. I am feeling as fine as ever."
> "Now you can't fool me," she said. "I knows something
> is wrong. Is it that we ain't doing things to please you?
> Or is it that the white folks is bothering you?"
> . . . Before he could say anything, she moved her face
> close to his and said loudly, "I done *told* you we is with
> you all the way. But even if we ain't with you, God's
> gonna take care of you." . . . Later, King said that with
> her consoling words fearlessness had come over him in
> the form of raw energy.[50]

A few minutes later King was informed that his house had
indeed been bombed as the caller had threatened three days
earlier. He went home and found an angry crowd ready for
revenge. King stepped to the front of the house and stated:
"We must meet hate with love. . . . I want it to be known the
length and breadth of this land that if I am stopped, this
movement will not stop. . . . For what we are doing is right.
What we are doing is just. And God is with us." The crowd
eventually dispersed peacefully into the night.[51]

Mother Pollard echoed the words that King had heard in
his mystical experience three days earlier: God would always
be there for him. King, now empowered, offered the same

encouragement to the angry crowd. The same God who spoke to Moses in a burning bush and to Saul on the Damascus road spoke to King in his inner consciousness. This God prompted Mother Pollard to approach King three days later as his house was being bombed, reaffirming God's message that everything was going to be all right. This is but one example of a countless number that could be shared. The God proclaimed in the Bible is both a social and personal liberator with experiential powers who will meet the needs of people in this age of diversity.

We must not disregard Vine Deloria, Jr.'s challenge. His comments are no doubt grounded in his observations of the faith experience of many Christians. There are many who call themselves Christians but have a faith devoid of any transforming power. Some who embrace the social dimension of biblical liberation fail to allow for the personal renewal that must accompany it for one to remain empowered in the struggle. Deloria's comments remind us that people need to be personally liberated and empowered in their lives. Martin Luther King, Jr.'s kitchen experience reminds us that a faith rooted in the God revealed in the Bible *does* have extraordinary experiential powers.

Merging Personal and Social Liberation

For many Christians, the problem is not one of too much emphasis on the social aspects of a liberating biblical faith but an exclusive focus on the personal aspects of faith in Jesus Christ. Many people consider faith a personal matter without implications for one's society. While this belief is held by some who are powerless in society, it is more pervasive among the powerful. People who face some form of injustice are more apt to seek out the Scriptures that speak of social liberation because of their individual circumstances. The sense of comfort experienced by those in power often blinds them to this message of the Bible because they have no felt need. Japanese American Lloyd K. Wake recounts an example of this: "Our Mennonite Brethren friends visited us while we were in the Concentration Camps in the Arizona desert during World War II. It was a compassionate act for which we were very grateful. But their religious faith never led them to speak against that injustice."[52] As we have demonstrated, a faith in God divorced from social concerns is not biblical.

The merger of a zeal for personal salvation with a commitment to social salvation could be found among many evangelical Christians during the 1800s in the United States. The revival meetings that called people to a personal conversion experience also called for the end of slavery, the right of women to vote, the need to address poverty, and, in some cases, the end of war.[53] Charles G. Finney was an outstanding example of this integration of personal and social liberation. He thought of himself as an evangelist inviting people to an experience of personal conversion, but he preached that conversion leads to new ways of acting regarding social issues. Speaking of what he believed was an ineffective Christian faith, Finney said, "Many churches have taken the wrong side on the subject of slavery, have suffered prejudice to prevail over principle, and have feared to call this abomination by its true name."[54]

Many North American denominations that started in the 1800s were born out of a marriage of personal and social liberation. Some examples of such denominations (and the social issues that were emphasized) include the Wesleyan Methodist Church (antislavery, women's rights);[55] Free Methodist Church (poverty, antislavery);[56] Christian and Missionary Alliance Church (poverty);[57] Church of the Nazarene (poverty, women's right to preach);[58] Church of God—Anderson, Indiana (unity along race and gender lines).[59] Two evangelical colleges of the 1800s, Oberlin and Wheaton, were important places where this marriage of social action and personal salvation was expressed.[60] In many of these cases, personal salvation later overshadowed any emphasis on social justice.

There were hopes for resurrecting this Finney-style evangelism in the 1950s. Martin Luther King, Jr., envisioned the possibility of joint crusades with Billy Graham. He could see the power of Graham preaching for personal conversion and King for social action. King's organization, the Southern Christian Leadership Conference, already had as its motto, "To redeem the soul of America." These two great Baptist orators could have preached to interracial audiences about the need for personal and social salvation, as well as called for repentance from racism as a personal and structural sin. King's counterpart was not ready.[61]

The challenge to bring together the personal and social dimensions of liberation, as well as the Hebrew Bible and the New Testament, is given impetus by the suggestion of Kosuke Koyama to merge the messages of these two biblical texts:[62]

> What does the LORD require of you but to do justice, and to love kindness, and to walk humbly with your God? (Micah 6:8).

> "Here is the Lamb of God who takes away the sin of the world!" (John 1:29).

For Koyama, these two texts capture the essence of what it means to be a follower of the God of liberation. The work of social liberation, "doing justice," needs a personal experience of liberation with "the Lamb of God who takes away the sin of the world," and vice versa. As Koyama writes, "Redemption cannot be complete without justice, nor justice without redemption."[63] Biblical liberation is both personal and social.

In this time of increasing diversity, the search is for a faith that liberates. This quest cuts across racial, cultural, economic, and gender lines. People who feel powerless want to be empowered. Some cry out for liberation at a systemic level. Others cry out for liberation from the daily grind of life. Even many of the powerful seek personal liberation from a life that is without ultimate meaning. The Bible is a source for discovering the God of liberation who desires to set people free.

We must embrace the Bible's emphasis on liberation and empowerment if our Christian faith is to be relevant for this generation. As James H. Cone writes:

> Many people think that religion has everything to do with an individual's personal relationship with God and nothing to do with society and one's fight for justice in it. . . . I contend that the depth of any religious commitment should be judged by one's commitment to justice for humanity, using the liberation activity of human beings as the lens through which one sees God.[64]

Questions for Discussion

1. How would you define *liberation?* How would you define *empowerment?* What in your definition is based on your understanding of God?

2. Do you agree that liberation is the central message of the Bible? Why or why not? What are some ways to address the biblical passages that seem to contradict the message of liberation?

3. What are the common themes in the Exodus event, the jubilee, and the life and message of Jesus Christ? How can these shared meanings impact our world today?

4. What do you think of Tissa Balasuriya's approach to liberating theology and the Bible? What are some other ways that our faith needs to be liberated?

5. Considering that so often when oppressed people are empowered they eventually become oppressors, what is needed to heal the souls of hurting people and break the cycle? What process can be put into place to accomplish this?

6. Take a moment and reflect on a time in your life when you have felt liberated, healed, or empowered. Describe the feeling.

7. Can religions other than the Christian faith provide liberating experiences? Are some better suited for this than

Christianity? Why or why not? Do we need to invite more people to experience the liberation, healing, and empowerment available in the God revealed in the Bible?

8. Why is it that personal and social liberation are often not integrated in an individual's life? How do we merge the personal and the social in our world today?

9. After reading this chapter, how would you answer the question, "Is faith in God liberating?" State the reasons for your answer.

10. Has chapter four influenced your understanding of faith in God? If so, how?

Chapter Five

No Justice, No Peace

The preceding chapter gave us an opportunity to consider the invitation of God to those of goodwill from all racial and cultural groups to experience liberation. We also heard the call to become free people who then liberate and empower others in our world. Perhaps there has been no other time in history when the message of God's liberation was needed more. Much of the violence and war in our world seems paradoxically and tragically fueled by our diversity. Fighting erupts over differences in religion, ethnicity, race, class, culture, gender, ideology, and the like. Jesus Christ came with a message of liberation and empowerment that, if practiced, can restore our sense of oneness, even in the midst of a broad mosaic of personalities and cultures. Unfortunately, the major questions regarding how we live together are being worked out on the battlefields and in the streets, not at peace summits and reconciliation rallies. The human family is at war with itself, and there is no peace.

In January 1994 I took my children, Rachel and Jonathan, sledding on one of the few days where the temperature had reached above zero that month in Minnesota. As we drove home, I turned on the radio and heard a news story about another group of children who had been sledding. They were sledding in the city of Sarajevo during a declared cease-fire in the midst of the Bosnian civil war. In the middle of what was a rare moment of fun, a bomb landed, killing several children. Their friends looked on in horror. One child saw a friend's head decapitated by the blast. The children of Sara-

jevo are innocent victims in a war being fought over long-nur-
tured hatreds and ethnic rivalries. In the face of such cruel-
ties, one wonders if peace is still possible.

Peace does seem to be an elusive ideal. There are those
who believe that if thousands of people think about peace at
the same time, it will somehow bring us closer to a world of
love. For them, possessing the right attitude about life brings
peace. This approach produces slogans like "think peace not
war." Others are convinced that peace is equivalent to the
absence of war. Therefore, military might ensures peace, and
weapon systems have even been called "peacekeepers" because of this mentality. Many people have just given up on
the possibility of peace. For them, peace is a fantasy and
completely unrelated to reality.

A popular chant in protest marches has been "no justice,
no peace." This phrase is often meant as a threat. If the group
making the demands does not receive the "justice" it wants,
then it will make sure that there is no peace for those who
are committing the "injustice." Yet the phrase also can be
understood as a sober reminder of a fundamental truth: If we
do not address the injustices in our world, there is no realistic
possibility of developing long-term peace. Like the prophets
have said, we must not cry "peace" when there is no peace
(see Jeremiah 6:14; Ezekiel 13:10; Micah 3:5; see also Luke
19:41-44). It is irresponsible to create false hopes for peace.
Peace is not the lack of violence; it is the absence of injustice
and oppression. More than that, though, peace comes when
we take redemptive and strategic action against injustice. As
people with a biblical faith, we should not forsake the goal of
creating a more peaceful society. But nonviolent coexistence
is not enough; we must pursue oneness through reconciliation. Peace results when a society is built on just and equal
relationships among its people. This vision caused the
prophet Amos to cry out, "Let justice roll down like waters,
and righteousness like an everflowing stream" (5:24). He
knew that justice was Israel's only hope for peace. Isaiah said
that only when "a spirit from on high is poured out on us" can

we find justice. He went on to make the connection between justice and peace: "Then justice will dwell in the wilderness, and righteousness abide in the fruitful field. The effect of righteousness will be peace, and the result of righteousness, quietness and trust forever" (32:15-17). Jesus blessed "the peacemakers" (Matthew 5:9) and considered justice among the "weightier matters of the law" (Matthew 23:23).

The calls for justice and peace are heard throughout the Bible. We cannot separate our allegiance to God from the biblical mandate to work for peace and social justice. Women and men from a wide range of experiences and backgrounds have embraced this call. The following people from the twentieth century are illustrative of a greater multitude of witnesses:

• Rigoberta Menchú, an indigenous activist in Guatemala, writes: "The work of revolutionary Christians is above all to condemn and denounce the injustices committed against the people."[1]

• Martin Luther King, Jr., an African American minister and social prophet, had so integrated a commitment to social justice with his faith that he described a conversion experience in terms of his commitment to justice: "And it seemed at that moment that I could hear an inner voice saying to me, 'Martin Luther, stand up for righteousness. Stand up for justice. Stand up for truth. And lo I will be with you, even until the end of the world.' . . . I heard the voice of Jesus saying still to fight on."[2]

• Mary John Mananzan and Sun Ai Park, Asian theologians, write: "Christian spirituality deals with . . . love and justice, community and individuals, religions and politics, peace and struggle toward holistic salvation."[3]

• Dietrich Bonhoeffer, a German theologian, said: "There are things for which an uncompromising stand is worth while. And it seems to me that peace and social justice, or Christ himself, are such things."[4]

• Oscar Romero, an archbishop in El Salvador, said just minutes before he was martyred in 1980 while serving Communion: "We may give our body and our blood to suffering and to pain—like Christ, not for self, but to bring about justice and peace for our people."[5]

In the Bible, peace and justice walk hand in hand as complimentary components of God's desire for this world. It is astonishing that more clergy and laity do not acknowledge this fact more often in their use and appreciation of Scripture. The biblical authors have much to say about the *shalom* or peace of God. But if peace requires justice, then we must strive to create a just society. We will focus our discussion on biblical strategies for responding to three forms of injustice in contemporary society: racism, sexism, and classism. While all forms of injustice are interrelated, these three require urgent and comprehensive analysis by the biblical activist in an age of diversity. Injustice exists both in the society and in the church. Therefore, biblical strategies for eliminating racism, sexism, and classism will have both an inward focus toward the community of God and an outward focus toward society. As Justo González writes, "Injustice thrives on the myth that the present order is somehow the result of pure intentions and a guiltless history."[6] Let us break the power of this myth by examining afresh the biblical resources that may inspire us to be people empowered by God. We must take action against injustice if we are ever to discover peace.

Racism

The pages of this book have repeatedly spoken of the effects of colonialism, slavery, genocide, and other injustices that have been perpetrated based on theories of racial superiority. There is hardly a place or a people in the past few centuries that have not been affected by racial injustice. Steve Charleston describes how racism has affected Native Americans:

> The most virulent form of the disease of racism has been used against Native America. Like other oppressed people, we have known slavery, poverty, and political conquest. We have also known something else—genocide. . . . Western

colonialism may speak of an American history. Native People speak of an American holocaust.[7]

People from other cultures and races could add their stories to his. Many people, particularly among the dominant group, would like to believe that racism should be spoken of in the past tense. This is because "there is a wide gulf today between what the majority group assumes and what the victim experiences."[8] But given the following working definition of racism, it is apparent that this plague on humanity still exists: an individual is racist when he or she believes in the innate superiority of one's own racial group and the inborn inferiority of others; an institution or a society's culture is racist when power is exercised to enforce the myth of racial superiority and inferiority.

The mission of the church has been affected by racism. Our oneness in Christ has been compromised by congregations and denominations that are segregated by race. *The greatest barrier to effective multicultural ministry is racism.* The missionary zeal and evangelistic outreach of the church will never achieve its full potential until it is addressed. Numerous individuals have rejected the Christian faith because of the racial prejudice of church people. E. Stanley Jones, speaking in reference to Mahatma Gandhi, wrote, "Racialism has many sins to bear, but perhaps its worst sin was the obscuring of Christ in an hour when one of the greatest souls born of woman was making his decision."[9]

As we have demonstrated in chapter one, people of all cultures and races are included in God's salvation story. Jesus himself was a racially mixed Afro-Asiatic Jew from Galilee. There were no social or economic systems based on race or skin-color designations in the biblical era. The Bible was composed in a time before racism and theories of racial types.[10] Racism is a latter-day aberration of God's creative design. It is an attempt to mutilate the image of God imprinted onto humanity. Racism is nothing less than a denial of the God of the Bible and therefore is apostasy. Infants are not born to be racists. It is a learned prejudice, an acquired taste. Racism is sin and, like all sin, requires repentance. The racism found in institutions, put in place intentionally for economic gain or power needs, affects whole groups of people in a society. Racism becomes ingrained in a culture as individuals and institutions instruct the next generation regarding their biases. Once it has become a part of the culture, racism is very difficult to root out and reproduces itself automatically. Racism becomes "normal." As followers of God we are compelled to fight racial injustice in all of its forms: individual, institutional, and cultural.[11] Even though the Bible was written in a time before racism per se, there is a wealth of information available for use in addressing it. People in biblical times were just as prejudiced as we are today. The way God addressed human bigotry in the Bible gives us insights as to how we should respond to prejudice's modern-day cousin, racism. Since earlier chapters have spent considerable time on this issue, we will focus on a few points needing elaboration.

Hebrew Bible

In chapter one, when discussing the inclusion of Africans in the biblical narrative, we singled out the so-called curses of Cain and Ham as the cornerstone for the argument that there is a biblical basis for white racial superiority.[12] This distorted use of the Hebrew Scriptures has undergirded much of the racial injustice in history. Few Christian leaders actively teach this "curse" mentality today. It is not necessary because this racist ideology has become a part of our culture. Let us examine two statements that describe the process of infusing racism into a culture. The first is from an African theologian and the second from a Latino theologian:

> One common factor uniting all such causes (negative views of Africans) is the misconception that the Euro-American world is the center of the universe. It is the model of what is good, just, and holy. It is the center of God's love and presence. As a consequence it possesses superior knowledge and wisdom, culture and civilization, dignity

and honor. When such a misconception is entertained for centuries and promoted in several ways, it becomes the heritage of the Euro-American. On the basis of such heritage, Africans look strange, unfamiliar, and dejected in appearance, behavior, environment, religion, and culture. Aspects of this heritage can be traced in Christian theology in relation to Africa.[13]

The conquest of the bronze peoples inhabiting the Americas and the subsequent wholesale uprooting and enslavement of hundreds of thousands of black Africans by white Europeans would engender and consolidate a racist mentality unprecedented in world history. As masses of persons were slaughtered or condemned to a life of abject misery and menial labor for the enrichment of others, a mentality justifying the inhuman treatment was built up, justifying the outrages and social despoliation of entire peoples. . . . The step from ethnocentrism to racism was an easy and even "logical" one: peoples are inferior because nature made them that way. . . . "We alone are fully human" became the basic cultural dogma of the European personality.[14]

Both of these statements describe the process of embedding racism into a society's self-understanding. While neither of the theologians mention Cain or Ham by name, the "curse" theology undergirds the process they describe. One group of people elevates themselves as the "chosen" people of God. They are created in the image of the Divine and are nearly divine themselves. The "other" group of people is portrayed as being created less than human (three-fifths human?), strange, abnormal, and godless. They are the progeny of the cursed ones. Yes, they are the children of a cursed Cain and a cursed Ham. Yet the theological case rarely needs to be made anymore. It is ingrained in the culture.

The curses of Cain and Ham do remain a part of the propaganda of white supremacist organizations and churches. Yet even there, an attention to the details is not necessary because the culture carries the seeds of racism from generation to generation. While I was in college, the

Knights of the Ku Klux Klan marched through the town. A student majoring in journalism interviewed a KKK member during the march. The Klansman attempted to tell the young journalism student about the origins of the black race by using the Genesis account about Cain killing Abel and then being sent away by God (Genesis 4:1-16). The Klansman said that "Gabe" killed his brother Abel. Because of the killing of Abel, "Gabe" was sent away by God and found an ape for a wife. This was the beginning of the black race. Even though the Klan member did not seem to know the right name for Cain, and stretched beyond the truth of the text into his own imaginings, he was certain that people who were not white were less than human. In fact, they were half ape!

Left unchallenged, such racist images dominate the cultural understandings of people around the globe. The myth of a racial hierarchy, which delineates who is inferior and who is superior, needs to be extracted from our cultural consciousness. In the United States, we must trumpet the message that "to be made to the image and likeness of God does *not* require the finishing touches of Anglo-American melting-pot assimilation."[15] Theories of racial superiority in all parts of the world must be dismantled. From a biblical perspective, this means undoing dogma like the so-called curses of Cain and Ham. Then new and truthful images can replace the racist mentality of our culture. Chapters one and two of this book have attempted to do just that.

Jesus

The society in which Jesus grew up had cultural biases not unlike the "curse" theology. Samaritans had been effectively marginalized by the first-century theology of Judaism. Many Jews avoided any contact with Samaria and Samaritans because they were considered "unclean," ritually impure. Jesus addressed the prejudice perpetuated by this "unclean" theology. He infused the culture with new and positive images of Samaritans that accurately declared their full humanity. Jesus began by refusing to permit any derogatory images of Samaritans. On one occasion, the people of a Samaritan village would not let Jesus and his disciples stay overnight in their village because they were traveling to Jerusalem for the Passover (Luke 9:51-56). This was due to the Samaritan belief that religious festivals should be held on Mount Gerizim (see Deuteronomy 11:26-30; John 4:20-24.) The people in this village chose not to support Jesus as he traveled to what they considered to be a false religious event. The disciples wanted him to call down fire on the village. Jesus refused to use this village's act of religious bigotry as an excuse to act in a way that reinforced existing stereotypes of Samaritans as a worthless people.

Another example of Jesus' refusal to buy into the "unclean" theology was when the Jewish religious leaders attempted to insult Jesus by saying he had a demon and calling him a Samaritan (John 8:48-49). The term "Samaritan" was meant as a derogatory ethnic slur. Jesus directly challenged their assertion that he had a demon. He informed the religious leaders that they had dishonored him. However, he did not respond at all to the "Samaritan slur." It seems that Jesus did not consider being called a Samaritan an insult or a sign of disrespect.

Jesus also challenged the prevailing cultural perceptions by publicly associating with Samaritans. He spent the night in Samaritan villages (John 4:39-42), conversed with both Samaritan men and women (Luke 17:11-19; John 4:4-26, 39-42), and reached out to Samaritans in a ministry of evangelism (John 4:39-42) and healing (Luke 17:11-19). After the Resurrection, Jesus sent forth his disciples to do the same (Acts 1:8), a commission they actively followed (Acts 8:5-25).

The most powerful way that Jesus addressed the prejudice against Samaritans that permeated the culture of first-century Palestine was the inclusion of positive images of Samaritans in his sermons and parables. In the story of the "good Samaritan," it was the Samaritan who demonstrated the neighborly compassion that was commanded of the Jews (Luke 10:29-37). The Samaritan was the hero of the story, helping someone who would have probably refused his help if he were not unconscious. It is interesting to note that while Samaritans were considered inferior in the first century, this story has made the name "Samaritan" a title of honor in our day. Jesus' story successfully changed the cultural image of the Samaritan from "unclean" to "good."

We must discard the negative images of people our culture tells us are "unclean" or "cursed." As we demonstrated in chapters one and two, when we lift up the biblical stories of Africans, Asians, and others who are marginalized by racism in our day, the process of restoring their human image in the culture begins. As people of faith, we start by changing our own racist images and practices. At the same time, we also confront the image makers of our own society—the media, the advertising world, the educational system, and others— and demand that racist images be replaced by positive and accurate portrayals.

Early Church

As the early church expanded into Asia, Europe, and Africa, the main source of ethnic tension was the relationship between Jews and Gentiles. This division was addressed regularly by the early church. This first became a problem for the early Jewish believers who had taken on aspects of Greek culture. There was a concern that the widows of the Greek-speaking Jews were not being treated with the same regard as the widows of the Hebrew-speaking Jews (Acts 6:1-7). The issue was resolved by appointing seven new leaders who were culturally Greek. One of the seven, Nicolaus, had been a Greek convert to Judaism before becoming a follower of Christ.

The appointment of leaders with an understanding of Greek culture did not end the tensions. Many of the original apostles themselves were struggling with prejudice against Gentiles. The apostle Peter is perhaps the best illustration of one who was biased against Gentiles. As we mentioned in chapter one, Peter had to struggle with his own ethnocentric perspective when the Good News began to be received by Europeans and others outside of his Jewish ethnic group. The author of Acts describes in great detail how Peter and the other apostles in the early church struggled with the conversion of Gentiles (Acts 10:1–11:18). God confronted Peter with his prejudice in a vision where he was asked three times to eat food that was considered unclean by Judaism. Each time Peter refused. So God responded, "What God has made clean, you must not call profane" (10:15). After the vision, Peter was summoned to the home of a Roman centurion to speak of his faith in Jesus Christ. At this point, Peter seemed to understand the message of the vision and proclaimed eloquently, "I truly understand that God shows no partiality, but in every nation anyone who fears him and does what is right is acceptable to him" (10:34-35). This was further confirmed when the Holy Spirit fell on these Romans while Peter was preaching. Later, when Peter was explaining to the cynical apostles what had happened to these Romans, he said, "If then God gave them the same gift that he gave us when we believed in the Lord Jesus Christ, who was I that I could hinder God?" (11:17).

After spending three years with Jesus, it is hard to conceive that Peter and the apostles still needed to address prejudice against Gentiles in their lives. As we demonstrated in chapter one, Jesus had interacted with Gentiles. He declared that a Canaanite woman had great faith (Matthew 15:21-28; Mark 7:24-30). Jesus had even described a Roman centurion's faith as greater than that of anyone in Israel (Matthew 8:5-13, Luke 7:1-10). Wasn't Peter paying attention to Jesus' remarks about this Roman? Perhaps since their next stop was Peter's home, Peter had gone on ahead to clean the house and missed this lesson (Matthew 8:14)! There was also the Roman at the cross who declared that Jesus was the Son of God. Peter evidently missed that one as well. He was perhaps too busy hiding in fear for his own life. He certainly couldn't have missed the fact that there were Romans at Pentecost (Acts 2:10). He was the main speaker. Maybe the crowd was too large.

Whatever reason Peter had for still harboring prejudice against Gentiles, his vision of God and experience at Cornelius' house should have been enough to set Peter free from his intolerance. As a Christian Jew and presumed leader of the apostles after Pentecost, he was painfully aware of the increased tension in the synagogues in a Roman environment growing increasingly hostile. Yet in Galatians, Paul described Peter's relapse into bigotry. Paul wrote:

> But when Cephas [Peter] came to Antioch, I opposed him to his face, because he stood self-condemned; for until certain people came from James, he used to eat with Gentiles. But after they came, he drew back and kept himself separate for fear of the circumcision faction. And other Jews joined him in this hypocrisy, so that even Barnabas was led astray by their hypocrisy. But when I saw that they were not acting consistently with the truth of the gospel, I said to Cephas before them all, "If you, though a Jew, live like a Gentile and not like a Jew, how can you compel the Gentiles to live like Jews?" ... if I build up again the very things that I once tore down, then I demonstrate that I am a transgressor (Galatians 2:11-14,18).

In Paul's interpretative report of this incident, it appears that Peter had backslidden into his "old" ways due to the pressure of those who were still hesitant about accepting Gentiles into the church. These "Judaizers" believed that Gentiles needed to convert to Judaism to become Christian. This meant being circumcised, following strict dietary regulations, and other changes. Peter's vision had declared that, according to God, Gentiles did not need to become Jews. It appears that the apostle had experienced a strategic memory loss when feeling coerced by "his own people." Peter's actions were introducing the concept of ethnic segregation into the life of the multicultural Antioch church. This would have created a situation much like that in North America where "on the one hand, we live in a society that contains a very diverse population of Christians; on the other, we go to church with people who are pretty much like us."[16] This would have had implications for the whole region because Antioch was the key church in the effort to reach out to Asia and Europe (Acts 11:26).

When someone of Peter's stature acts in prejudicial ways, it leads others astray. Even the great encourager, Barnabas, followed Peter in this separation. Paul illustrated what needs to happen when individual racists get in the way of God's will: "I opposed him to his face." Paul publicly challenged the leader of Jesus' disciples and was not afraid to state that his own partner in ministry, Barnabas, had been led astray. Paul challenged Peter at the core of his faith understanding. Their common profession of Christ as Lord gave them a point of departure in such a discussion. This has to be the source of discussions about racism today in the church. The racist and the one fighting racism are reading the same Bible. According to Heribert Adam and Kogila Moodley, this was what inspired hope for change in South Africa:

> When popular spokespersons for the oppressed affirm the common Christianity of the oppressors, they cannot be seen as a dehumanized personal enemy to be eliminated with callous ruthlessness. . . . The racial outsider remains simultaneously a Christian insider who must be enlightened, cajoled, or even threatened but who cannot be destroyed. . . . Praying together to the same God, be it for rain or the dismantling of apartheid, binds the rulers and the ruled, in a situation unique in the annals of contemporary oppression.[17]

The tension between Jews and Gentiles in the church did not go away. It was the main topic at a leadership council in Jerusalem (Acts 15:1-35). Paul reports that he often had to disarm this prejudice in the congregations he founded. He wrote to many of the churches that in Christ there was neither Jew nor Greek (Romans 10:12; 1 Corinthians 12:13; Galatians 3:28, Ephesians 2:11-16; Colossians 3:11). The church in Antioch was a model of the inclusiveness that Paul preached about (Acts 13:1). The apostle Paul apparently was

right to intervene and confront Peter in Antioch. He saved
the witness of this church. As we stated in chapter one, the
leadership of the church in Antioch was multicultural. This
had influenced the ministry of Paul and all of those serving
in the region. E. Stanley Jones noted that

> the Antiochan church made Simeon called Niger a
> prophet and teacher who laid the hands of a black man on
> Barnabas and Paul to commission them to preach the
> Gospel to Asia and white Europe. And they did it without
> comment as though it was the normal Christian attitude.
> It was. The present-day attitudes on race are subnormal
> and sub-Christian and anti-Christian.[18]

Jones was right when he described racism as "subnormal,"
"sub-Christian," and "anti-Christian." The Bible defies the
evil of prejudice. The prejudice of individuals such as Peter
and Barnabas is directly confronted. The prejudice was displayed in a public setting, so Paul confronts these apostles
publicly. Often the racism of individuals can be addressed
privately. The message of Paul is that racism must not be
ignored in the church or it will become like a festering cancer
spreading throughout the body of Christ.

Confronting racism constructively involves more than cor-
recting individuals. Christian organizations can be some of
the most racist institutions in the world. The Antioch church
reminds us that it is possible for the church, as an institution,
to be organized in ways that model and promote inclusiveness. Institutional racism must be exposed in congregations,
denominations, academic institutions, parachurch organizations, and any other associations claiming to be "Christian."
Then it must be eliminated. Sadly, it is only when this
happens that we can expect to be successful in changing the
institutions of the broader society.

The God of the Bible calls us to address the racism of
individuals, institutions, and culture. As stated earlier, when
racism is entrenched in the culture, it not only appears to be
a normal part of society; it also replicates itself without any
effort. In the case of the "unclean" Samaritans in first-cen-

tury Palestine or the "cursed" people of color of this modern age, the implication of inferiority is passed down from generation to generation as though it was the truth. Our challenge is to extricate racism from the entanglement of culture's web and then reintroduce into society the truth that God's loving regard is applied equally to all women, men, and children in the human family.

Sexism

Although racism based on skin color was not a part of the biblical world, sexism was deeply woven into the fabric of the times. Women in this period had very few rights. They generally were considered the property of men. They began as the property of their father and at the time of marriage became the property of their husband.[19] The Bible was written by men in a male-dominated and male-oriented society. This has no doubt affected the interpretation of God down through the centuries.[20] The effect has not gone unnoticed. A new generation of women scholars are speaking the hard, yet honest, truth about this biblical legacy.[21] Renita J. Weems writes that "specific texts are unalterably hostile to the dignity and welfare of women."[22] Elsa Tamez adds that "women find clear, explicit cases of the marginalization or segregation of women in several passages of both the Old and the New Testaments."[23] Elisabeth Moltmann-Wendel simply concludes that the Bible "contains a number of sexist remarks."[24] The sexism of the times influenced, and was often unchallenged by, the authors of the Bible. This has been well documented by these and other scholars.

One example of the lack of regard for women in Israel and how sexism went unchallenged by biblical authors is found in Judges 19–21.[25] A group of men from the tribe of Benjamin living in the city of Gibeah gathered outside of a house where a Levite from another city and his entourage were staying. They were intent on raping this man. In order to save himself, the man pushed his female companion out of the house and into the crowd. The men "wantonly raped her, and abused her all through the night until morning" (19:25). She was found dead the next morning in the doorway of the house. The man took the body of his female partner, cut it into twelve pieces, and sent it out to each of the twelve tribes of Israel as a protest of what had happened. The result was that the Israelites took an oath not to give their daughters to the men of the tribe of Benjamin. Knowing that the Benjaminites would still need wives, the Israelites went out and kidnapped some virgin girls from a neighboring people (as one of the tribes of Israel, the Benjaminites' line needed to continue). This story illustrates that the lives of women were considered expendable and obviously inferior to men. A woman's life could be sacrificed to save a man from degradation and death, and women could easily be replaced by going out and hunting for some new ones (see also Genesis 19:1-11).

Such a lack of regard for women in biblical times under-girded the development of an image of God as exclusively male. (The effects of this in the modern era were briefly referred to at the beginning of chapter two.) A male image of God led to many incidents down through history that parallel the incident in the book of Judges. The life of Elizabeth Hooten, the first Quaker convert, is an example. The Quakers believed that the Bible taught that God created women equal to men, and therefore women were able to preach. Imagine how men who believed that God was male felt about women preachers! Elizabeth Hooten experienced the brunt of anti-women sentiments. For attempting to spread the faith into Massachusetts, Hooten "was sentenced to the savage punishment of being tied to the tail of a cart and forced to walk to the whipping posts . . . At each post she was stripped to the waist and beaten with a three-corded whip. Finally she was taken deep into the wilderness on horseback."[26] Hooten described what happened next: "So they put me on a horse and carried me into ye wildernesse many miles, where was many wild beasts both bears and wolves & many deep waters where I waded through . . . but ye Lord delivered me."[27]

For many women, the experience of Christianity, while not

as physically brutal as described above, has been disappointing and devastating. Renita Weems describes the experience of many:

> Dutifully, we have sat through sermons, lectures, and Bible study lessons, nodding when appropriate, copiously taking notes when expected and, when called upon, obediently recapitulating what we have been told. All the while our souls have starved for a new revelation on the role of women in salvation history. Surely, God did not mean for us to be a footnote to redemption.[28]

Sexist interpretations of the Bible have created a church that "mirrors the blasphemous duplicity of a society that proclaims that all are created equal, but excludes certain groups from access to justice and opportunity."[29] Cheryl Sanders writes, "This state of affairs is blasphemous insofar as it is grounded in the belief that God favors the white male, who alone bears God's image."[30] Because much of the church has accepted uncritically the sexism of society, we must seriously consider how biblical interpretation has been affected.

Could the fact that some in the church interpret the sin of a woman (Eve) as applicable to all women, while the sin of a man (Judas) who betrayed the Savior of humanity as applicable only to himself, be attributed to sexism? We might also ask, is it possible that many in the church prefer the term "born again" because it was used when evangelizing a man, Nicodemus? Certainly the phrase "born again" (literally "born from above") was not very effective in communicating the message of salvation to the theologian Nicodemus. So Jesus coined a new word picture for salvation while sitting by Jacob's well. The phrase "living water," which was so effective that it led to the conversion of a whole town, was used for evangelizing a woman (see John 3 and 4).

In chapter one we demonstrated that even in the midst of ancient strands of Israel's ethnocentrism, the oneness of the human family kept emerging in the Bible. The same is true in regard to women. Despite the sexism of the time and the fact that the authors of the Bible were all male, God kept calling and empowering women as equals and as sources of God's power. Since we have not yet given sustained focus to sexism and the role of women in previous chapters, an overview of the biblical passages that speak to gender equality and the leadership of women should be most instructive.

Hebrew Bible

When one opens the Bible and encounters the first reference to humanity, the reader finds that both men and women were created equally in the image of God. Here, the image of God includes both the feminine and the masculine: "So God created humankind in his image, in the image of God he created them; male and female he created them" (Genesis 1:27). There is no suggestion of the subordination of women. Even though the man was created first, according to the second chapter of Genesis, it was not meant to convey the message that men should dominate. That would invalidate the image of equality presented in chapter one of Genesis. One could easily argue that the woman should hold the upper hand because usually the prototype has flaws that are corrected in a second phase of the creative process.[31]

Throughout the Hebrew Bible there are examples of women who heard the call of God and served in the same ways that men did. The prophet Joel acknowledged this equality: "I will pour out my spirit on all flesh; your sons and your daughters shall prophesy . . . Even on the male and female slaves, in those days, I will pour out my spirit" (Joel 2:28-29, see Acts 2:17-18). According to biblical scholar Marie Strong, it was "very radical" for Joel to suggest that sons would prophesy because nothing happened without the permission of the oldest male in the family. It was "radical in the extreme" for women to prophesy. Even the female slaves were included.[32]

Although Joel appears to be speaking of a future event, God was already speaking through women prophets in the male-oriented Israelite society. Miriam, who was often overshadowed by her brother Moses, was a prophet (Exodus

15:20-21). Two chapters of the Bible are devoted to the work of Deborah, a prophet and a judge (Judges 4 and 5). Huldah prophesied the word of the Lord to the king of Judah (2 Kings 22:14-20; 2 Chronicles 34:19-28). Noadiah was among the prophets that Nehemiah feared (Nehemiah 6:14). Isaiah's wife was a "prophetess" (Isaiah 8:3). Then there was Anna, an eighty-four-year-old prophetess in the tradition of the Hebrew Bible. When she saw the infant Jesus in the temple, she "began to praise God and to speak about the child to all who were looking for the redemption of Jerusalem" (Luke 2:36-38).

Parallel to the prophetic tradition of Israel, the Hebrew Bible includes the stories of strong women like Hagar (Genesis 21:14-21); Naomi and Ruth (Ruth 1:1–4:17); Hannah (1 Samuel 1:2-2:10); Abigail (1 Samuel 25:2-42); the queen of Sheba (1 Kings 10:1-10,13; 2 Chronicles 9:1-9,12); the Shunammite woman (2 Kings 4:8-37); Esther (Esther 2:5–9:32) and others. One woman, Athaliah, even ruled Judah for a while (2 Kings 11:1-3). The ideal wife, according to Proverbs 31:10-31, was a strong and self-sufficient woman. The woman in the Song of Solomon was presented as an equal to the man in understanding and initiating the intimacies of love.

In addition to illustrating the leadership abilities of women, the Hebrew Bible contains feminine images of God.[33] The prophet Isaiah, speaking for God, said: "As a mother comforts her child, so I will comfort you; you shall be comforted in Jerusalem" (Isaiah 66:13). Some other examples of feminine images of God include presentations of the Lord as pregnant and giving birth (Numbers 11:12; Deuteronomy 32:18; Isaiah 42:14, 46:3-4, 49:15, 66:9); nursing (Numbers 11:12; Isaiah 49:15); and serving in the role of the traditional Israelite mother (Hosea 11:1,3-4).

Perhaps the most powerful commentary found in the Hebrew Bible regarding sexism is the story of David and Bathsheba (2 Samuel 11:1–12:13). The author described how King David ordered Bathsheba to have sexual intercourse with him. His behavior was sexist as well as adulterous. Also, as the king, David was in effect ordering Bathsheba to have sexual relations with her husband's employer. (Uriah, Bathsheba's husband, was a soldier in David's army.) If she refused, it could affect her husband's job. By today's Western standards, this would be tantamount to sexual harassment. Beyond any doubt, it would today be considered an act of rape. Had Bathsheba refused, the king could have ordered her death. David had abused his power and violated Bathsheba's marriage. In the face of such blatant sexism, God sent the prophet Nathan to confront King David powerfully with his sin: "You are the man! . . . Why have you despised the word of the LORD, to do what is evil in his sight?" (2 Samuel 12:7,9).

Jesus

The life and ministry of Jesus significantly influence how we understand God's view of women and how men are to relate to women. Anne Nasimiyu-Wasike writes, "The original relationship between women and men first established by God at creation was restored in Jesus Christ."[34] Jesus related to women as equals. "The fact that this impression has been transmitted through the writings of men who shared the assumptions of their culture indicates how strong this feature was in the ministry of Jesus," states Barbara J. MacHaffie.[35]

Jesus affirmed women in many ways. In a society that strictly segregated the relationships of men and women, he was very comfortable in the presence of women. Jesus was not afraid to touch women physically. He offered a healing touch to a woman who had been bent over for eighteen years (Luke 13:10-17). Then he called her a "daughter of Abraham," and her dignity was given new life. Men were called sons of Abraham, but it was unheard of to call a woman a "daughter of Abraham." Women also touched Jesus, and he was neither embarrassed nor dismayed by this action. There was a woman with an issue of blood who touched his garment, hoping to be healed (Matthew 9:20-22, Mark 5:25-34, Luke

8:43-48). Jesus did not scold her for touching a rabbi. He celebrated her faith. Once a "sinful" woman bathed Jesus' feet with her tears, dried them with her hair, kissed them, and anointed them with ointment. When others questioned her intimate actions, Jesus accepted this act of love as born out of her gratitude for God's forgiveness (Luke 7:36-50).

Jesus often talked with women about matters of faith. Most men considered this to be inappropriate and a waste of time. Jesus considered these discussions about faith to be at the center of his ministry—a ministry that was directed equally to women and to men. So he conversed about godly matters with a woman from Samaria (John 4:7-26), a Canaanite woman (Matthew 15:21-28; Mark 7:24-30); Martha of Bethany (John 11:21-27); Mary of Bethany (Luke 10:38-42); Mary Magdalene (John 20:17); and others. Among those who followed Jesus in his ministry were women (Matthew 27:55-56; Mark 15:40-41; Luke 8:2-3). There was Mary Magdalene, Mary the mother of James and Joseph, the mother of the sons of Zebedee, Salome, Susanna, Joanna (the wife of Herod's steward), and many others who were left unnamed. Biblical scholar Joachim Jeremias called this "an unprecedented happening in the history of that time."[36] Barbara MacHaffie adds that "these women broke with Jewish custom in order to leave their homes and travel openly with Jesus."[37] It was women followers who funded Jesus' itinerant ministry (Mark 15:40-41; Luke 8:2-3). Jesus often stayed as a guest at the home of two sisters, Mary and Martha of Bethany, who were also most likely among the women who followed Jesus (Luke 10:38-42; John 11). The call to follow Jesus was very demanding and required great sacrifice. It meant leaving behind family members. Among the sacrifices of discipleship, Jesus included leaving behind sisters (Matthew 19:29; Mark 10:29-30). In male-oriented Palestine, leaving behind a brother, a father, and perhaps a mother brought a sense of loss. Leaving behind your sister was not worth comment or consideration.[38] Yet Jesus thought it was significant.

Women played some of the most important roles in the life and ministry of Jesus. The first person to receive the knowledge that Jesus was the Messiah was a woman in Samaria (John 4:25-26). While Peter is best known for his declaration that Jesus was the Christ (Matthew 16:16), Martha of Bethany also professed that Jesus was the Messiah (John 11:27). The first evangelist of the Christian era was a woman (John 4:28-30,39-42). It was a woman, Mary of Bethany, who was the first to be aware that Jesus was going to die (Matthew 26:6-13; Mark 14:3-9; John 12:3-8). Those who stayed with Jesus through the crucifixion were all women, except for "the disciple whom Jesus loved" (Matthew 26:56; Mark 14:50; John 19:25-27). Women were the first to discover the empty tomb (Matthew 28:1; Mark 16:1-2; Luke 24:1-12; John 20:1-10). The first people to see Jesus resurrected were women (Matthew 28:8-10; Mark 16:9-11; John 20:11-18). In fact, as Elisabeth Moltmann-Wendel reminds us, "The most important traditions, i.e. those of the death, burial and resurrection of Jesus, go back to women, because they were the only followers of Jesus who were there at the time."[39]

The equality of women can also be observed in how Jesus balanced his teachings and illustrations between the life experiences of both men and women.[40] Jesus said that the kingdom of heaven was like a mustard seed planted by a man and the yeast used by a woman in baking (Matthew 13:31-33). He compared the kingdom of heaven both to ten bridesmaids and to a man and his servants (Matthew 25:1-30). The joy in heaven when a sinner repents was likened to a shepherd that left behind ninety-nine sheep to find the one that was lost and to a woman who swept her house looking for the coin she lost (Luke 15:3-10). When talking about prayer, Jesus equated the act to a widow who constantly demanded justice from a judge and to the attitude of two men, a Pharisee and a tax collector (Luke 18:1-14). In a sermon about the end of time, Jesus said that two people would be together with one being taken and the other left behind. He first illustrated this with two men in a field and then with two women grinding meal (Matthew 24:41-42). In addition to using the experiences of women as illustrations for teaching, Jesus used feminine imagery in his evangelism. When Jesus spoke to the theologian Nicodemus about his spiritual need, he used the image of giving birth to describe the spiritual transformation that Nicodemus needed in his life (John 3:3-7). On another occasion, Jesus compared his own mission to a hen gathering her chicks under her wings (Matthew 23:37; Luke 13:34).

Jesus addressed the various forms of sexism of his day. The laws on divorce were biased in favor of men; only men could divorce their wives. This was because the wife was essentially the property of the man.[41] While Jesus did not endorse divorce, he allowed that a woman had the same right as a man to initiate a divorce (Mark 10:11-12). In another setting, Jesus challenged the perception that only women could commit adultery (John 8:3-11). The religious leaders were ready to stone a woman they had caught in the very act, yet they had showed little interest in identifying the man. Jesus disarmed their sexism at the point of their own sin. He also confronted the sexism of the culture in first-century Palestine, where women were seen as objects of lust (Matthew 5:27-29).

The fact that the Jesus of history was born a male causes concern for some who seek to hear the feminine voice of God. Yet, considering the male-dominated society of the first century, sending Jesus as a man could be perceived as a stroke of genius. Jesus could respond to sexism by modeling how men (and society in general) should relate to women. Virginia Fabella writes that "by being male, Jesus could repudiate more effectively the male definition of humanity and show the way to a right and just male-female relationship, challenging both men and women to change their life patterns."[42] Kelly Brown Douglas adds that Jesus "was able to reject the privileges of being male in a patriarchal world."[43] Ultimately, Jacquelyn Grant is correct when she states that "the significance of Christ is not his maleness, but his humanity."[44]

Early Church

Women were at the forefront of leadership in the early church. This was displayed clearly in Saul's eagerness to put them in jail to end the Jesus movement (Acts 8:3, 9:2).[45] After Saul became Paul, he was smart enough to make sure that many of his co-workers were women. Of the thirty-four people Paul mentioned at the end of his letter to the Romans, sixteen were women (Romans 16). Many women were leaders of house churches. Among those listed in the New Testament are Mary (Acts 12:12); Lydia (Acts 16:14-15,40); Prisca (Romans 16:3-5; 1 Corinthians 16:19); Chloe (1 Corinthians 1:11); Nympha (Colossians 4:15); and Apphia (Philemon 2).[46] Euodia and Syntyche probably were among the leadership of the church in Philippi since Paul singled them out with a plea for them to resolve their disagreement (Philippians 4:2-3).

Prisca (sometimes referred to as Priscilla) was a prominent woman leader. She worked in a team ministry with her husband, Aquilla. Prisca was probably the lead partner in this ministry. Her name is mentioned first four times out of the six occurrences (Acts 18:2,18,26; Romans 16:3; 1 Corinthians 16:9; 2 Timothy 4:19).[47] Since it was common to mention the man's name first, this was most likely a way of declaring her leadership. Prisca and Aquilla were involved in teaching Apollos, the African preacher from Alexandria, about the way of God, and "since Prisca is mentioned first in Acts 18:26, it was probably she who was primarily responsible for Apollos' conversion."[48]

There were women whose titles suggested they had significant positions among the leadership of the early church. Philip's four daughters were prophets (Acts 21:9). Phoebe was a minister in the church at Cenchreae (Romans 16:1-2). Junia was "prominent among the apostles" (Romans 16:7). Fourth-century church leader John Chrysostom, writing about Junia, said, "Oh how great is the devotion of this woman that she should be counted worthy of the appellation of apostle."[49] While Junia is the only woman who was listed using the title "apostle," others were qualified. The qualifications were that one had seen Jesus resurrected and had been commissioned to preach (Acts 2:21-22; 1 Corinthians 9:1; Galatians 1:1,11-12). As Virginia Fabella writes, "Paul's claim to be an apostle because he had seen the risen Jesus and received a direct commission to preach the good news applies equally to Mary Magdalene."[50]

Although the Pauline letters are often quoted in support of the dominance of men, portions of these writings demonstrate an understanding of the equality of women. The apostle Paul's statement in Galatians 3:28 that "there is no longer male and female; for all of you are one in Christ Jesus" captured the theme. Another interesting passage that demonstrates an understanding of unity is where Paul discussed marriage and the single life in light of the expected return of Jesus Christ (1 Corinthians 7:1-40).[51] He addressed his remarks to both men and women in a fashion that was mutual: husbands and wives both had equal conjugal rights (vv. 2-5); men and women both were allowed to divorce if their unbelieving spouse wanted out of the marriage (vv. 10-16); single women and single men were both encouraged to remain unmarried in order to focus on ministry (vv. 25-28,32-35).

In the act of creation, God presented to the world a man and woman both equally possessing the image of the Almighty. Even in the midst of a highly sexist society, God just kept calling, liberating, and empowering women as demonstrated by the extensive involvement of women as leaders in the biblical narratives. The actions of Jesus, as the Incarnation of God, speak forcefully in favor of the equality of women and men. Given the evidence, it is hard to believe that anyone can doubt this. The biblical texts that reflect the sexist attitudes of earlier times and undergird sexist tendencies in the church today seem contrary to the reality of the biblical record we just perused. Yet, as Carolyn Osiek writes, "a headache for biblical conservatives and an embarrassment for biblical liberals, the problem of oppressive texts will not soon go away."[52] But to say that women are less than equal to men is to demean the image of a just and righteous God.

How can we deal with the incongruity of the Bible on the issue of women? Perhaps we can follow a route similar to that suggested in the previous chapter regarding those passages that contradict the Bible's proclamation that God is a liberator. We must be willing to struggle with the seeming discrepancies in the Scriptures, which really point out the evolution of different ancient traditions, without losing sight of the fact that God created women as equal partners to men in the human endeavor. The men who wrote the Bible were attempting to recount the story of God's salvation, while often at a human level they were wearing the blinders of a sexist culture. Much of the time they captured the truth, as in the passages delineated above. Sometimes they fell prey to their human limitations. Both men and women need to embrace the approach to the Bible suggested by Osiek, when she states, "To read the Bible as women is to participate in a long and rich tradition, to be ready to critique the parts of that tradition that no longer serve, and to celebrate our belonging in a way that will make our contribution to generations to come."[53]

Classism

Like racism and sexism, classism inhibits the world's ability to be just. We live in a society that values people based on their status, power, appearance, celebrity, and wealth. In the class-conscious United States, people are ranked as upper class, upper middle class, middle class, lower middle class, working class, lower class, and under class. Other countries have their own class distinctions or caste systems. Unfortunately, many churches reflect this class division. The first-century followers of Jesus—fishermen, tax collectors, militant activists, prostitutes, tentmakers, and other poor and working people—would not feel comfortable in some congregations today. In fact, the carpenter-turned-preacher Jesus would not be welcome in some churches.

The Bible has much to say about the issue of social class.[54] Ronald Sider states that "the sheer volume of biblical material that pertains to questions of hunger, justice and the poor is astonishing."[55] The Scriptures lift up those who are oppressed (the poor, widows, orphans, sojourners, the sick, women, Samaritans, and others) and challenge the powerful and the rich to practice justice and equality. It is hard to believe that the Bible has been used to support economic domination when it has so much to say about God's concern for the poor. There are over two hundred and fifty references to the poor.[56] "The variety of the terms used to describe the poor in the Bible and the frequency of their occurrence is striking, and gives a unique flavour to the religiosity of the Bible," writes George M. Soares-Prabhu. "No other religious tradition I know of gives such importance to the poor or assigns to them so significant a role."[57] In our discussion of classism, we will use George M. Soares-Prabhu's definition:

> The poor of the Bible are all those who are in any way, and not just economically, deprived of the means or the dignity they need to lead a fully human existence; or who are in a situation of powerlessness which exposes them to such deprivation. . . . But whatever its form, poverty in the Bible is experienced not as a natural phenomenon . . . It is always identified as the avoidable and undesirable consequences of injustice and exploitation.[58]

Much of the discussion on liberation in chapter four related directly to classism. What follows will examine some biblical material not addressed in the previous chapter.

Hebrew Bible

As we demonstrated in chapter four, the Hebrews had integrated the need for just relationships into their faith statements and legal codes. Cain Hope Felder confirms this when he notes that "the earliest traditions of Hebraic thought or ancient Judaism do not separate social ethical obligations and religious observances."[59] The Hebrews served a God who had liberated them from the oppression of slavery and "low" social status. God expected Israelite society to treat others within society who were vulnerable with the same compassion. As the author of Exodus stated, "You shall not wrong or oppress a resident alien, for you were aliens in the land of Egypt. You shall not abuse any widow or orphan" (22:21-22).

The liberation of the Hebrews was vitally important to their understanding of how Israelite society should operate. John R. Donahue writes that for Israel, their treatment of "the marginal groups in society—the poor, the widows, the orphans, the aliens—become[s] the scale on which the justice of the whole society is weighed."[60] The author of Deuteronomy summed up the promise of Israel's social legislation: "There will, however, be no one in need among you, because the LORD is sure to bless you . . ." (15:4).

As a study of the Hebrew Scriptures makes clear, the nation of Israel did not translate its stated commitment to the poor and oppressed into concrete action. The people set free by God from slavery eventually enslaved others, including many of their own people, economically and socially. Classism was alive in the land of the "liberated" Hebrews. The fact that "the poor continue to exist becomes a scandal to the conscience of Israel and a warning that it has failed to live up to its calling."[61]

There were individual acts of kindness imparted upon people who found their lives molded by class distinctions. Even the king, David, reached out to Mephibosheth, the grandson of the former king, Saul (2 Samuel 9). Mephibosheth was marginalized by society for at least two reasons: he was a family member of the deposed king, and he was physically disabled with two lame feet. David invited him to eat at the king's table regularly. Compassionate actions directed at select individuals, while vitally important to that person's well-being, do not create by themselves a just and righteous society. Despite the suggestion of the author of Deuteronomy, one would be hard-pressed to demonstrate a time during the reign of Israel's monarchs when there were not persons in need.

In the midst of oppression and poverty, God does not forget those who cry out in their misery. The psalmist and the prophets spoke of God's love for the poor. The following two verses capture these sentiments:

> "Because the poor are despoiled, because the needy groan, I will now rise up," says the LORD; "I will place them in the safety for which they long" (Psalm 12:5; see 35:10).

> When the poor and needy seek water, and there is none, and their tongue is parched with thirst, I the LORD will answer them, I the God of Israel will not forsake them (Isaiah 41:17).

The lack of social justice in Israel and the concern of God for the vulnerable gave rise to the prophets and their mission. It was the prophets in the Hebrew Bible who challenged Israel to live up to its calling to be a model of justice. The prophetic books speak at length regarding the issue of classism. The prophets warned Israel's leaders of the dire consequences of their disobedience. These words of Isaiah, Ezekiel, and Amos represent the concern expressed by many of the prophets:

> Ah, you who make iniquitous decrees, who write oppressive statutes, to turn aside the needy from justice and to rob the poor of my people of their right, that widows may be your spoil, and that you may make the orphans your prey! What will you do on the day of punishment, in the calamity that will come from far away? To whom will you flee for help . . . ? (Isaiah 10:1-3; see 3:15).

> This was the guilt of your sister Sodom: she and her daughters had pride, excess of food, and prosperous ease, but did not aid the poor and needy (Ezekiel 16:49; see 22:29).

> I will not revoke the punishment; because they sell the righteous for a piece of silver, and the needy for a pair of sandals—they who trample the head of the poor into the dust of the earth, and push the afflicted out of the way . . . (Amos 2:6-7; see 8:4-7).

Not only did the prophets shout loudly the warning of God to those who were acting unjustly; they also called forth to

the people of Israel, inviting them to return to a right relationship with God. Any relationship with God that was
judged righteous had the practice of justice as its prime
component. Isaiah, Jeremiah, and Micah summed up the
perspective of these voices crying out in the wilderness:

> Is not this the fast I choose: to loose the bonds of
> injustice, to undo the thongs of the yoke, to let the op-
> pressed go free, and to break every yoke? Is it not to share
> your bread with the hungry, and bring the homeless poor
> into your house; when you see the naked, to cover them,
> and not to hide yourself from your own kin? . . . Then you
> shall call, and the LORD will answer; you shall cry for help,
> and he will say, Here I am (Isaiah 58:6-7,9).

> For if you truly amend your ways and your doings, if you
> truly act justly one with another, if you do not oppress the
> alien, the orphan, and the widow . . . then I will dwell with
> you in this place . . . (Jeremiah 7:5-7; see 22:15-16).

> He has told you, O mortal, what is good; and what does
> the LORD require of you but to do justice, and to love
> kindness, and to walk humbly with your God? (Micah 6:8).

The nation of Israel was a study in contradictions. It
worshiped a God of liberation yet oppressed its own people.
The nation's laws required justice, yet the government allowed unjust practices to thrive. Israel demanded a king to
be the representative of God to lead the Hebrew people, yet
the true voice of God's heart—justice and righteousness—
was heard through the prophets. The prophets, in the name
of God, denounced classism!

Jesus

Jesus came as the Incarnation of God's love for the poor
and despised. Like James H. Cone has stated, "To understand
the historical Jesus without seeing his identification with the
poor as decisive is to misunderstand him and thus distort his
historical person."[62] As we demonstrated in chapter four,
Jesus' message and lifestyle effused liberation. The message

of justice for the poor and oppressed was prophesied over Jesus even while he was still in the womb of his mother. It was his mother, Mary, who proclaimed, "He has brought down the powerful from their thrones, and lifted up the lowly; he has filled the hungry with good things, and sent the rich away empty" (Luke 1:52-53).

The Savior of humanity was reared in a "working-class" home. Jesus' first sermon spoke of "good news" for the poor and oppressed (Luke 4:18-19). He chose his disciples from among the powerless and despised of society, in effect lifting up the lowly.[63] Jesus echoed the words of his mother's prophesy in his Sermon on the Plain when he proclaimed blessings on the poor and woes on the rich (Luke 6:20-26). He lived a life of solidarity with those who were considered outcasts. He often slept outside because he had "nowhere to lay his head" (Matthew 8:20; Luke 9:58).

Jesus had little patience for classism. He challenged individuals whose egos were intertwined with class-based needs for wealth and status. Two such individuals were a rich young ruler (Matthew 19:16-30; Mark 10:17-31; Luke 18:18-30) and Zacchaeus (Luke 19:2-10). Jesus invited them to let go of worldly wealth and become "spiritually rich." Jesus also addressed institutional classism. His most dramatic effort was the clearing of the money changers from the temple (Matthew 21:12-17; Mark 11:15-19; Luke 19:45-48; John 2:13-17). Jesus confronted the classism of the culture by exalting people like the widow who contributed all she had to the temple offering (Mark 12:41-44; Luke 21:1-4). He also told parables like that of the rich fool (Luke 12:13-21) and the rich man and Lazarus (Luke 16:19-31) to address class issues. When Jesus washed the feet of his disciples, he powerfully exalted the role of the servant (John 13:1-20). Every aspect of his life and ministry contradicted the nature of class structures. Jesus reached out to those pressed down by social class and confronted those benefiting from class at the expense of others. Jesus lived and taught the ethic of the intrinsic equality of all people and the creation of all in the image of God. In the final judgment, according to Jesus, salvation is directly equated with one's concern for the vulnerable (Matthew 25:31-46). Caring for the poor was like ministering to the Lord directly. According to Jesus, the classist will find herself or himself responding in the following manner:

> "Lord, when was it that we saw you hungry or thirsty or a stranger or naked or sick or in prison, and did not take care of you?" Then he will answer them, "Truly I tell you, just as you did not do it to one of the least of these, you did not do it to me." And these will go away into eternal punishment, but the righteous into eternal life (Matthew 25:44-46).

Early Church

Obviously, the early church included many who were poor or marginalized by society because it was initiated by those who followed Jesus during his ministry. When some congregations began to prosper economically, there remained a commitment to serve the poor. This was illustrated by Paul's effort to collect money from a number of congregations to help the poor believers in Jerusalem (Acts 11:29-30; 24:17; Romans 15:25-27; 1 Corinthians 16:1-3; 2 Corinthians 8:1-9:15; Galatians 2:10). Also, Paul regularly reminded the churches that in Christ there were to be no class distinctions (1 Corinthians 12:13; Galatians 3:28, Colossians 3:11).

Of the books of the New Testament, the Letter of James provides the strongest rebuke of classist behavior (2:1-13) and perhaps the most stringent statement directed at the rich (5:1-6). In his letter, James challenged the faith of his readers when he wrote:

> My brothers and sisters, do you with your acts of favoritism really believe in our glorious Lord Jesus Christ? For if a person with gold rings and in fine clothes comes into your assembly, and if a poor person in dirty clothes also

comes in, and if you take notice of the one wearing the fine clothes and say, "Have a seat here, please," while to the one who is poor you say, "Stand there," or "Sit at my feet," have you not made distinctions among yourselves, and become judges with evil thoughts? (2:1-4).

James questioned whether one can truly be a Christian if one exhibits such classist behavior. His question should cause many of us in our time to reexamine our attitudes and how our faith is lived. James continued his commentary on the classism that was seeping into the church:

Has not God chosen the poor in the world to be rich in faith and to be heirs of the kingdom that he has promised to those who love him? But you have dishonored the poor. Is it not the rich who oppress you? Is it not they who drag you into court? Is it not they who blaspheme the excellent name that was invoked over you? You do well if you really fulfill the royal law according to the scripture, "You shall love your neighbor as yourself" (2:5-8).

James challenged his readers to observe the rich faith of the people they were treating with such disregard. Then he reminded these believers that they were placing favor on the very people who had oppressed them. So often we seek acceptance from the very people who are hurting us. The systems of our world are often in direct contradiction to the faith we claim.

Both the Hebrew Bible and the New Testament inform us that there will always be poor and needy people (Deuteronomy 15:11; Matthew 26:11; Mark 14:7; John 12:8). This is simply an honest recognition of the fact that evil pervades our world through the practices of unjust individuals and oppressive systems that keep people poor. For this reason, throughout the Hebrew Scriptures there is a constant refrain condemning classism and expressing God's love for the poor. This theme remained a priority in the ministry of Jesus and the early church. The book of Revelation also speaks of the future judgment of those who lived in luxury at the expense of the poor and downtrodden (Revelation 18–19). While the biblical record on sexism is at times incongruent, Scripture makes it very clear that classism is contrary to the will and the nature of God.

No Justice, No Peace

As we stated at the outset, racism, sexism, and classism intersect. All injustice is intertwined. The woman that Jesus conversed with at Jacob's well in Samaria was affected by racism, sexism, and classism (John 4:4-18). She experienced prejudice as a Samaritan, sexism as a woman, and classism because of her lifestyle. This woman had been married five times and was living with a man who was not her husband. So intense was her shame and rejection that rather than getting water in the cool of the morning or evening, she drew water from the well in the heat of the day. The Samaritan community experienced life as outcasts. This woman from Samaria had been cast out of a community of outcasts. Jesus reached out in compassion and empowered her in the presence of his disciples and her community.

Jesus broke nearly every social taboo of first-century society by liberating the victims of injustice and by challenging the individual, institutional, and cultural forms of injustice. Our biblical faith calls us to follow his example. Let our sentiments be like those of Mercy Amba Oduyoye:

> I have arrived at a point where I no longer wish to be patient with sexism, racism, and injustices against the dignity that rightly belongs to beings made in the image of God. These labels are losing their force, but the realities they point to, the burden and the evil we are naming, continue.[64]

Peace, peace, but there is no peace. There will be no peace until we take seriously the biblical mandate to work for social justice, specifically against racism, sexism, and classism.

Questions for Discussion

1. Define the following terms: *justice, peace, prejudice, racism, sexism,* and *classism*.

2. Describe the relationship of peace and justice as understood in the Bible. Is it possible to create a peaceful environment without giving attention to social justice? Why or why not?

3. Identify how racism is affecting your community. Is there a "curse" mentality at work? What are some of the ways that we can remove racism from our communities?

4. In your opinion, why did the apostle Peter have such a difficult time with ethnic prejudice? Was it appropriate for Paul to confront him? How would you handle a similar situation today?

5. Do you think of God as a male? If so, why? If not, how do you think of God?

6. How do we come to terms with the incongruity of the Bible on the issue of women?

7. If classism is so clearly stated as wrong in the Bible, why is it such an issue for modern Christianity?

8. Racism, sexism, and classism are all injustices. In what ways are they interrelated? How do they differ from each other? Can someone who experiences racism still be a classist or sexist? Can someone who is affected by sexism still practice racism or classism? Can someone victimized by class still hold sexist and racist attitudes? Why or why not?

9. Racism, sexism, and classism can be found in at least three forms: individual, institutional, and cultural. Identify some strategies for addressing these "isms" in each of their forms in personal attitudes, the community, and the church.

10. After reading chapter five, in what ways are you committed to work for peace and justice in society and in the church?

Chapter Six

Community in the Midst of Diversity

Throughout this book we have examined the ways in which cultural perspectives enrich our understanding of the Scriptures. God, as revealed in the Bible, is a God of liberation who calls us to confront injustice. Racism, sexism, and classism are barriers to peace and reconciliation. Our biblical faith invites us to follow an Afro-Asiatic Jesus of history who was, by the Resurrection, transformed into the universal Christ. As such, Christ embraces, critiques, and transcends all cultures. We have consistently lifted up the biblical passages and themes that proclaim the oneness of the human family, as well as those that celebrate the rich mosaic of our cultural expressions.

Although we may be one family, it is easy to demonstrate that "community" is a rare experience in society. In many parts of the world, we find people isolated by the unique aspects of their humanity. Men and women, even in marriage, can find themselves lonely for someone who truly understands their journey. Parents and children under the same roof often live in worlds with dramatically different value systems. The opportunities of the rich versus those of the poor, the experiences of whites versus those of people of color, the perspectives of East versus those of the West, and the histories of indigenous peoples versus those of immigrants—all contribute to a multitude of differing cultural world-views. Our lifestyles are often barely comprehensible to each other. These different, and sometimes conflicting, ways of understanding human existence have led to an experiential separation by race, culture, nationality, gender, age, economic status, and the like. The breakup of the human family leads to using the "other" as a scapegoat for all the world's problems. It has brought us ethnic cleansing, holocaust, genocide, and a host of other ills. Discovering a humane and beloved community in the midst of such human diversity is indeed an imposing proposition.

Even among people who are "alike" we discover very little real community. In the so-called advanced societies in our world, modern technology has made direct human interaction nearly unnecessary. We can now work exclusively through computers and fax machines, eat food delivered to our doorstep, shop for material needs on cable television, relate intimately with images of people created by virtual reality, seek counseling by phone, and get religion through television. Too many people's lives are structured by a daily existence that isolates them from others.

Community is also an uncommon experience for people of faith. We have not heeded Martin Luther King, Jr.'s call "for a world-wide fellowship that lifts neighborly concern beyond one's tribe, race, and nation . . . an all-embracing and unconditional love" for all people. King wrote, "When I speak of love, I am speaking of that force which all the great religions have seen as the supreme unifying principle of life." For King, community was "an absolute necessity" for the survival of humanity.[1] A generation later, the faith community remains fraught with division and mistrust. At times it actually foments animosity. Our limited attempts at togetherness have been defined by very narrow parameters.

A 1991 report, *Milwaukee's Faith Community Speaks*,[2] collected the thoughts of leaders in the faith community of Milwaukee, Wisconsin. The insights of eighty-one leaders from different religious persuasions were compiled.[3] The report hoped to initiate a process that would lead to a spirit of cooperation and unity among the city's community of faith. It produced a meaningful consensus on the need to address racism and poverty, as well as challenging people of faith to hear the parallel calls from their Scriptures to pursue unity and justice. The report spoke even louder, though, of the fragmented condition of the faith community, stating, "Achieving unity within the faith community could prove to be difficult. Religious leaders said they would need to set aside theological differences, historical conflicts, personality clashes, jealousies, and individual goals if unity were to be achieved . . ."[4] Adding the separation that results from racism, sexism, classism, cultural insensitivity, religious belief, and the like, it would almost seem that we do not really want to live together.

Even though bona fide community is an unusual occurrence in our world, people still long for a sense of belonging and togetherness. We need community, a place to call home, and a relational web built on trust and support.[5] As Howard Thurman has mused, "Every person is at long last concerned with community. There is a persistent strain in the human spirit that rejects the experience of isolation as being alien to its genius. . . . community is the native climate of the human spirit."[6] Without the experience of community, our life is deprived of meaning.

The Bible and Community

The Bible has much to say about community. In the very act of creating humanity, God initiated community. When God created humanity, the spiritual aspect of community began (God and human forging a relationship). In creating Adam and Eve, God initiated human community. From the beginning, God determined that community is indeed "the native climate of the human experience." In general, the book of Genesis views the extended family as community. It began with the union of Adam and Eve and continued through the families of Noah, Abraham, Isaac, and Jacob. The biblical concept of community expanded during the days of enslave-

ment in Egypt from consisting of the extended family of Jacob
to including a community of people, the Hebrews. After the
Exodus from Africa, community came to be understood as
encompassing the whole nation of Israel. In the Hebrew
Scriptures, community proceeded from the relationship of a
man and a women and their immediate family, to an extended
family, to a cultural understanding (the Hebrews), to an
ethnic understanding (the nation of Israel). Finally, some of
the prophets began to tentatively speak of a more universal
understanding that was inclusive of people from all nations
(Isaiah 2:2-4; 19:24-25; Hosea 2:23; Amos 9:7; Zephaniah
3:9-10).

Jesus' ministry, and that of his disciples, was concerned
with redefining and expanding the notion of community
based on the prophetic understanding of God's love for all
of humanity. One way of looking at Jesus and his followers
is to view them as a community of men and women who
had been cast aside by society. This fact, combined with
the understanding of the prophets, greatly influenced the
shape of the Jesus community. The early church understood community to be made up of those persons who had
a relationship with a resurrected and living Jesus Christ.
This was acknowledged at their gatherings when they
proclaimed, *"Maranatha"*—"Come, Lord Jesus." The early
Christians believed that the risen Christ was present when
they gathered together.[7] Their understanding can be summed
up by the words of Dietrich Bonhoeffer when he wrote,
"Christianity means community through Jesus Christ and in
Jesus Christ."[8]

Probably the most commonly used word for the community
of God's people, in the Christian era, has been "church"
(ekklesia), those who were "called out." In Matthew 16:18,
Jesus declared that he would build his church on the faith of
the disciples. The early disciples thought of themselves as
the people of Jesus, the church.[9] It is interesting to compare
two very distinct ways that the apostle Paul described the
church of God in Corinth.[10]

To the church of God that is in Corinth, to those who are sanctified in Christ Jesus, called to be saints, together with all those who in every place call on the name of our Lord Jesus Christ . . . (1 Corinthians 1:2).

Consider your own call, brothers and sisters: not many of you were wise by human standards, not many were powerful, not many were of noble birth. But God chose what is foolish in the world to shame the wise; God chose what is weak in the world to shame the strong; God chose what is low and despised in the world, things that are not, to reduce to nothing things that are, so that no one might boast in the presence of God (1 Corinthians 1:26-29).

In the span of some twenty verses, Paul went from calling the church a community of sanctified and holy people to describing it as a group of folks who were foolish, powerless, low, and despised. Through the use of these two apparently diametrically opposed descriptions, Paul demonstrated his genius for understanding how God's power operates in community. The essence of the image of the church was that when the people of God assembled together, they were no longer defined by the standards of society; they became a people called out of the world by God. They were set apart and made holy.

For some, the image of "the church" remains compelling. For others it has become a stumbling block to faith. The following comments represent these two divergent views on the church today:

People whose humanity is often denied in society at large—and for whom the memory of slavery, segregation, exile, and refugee camp is very vivid—find in the church an atmosphere that not only welcomes them, but grants them full citizenship. If our people have an experience of deliverance, it is often through worship that such an experience is experienced and expressed. The churches are the most stable institutions in most of our poorest neighborhoods, and the only ones that remain there when public or private funding falters. They have been and still are the place where most autochthonous ethnic minority leadership is trained . . .[11]

Despite the many impressive cathedrals of Europe and America, and the highly visible, vocal and commercial nature of so much of American religiosity, many people perceive the Church as irrelevant to the on-going, vital concerns of daily life. For these, the Church has become too closely identified with national culture and the economic-political establishment. The realities of the church's own institutional self-interest and role as conservator of socio-cultural values have, perhaps unwittingly, caused her to function almost as priest—at times even royal priest—to the *status quo,* while tending to forget her call to prophetic witness.[12]

These statements report two realities, both of which call themselves "church."[13] One sounds much like the community of faith described in the New Testament. The other describes a state or civic church that has lost its relevance. It does not have the vibrancy necessary to motivate people to come together in community. In today's world, the term "church" evokes differing images and, therefore, sends mixed signals.

Another image used by the apostle Paul to describe the community of faith was "body of Christ" *(soma Christou).* Paul's image revealed that every member of the community had something to give, and all gifts were valued (1 Corinthians 12:12-27). Paul Minear saw in the image of the body of Christ "a way of describing a social revolution." He wrote, "The image of the head and its body was thus used to attack at its deepest cosmic and psychic roots the perennial human habit of accepting as ultimate the world's way of dividing mankind into competing societies, whether religious, racial, cultural, or economic."[14] Unfortunately, in our day, the concept of the head and its body has been used to support domination: husbands over wives, men over women, pastors over congregations, and so on. The image of the "body of Christ" no longer tends to communicate the biblical vision of community in some circles.

There are a number of images of community in the Bible. (As we have illustrated, some have been robbed of their ability to convey the quintessence of the people of God.) We will peruse four such images that have great potential and particular relevance in our time for portraying what God's community should be like. They are: Israel as a contrast community, the household of God, the *koinonia* fellowship, and the table fellowship of Jesus.

Contrast Community

The Hebrew people were set free from slavery in Egypt by God for the express purpose of creating a community that would be a model to the other peoples in the region. This is the contention of George M. Soares-Prabhu when he calls Israel a "contrast community."[15] He writes, "Biblical history thus begins with the liberation of the poor. A group of utterly powerless bonded labourers rescued by Yahweh are summoned to be the nucleus of his contrast community."[16] Israel was to offer an alternative, a contrast, to the ways of other nations. Soares-Prabhu supports his assertion when he states:

> The Sinai covenant spells out the new social order which Israel is to adopt in order to become Yahweh's people, that is, to form the free, just, non-exploitative community that will serve as a "contrast community" to the oppressive, violent and power-hungry city states among which Israel lives.[17]

The laws given in Exodus, Leviticus, and Deuteronomy emphasized social justice and human relations.[18] As stated in chapter four, the jubilee year was an exemplary ideal of placing just relationships at the core of Israel's community life. It would seem that God wanted to demonstrate that, in order for community to flourish, it must integrate equality and justice into the formation of its organizational principles and ways of daily living.

This image of the contrast community is exemplified well by Steve Charleston's understanding of the tribe, which he calls "a metaphor for community."[19] He maintains that

> Native civilization in North America represented a political, social, and economic system that radiated out from a religious center through the communal network of ex-

tended family and kinship. . . . Native People do not share
the assumptions and mythologies of their oppressors. They
do not simply want a higher place on the pyramid of
capitalism; they do not want a bigger piece of the action for
themselves; they do not aspire to joining the middle class.
They do not want *more*. As the tribe they want enough for
all to share equally.[20]

This captures what the Hebrew people, as a contrast community, were to model for their neighbors. They were to be a
community that emphasized liberation, social justice, equality, and human dignity by refusing to assimilate to the ways
of governing found in Pharaoh's court or among the nations
in Palestine.

The experimental use of Israel as a model of God's justice
and liberty did not last long. Soares-Prabhu believes that it
ended when Israel asked for a king.[21] I would suggest that
the contrast community probably was never implemented.
The underlying concepts for this contrast community were
developed in the wilderness years during the charismatic
leadership of Moses. But when Joshua led the Hebrew people
into the "Promised Land" of their new communal home, the
children of Israel certainly did not model this sense of justice
when relating to their new neighbors. Soares-Prabhu concludes that "the dream of one day realizing this 'contrast
community' remains an inalienable part of Israel's hope."[22]

Had the contrast community been actualized, it would
have revolutionized biblical—indeed, world—history. It
would have been much like Charleston's vision of the tribe.
He issues the following invitation:

The tribe as a metaphor for community is dangerous. It
is dangerous to colonial capitalism. It is dangerous to
racism. It is dangerous because it is a symbol for the
strength of the oppressed. It is an inclusive symbol for all
women and men who want to wake up from the dream. It
says to people of all colors and cultures: There is a better
way. Let go of the myths and the images and the empty
promises. Join hands in the strong bond of kinship. Become
a tribe.[23]

Charleston's challenge to people of faith to become a tribe resonates with the understanding that Jesus and the early church had of community, as we shall see in the following images of God's community.

Household of God

The vision of a contrast community expressed the need for people to be organized in nonoppressive ways. Any attempt today to create a sense of togetherness should begin with this understanding. Since a community of justice was never actualized, God sent Jesus to incarnate the jubilee spirit of the contrast community. The biblical community of God was not only called to offer a contrast to the way society was organized; it proclaimed that relationships needed to be reordered. The household of God *(oikeioi tou Theou)* is an image that conveys powerfully these new ways of understanding relationships that are needed for a sense of community to thrive. In the New Testament, the image of the household of God was used to depict the followers of Jesus Christ in the Petrine literature (1 Peter 4:17) and the Pauline literature (Galatians 6:10, Ephesians 2:19). The apostle Paul captured the essence of the household when he wrote:

> So then you are no longer strangers and aliens, but you are citizens with the saints and also members of the household of God, built upon the foundation of the apostles and prophets, with Christ Jesus himself as the cornerstone. In him the whole structure is joined together into a holy temple in the Lord; in whom you also are built together spiritually into a dwelling place for God (Ephesians 2:19-22).

In the household of faith, our relationship with God takes priority over our relatedness to family, race, culture, nation, gender, or any other group we belong to. This reordering also transforms how we relate to each other. The concept of family was reconstrued in the household of God. The terms *sister, brother, mother, father, friend,* and *neighbor* were all reinterpreted and redefined by Jesus. When we enter into and live in the household of God, "no longer are blood relations to be the people of God's decisive criterion for determining family relations."[24] As Jesus said, "For whoever does the will of my Father in heaven is my brother and sister and mother" (Matthew 12:50). Discussions about "family values" are enriched when they begin with the image of the household of God as the foundation of Jesus' understanding of family. The family that Jesus envisioned was not held captive by the boundaries of tradition and society. Modern families are falling apart and neighborhoods are disintegrating because they have not been built on the foundation of the household of God. Only when we revitalize the family of God will there be hope for our families and neighborhoods.

In the story of the prodigal son (Luke 15:11-32), Cain Hope Felder suggests that the

> householder epitomizes the work of Jesus, who—unlike many other ancient Jews—forgives and shows extraordinary compassion for all who languish in the margins of ancient Jewish society: women, children, slaves, outcasts, tax collectors, prostitutes, paralytics, the blind, epileptics, the mentally ill, and even Gentiles.[25]

Jesus, as God Incarnate, demonstrated that the family of God included even those our society refuses to consider as family. God invites all members of the human family to enter into the household. God welcomes into the household those who do not belong anywhere. With God as the head of the household, we are guaranteed a parental figure who loves us unconditionally and always has our best interest at heart.

The household of God includes people from diverse cultures and life experiences. According to Felder, "Because of Christ's blood, all believers are supposed to be transported into a new Household of reconciliation and solidarity."[26] This calls us back to our oneness. African theologian Anselme T. Sanon illustrates this concept:

> In the tradition of a region of my tribe, a new village is always founded on the banks of two currents of water, so that, at their confluence, the root, or place of rooting, of the

village is found. In the new community of Christ, which must be founded on all shores of the world, a junction must be struck, under penalty of treason, at a confluence—to drain the rich alluvions of all peoples of all lands of the great river, to the shore of shores, the face of Christ.[27]

The household of God is an image that beckons the community of Jesus Christ to be a place of convergence for the great rivers of humanity. People of all cultures, races, languages, nations, tribes, and clans reside in the household of faith. The household of God is analogous to the theme of the Kendall Community Church of God in Miami, Florida, which proclaims that they are "inter-national, inter-cultural, inter-denominational, and interesting."[28]

Koinonia

God's community is meant to be a model of justice. Its household includes a rich mosaic of people who are invited by God. The people of God are also summoned to be a fellowship based on equal sharing. The biblical image of *koinonia* epitomizes a quality of fellowship that encourages participation and togetherness that is linked by a common cause. It is a fellowship with each other and with God as we walk in the light of Jesus Christ (1 John 1:3,6-7). The use of *koinonia* as an image of the community of God was modeled in the communal life of the believers after Pentecost. The author of Acts described their way of life:

All who believed were together and had all things in common; they would sell their possessions and goods and distribute the proceeds to all, as any had need. Day by day, as they spent much time together in the temple, they broke bread at home and ate their food with glad and generous hearts, praising God and having the goodwill of all the people. And day by day the Lord added to their number those who were being saved. . . . Now the whole group of those who believed were of one heart and soul, and no one claimed private ownership of any possessions, but everything they owned was held in common. With great power the apostles gave their testimony to the resurrection of the

Lord Jesus, and great grace was upon them all. There was not a needy person among them, for as many as owned lands or houses sold them and brought the proceeds of what was sold. They laid it at the apostles' feet, and it was distributed to each as any had need (Acts 2:44-47, 4:32-35).

This passage informs us that true community is possible only when there is sacrifice and substantial sharing. Many may want to discount the importance of this passage. Perhaps because we live in a time of selfishness, we can hardly conceive of economic sharing as the will of God for the Christian community. We have heard too many sermons claiming that the evidence of God's blessing is financial prosperity. A look at much of the church in twentieth-century America could convince one that consumerism has become a form of spirituality. Paul Minear declares that the early followers of Jesus Christ exhibited the spirit of *koinonia:*

Being possessed by the same spirit, they no longer considered their own possessions as their own . . . they had everything in common. . . . believers were introduced by their faith into a radically new kind of fellowship, which rightly should confer upon them all a freedom from fear of external enemies and from the tyranny of private possessions.[29]

A spirit of *koinonia* brings great freedom. Individuals can be set free from the emptiness of material prosperity or the desperation of poverty by meeting at the common ground of *koinonia*.

Koinonia includes more than economic sharing. It is "a cooperative sharing of talents and spiritual gifts toward the creation of an integrated, healed, and whole body."[30] The *koinonia* community is embodied in the Native American understanding of the circle. The symbol of the "circle is self-defining; it defines the limits of the people."[31] George Tinker writes:

The fundamental symbol of Plains Indians' existence is the circle, a symbol signifying the family, the clan, the tribe, and eventually all of creation. Because it has no

beginning and no end, all in the circle are of equal value. . . .
Native American egalitarian tendencies are worked out in
this spatial symbol in ways that go far beyond the classless
egalitarianism of socialism.[32]

God's *koinonia* invites us to a radical sharing of all of our
resources: finances, education, skills, gifts, wisdom, time,
and the like. As the circle has no end, so our sharing is to be
measureless. We are all equal in the *koinonia* community,
needing both to give and to receive.

Table Fellowship

Community emerges in the midst of diversity when all are
invited, embraced, accepted, and included. The most provocative image of community that Jesus modeled in his life was
his fellowship around the table with people who were considered sinners and outcasts in society.

> And as he sat at dinner in Levi's house, many tax
> collectors and sinners were also sitting with Jesus and his
> disciples—for there were many who followed him. When
> the scribes of the Pharisees saw that he was eating with
> sinners and tax collectors, they said to his disciples, "Why
> does he eat with tax collectors and sinners?" (Mark 2:15-
> 16).

Sharing a meal in first-century Palestine indicated the acceptance of those around the table. As Albert Nolan explains:

> In societies where there are barriers between classes,
> races or other status groups, the separation is maintained
> by means of a taboo on social mixing . . . The scandal Jesus
> caused in that society by mixing socially with sinners can
> hardly be imagined by most people today. It meant that he
> accepted them and approved of them and that he actually
> wanted to be "a friend of tax collectors and sinners" (Mt
> 11:19). The effect upon the poor and the oppressed them-
> selves was miraculous.[33]

Jesus intentionally shattered the boundaries instituted by
society and fashioned a new understanding of community
rooted in the grace of God. He boldly reached out to those

who were shunned by society and brought them to his table. Jesus publicly ate meals with individuals like Zacchaeus, "a chief tax collector" (Luke 19:2-10), and others who had been ostracized and isolated by society and religion. The personal implications for the people around the table were significant. As Marcus J. Borg writes, "It must have been an extraordinary experience for an outcast to be invited to share a meal with a man who was rumored to be a prophet. . . . and therefore his acceptance of them would have been perceived as a claim that they were accepted by God."[34] This indeed was the statement that Jesus was making. The table of God's community was open to everyone!

Jesus gained quite a reputation because of the people he invited to join him around the table. He was called "a glutton and a drunkard, a friend of tax collectors and sinners!" (Matthew 11:19, Luke 7:34). Religious leaders denounced Jesus by exclaiming, "This fellow welcomes sinners and eats with them" (Luke 15:2). As Nolan reminds us, "All the men of religion, even John the Baptist, were scandalised by the way he mixed socially with sinners, by the way he seemed to enjoy their company . . . In terms of group solidarity his friendship with sinners would classify him as a sinner."[35] Jesus was not your normal teacher. He taught about community by living in the presence of those who hungered for it most. No one was excluded from the table. Jesus even shared a table with Judas, who was preparing to betray him in a few hours (John 13:25). The concerns of the religious leaders did not intimidate Jesus. In fact, he allowed a woman who was considered a "sinner" to anoint his feet with tears and kiss them right at the table of a Pharisee (Luke 7:36-39). Again Albert Nolan indicates the significance of such acts when he writes:

> It would be impossible to overestimate the impact these meals must have had upon the poor and the sinners. By accepting them as friends and equals Jesus had taken away their shame, humiliation and guilt. By showing them that they mattered to him as people he gave them a sense

of dignity and released them from their captivity. The physical contact which he must have had with them when reclining at table . . . and which he obviously never dreamed of disallowing . . . must have made them feel clean and acceptable.[36]

Jesus' table fellowship also had implications for the broader society. The meals of Jesus "became a vehicle of cultural protest, challenging the ethos and politics of holiness, even as it also painted a different picture of what Israel was to be, an inclusive community reflecting the compassion of God."[37] The table fellowship of Jesus truly gave birth to the contrast community for which the Hebrew Scriptures had expressed hope. Jesus' parable of the great banquet described this revolutionary reordering of community by inviting the oppressed to the table (Luke 14:15-24). In the story of the rich man and Lazarus (Luke 16:19-31), Jesus made it clear that excluding the poor from one's table of fellowship could lead to one's exclusion from God's table in the life after death. (The reordering of community was evident in the fact that Lazarus was at the heavenly table.) The table fellowship of Jesus "must be seen both as a protest against a religious zeal that is judgmental and exclusive and as a lived-out expression of the openness of God's grace."[38]

It is clear that Jesus' table fellowship turned first-century Jewish society upside down. As Virginia Fabella writes, "His message included what others have never taught: the inclusive character of God's reign. Jesus lived out his teaching by freely associating with, and showing preference for, the poor and marginalized—sinners, outcasts, women. They were the last who had become first; the humble who had become exalted."[39] It has been said that "Jesus was killed because of the way he ate."[40] It would be hard to dispute that as a partial truth. Jon Sobrino summarizes the importance of the table fellowship of Jesus as an image for God's community when he writes:

Jesus states that solidarity does not exist in his society, and then moves toward those whom that society has ostracized. He defends prostitutes, he speaks with lepers and the ritually impure, he praises Samaritans, he permits ostracized women to follow him. These are positive actions of his, calculated to create a new collective awareness of what solidarity is, that it actually exists, and the partisan way in which it ought to develop. Jesus' meals with the poor have special importance for this point. Of course they are only symbolic. But symbols are effective. Correspondence with a kingdom of God "at hand" is had when human beings feel solidarity with one another around a common table. Jesus approaches the ostracized not only individually, but in their community, re-creating them as a social group through the materiality of the dining table.[41]

The early church carried on with the tradition of table fellowship that was instituted by Jesus.[42] Certainly the act of breaking bread together by the Jerusalem believers (Acts 2:46) and the love feasts of the early church (1 Corinthians 11:20-21; Jude 12; also see 2 Peter 2:13) were a continuation of the tradition. Also the Lord's Supper no doubt had its roots in the table fellowship of Jesus.[43] This table fellowship must have been highly valued. In 1 Corinthians 11 and Jude, the writers are challenging the community to address serious breaches in the fellowship at these love feasts. In Corinth, the poor were not getting anything to eat (while others in the community were getting drunk). Jude was concerned that people claiming to be Christians but intent on dividing the community were participating in the love feasts. In both of these cases, the table fellowship of Jesus was being compromised and losing its power as a symbol of God's grace.

Among the modern tables of fellowship are even some barbershops and beauty salons. I get my hair cut at Classy Cuts in Minneapolis, Minnesota. This salon captures some of the nuances of Jesus' table. Classy Cuts was opened in 1991 by Becky and Hop. Hop is from Vietnam, and Becky is from Mexico. Who would have ever imagined that a woman of Mexican heritage and a woman of Vietnamese heritage would start a business together in the cold climate of Minnesota? This small, storefront operation attracts a wide diversity of customers. It is common to hear Vietnamese, Spanish, Hmong, Lao, English, and other languages spoken in the course of a few hours at the salon. Every day Hop and Becky attract people across the boundaries of language, race, culture, gender, denomination, and economic status for the common purpose of getting a haircut. The household of God is called to cross similar boundaries in order to build a visible representation of Jesus' table fellowship. It happens every day at Classy Cuts. It will happen in the community of God when we stop preventing people from joining us at the table of *koinonia* fellowship with Jesus.

A Fresh Vision of Community

We have encountered four powerful biblical images, yet community remains so elusive in our society as a whole or even regionally because "where there is no vision, the people perish (Proverbs 29:18, KJV). Our world is decaying because the bold and creative voices declaring a new way for the human family are becoming fewer in number. A fresh vision of community needs to emerge if we are to prosper. We need to "see visions" and "dream dreams" again (Acts 2:17). The biblical images we have presented can inspire and ignite our envisioning process. It is time to develop the contrast community of God, where, as C. S. Song says, people "can now laugh because their human rights are restored."[44] It is time to build the household of God, where, as Stephen S. Kim writes, there is enough room "to accommodate the wide spectrum of racial, cultural, and theological differences found in our society, in our new homeland where we mean to build an authentic community with God's help."[45] It is time to embrace the spirit of *koinonia*, where, as Howard Thurman says, we can experience "a way of life transcending all barriers alien to community."[46] It is time to join Jesus at the table, where, as Ivone Gebara states, "men and women will eat the same bread, drink the same wine, and dance together in the brightly lit square, celebrating the bonds uniting all humanity."[47]

A fresh vision of community requires that ineffective and oppressive systems be removed so that brand-new approaches can originate. Often it is the old and barren structures that are blocking novel and innovative designs. Vincent Harding has said that this is the problem in the United States where

> . . . for years white America was busy building this house, and then had people from different cultural groups living in the yards or shanties around the house. The liberal contribution since the civil rights activity of the '60s has been to say, "We have to open our house and invite these people to come in and stay." But the problem . . . is [it's] still their house. We're still guests.[48]

The systems on which we build our society need to be evaluated. They are not sacred. If the systems are unjust, then something needs to change. Often the problems we struggle with in our world are the result of a faulty foundation for our life together.

The biblical images we examined offer a blueprint for God's house where the foundation is the justice of God and all are invited to share in the development of God's community. As George Tinker says, "We need to think about building a new house where everybody gets equal say in its design and has equal ownership. Then we need to tear that old house down."[49] Naomi P. F. Southard, using an image from an essay by Audre Lorde, states, "In order to build a new kind of house, one in which we will be truly at home, we must not only dismantle the master's house, but design new tools to create our dreams."[50] Naomi Southard's comments are reminiscent of Jesus' parable about the new wineskins, in which he said:

> And no one puts new wine into old wineskins; otherwise the new wine will burst the skins and will be spilled, and the skins will be destroyed. But new wine must be put into fresh wineskins. And no one after drinking old wine desires new wine, but says, "The old is good" (Luke 5:37-39; see also Matthew 9:17).

Jesus told his followers that new understandings cannot be contained by old structures. Southard's statement about designing new tools for creating our dream of community is critical. The old tools were developed for the purpose of building the old structure. A fresh approach to community entails new methods and skills, that is, new tools. Some of the new tools that are needed are outlined in the rest of this chapter.

Spiritual Transformation

The community ideal begins with God's initiative in reaching out to humanity for a particular kind of relationship. This is the starting point for any attempts at building community. One must be transformed spiritually before one can sustain human relationships that are healthy and empowering. These relationships of belonging need a spiritual core, a divine center, in order to be held together. Dietrich Bonhoeffer helps us recall where this focus needs to be: "The more genuine and the deeper our community becomes, the more will everything else between us recede, the more clearly and purely will Jesus Christ and his work become the one and only thing that is vital between us."[51] It is in God's household and at Jesus' table where we gather.

Centering our communal relationships in God produces a spirit in life that "makes for wholeness and for community."[52] Howard Thurman said that this spirit "knows no country and its allies are to be found wherever the heart is kind and the collective will and the private endeavor seek to make justice where injustice abounds, to make peace where chaos is rampant, and to make the voice heard on behalf of the helpless and the weak."[53] The spirit that produces community is the Spirit of God. It is each individual's relationship with God that prepares her and him for the experience of building a sense of community because "the work for harmony and wholeness in the world cannot be accomplished without the cultivation of the inner life."[54] God awakens the desire for community through spiritual transformation.

In the early 1980s, I was a member of the Covenant House Faith Community[55] in New York City. We lived a communal life that embraced prayer as central to our life together. Our work was with youth and children who were homeless. So our prayers often focused on the young people we served. One evening, a teenage girl who had run away from home and had become trapped in prostitution came to our shelter badly beaten by her pimp. (She had been in and out of the shelter up to this point.) After spending a few days there attempting to heal from the physical and emotional scars of her ordeal, she asked me if I still prayed. She was aware that I lived in the faith community. I responded to her query by assuring her that I did. She asked me to pray that she could go home. (Her parents were not receptive to her return, believing that she would be a bad influence on a younger sister.) Due to persistent prayer and the fine work of social workers, she went home in a few months. I learned a few years later that she had turned her life around and was in nursing school.

This encounter took on greater meaning upon reflection. I believe that what the young woman ultimately wanted was the unconditional love of God and a place to belong. As she was asking me if I still prayed, she was kneeling down before me tying a piece of ribbon on the lace of one of my sneakers. It frightened me a bit, for I could not help viewing her actions as an act symbolically reminiscent of the woman who kissed and anointed Jesus' feet (Luke 7:36-39). It was a gesture of profound gratitude for possible grace. It was a cry for God. It was a plea for community. Whether one has experienced the desperation of life on the streets or the loneliness of a bleak night of the soul, there can be an inward crying out by our spirit for communion with the Spirit of God.

Experience of Community

In addition to the need for spiritual transformation, one of the greatest barriers to the formation of community is that many do not understand community experientially. When

Howard Thurman reflected on his experience of developing a multicultural congregation, the Church for the Fellowship of All Peoples, he wrote that

> . . . one basic discovery was constantly surfacing—meaningful experiences of unity among peoples were more compelling than all that divided and separated. The sense of Presence was being manifest which in time would bring one to his or her own altar stairs leading each in his own way like Jacob's ladder from earth to heaven.[56]

The experience of togetherness, even if brief, awakens a desire for and inspires hope in the possibility of community.

Recently I was facilitating a coalition-building process for a group of people who all worked on issues related to commercial sexual exploitation. The people in the room represented the widest possible range of political and theological viewpoints. Yet in the midst of this broad spectrum of allegiances and identities, a spirit of community began to emerge. The common bond of caring about vulnerable women and children who had been exploited transcended the differing opinions and diverse value systems in the room. For those few hours we experienced the sense of community that Jesus told his disciples to pray for: "Your kingdom come. Your will be done, on earth as it is in heaven" (Matthew 6:10). It could not be preserved because the common center of Jesus Christ was not shared by all who were there. Yet the experience brought a foretaste of what is possible.

Local congregations should be places where the kind of community described in the biblical images exists. Yet there are people who have attended church all of their lives who have never experienced a sense of togetherness. Experiences of community exhibit themselves in unusual ways and at unexpected times. The experience may be a brief moment in a service or a meeting when the Spirit of God brings reconciliation. It may also occur when an unlikely group of people finds themselves thrown together by circumstances. Those who hunger for community need to seek opportunities for experiencing togetherness by taking the second step, after acknowledging God's initiative, to go to where community exists. If we are open to the unfamiliar and to others, God will lead us to experiences of community.

Everyone Has a Voice

Sustained social action and community formation requires that each of us become spiritually transformed. For community to have the equality that God expects, everyone must have a voice. Stephen S. Kim envisions this as "an invitation to gracefully transcend racism, bigotry, superiority complex, and landlord complex, and to cooperate in our common task of the humanization of institutions, divinization of humanity, and ordination of a veritable community, a community of grace and mercy which our Lord envisioned."[57] This means that those who have power in society (or the church), and thereby already have a voice, will need to listen more. Those who have been voiceless in society will have to become emboldened by the Spirit to speak because very likely "the answer for a more livable society rests with those whose voices are too often unheard and rarely sought."[58] The challenge is to find ways to hear from everyone. Sadly, many among the ranks of the voiceless, crushed, and alienated will not speak unless invited.

For everyone to have a voice, a *koinonia* spirit of sharing is necessary. Those of us who have a strong psychological need for receiving credit for our ideas and contributions will want to learn how to place the need for community above our own ego. A focus on individual accomplishments should be replaced by a community-centered agenda. This will be a challenge for persons trained in settings where individualism is highly valued. Naomi Southard states that "in the Asian context, decision making and discussion is a community enterprise, not the task of one person to lay out and the rest react to."[59] Justo González adds: "In most traditional cultures, an idea belongs to the community, not to the individual who somehow was the channel employed by the spiritual powers to communicate the idea to the community."[60]

When ideas are considered community property and no one needs to claim ownership of what they share, we are closer to realizing *koinonia*. In such a community, roles are based on gifts with individuals leading in the areas of their giftedness. Everyone has a voice, and all the glory goes to the householder, Jesus Christ.

The Discipline of Dialogue

In order to create an environment where everybody's voice is heard, we will need to become skilled at what James Earl Massey calls "the discipline of dialogue."[61] Massey describes it this way:

Dialogue is the way of community. It is the personal dimension of sharing. Dialogue concretizes the will to be in relation with another person. It is the self-conscious response of an individual with another self. It is the form of the personal; it is the way of the willed encounter, a means of grace, a celebration of shared meaning. Dialogue is the way of explored intention, the way of God who is always seeking to share himself with others.[62]

In order for a community that values equality to develop, we must take "others seriously as persons."[63] Every person is created in the image of God and therefore has dignity, worth, and something of value to share. So we must develop the art of listening. This will be particularly challenging as we try to listen to those whose experience in life is very different from ours. As we dialogue with people from different cultural perspectives, we will need to "learn how to listen to voices and melodies that are unfamiliar to us."[64] These voices may hold the keys to unlocking the doors that open our minds to the essential components for creating our desired unity.

The more inclusive the dialogue, the richer the content and the stronger the outcome. Delores S. Williams says that womanist theologians use a "multidialogical" approach where one participates "in dialogue and action with *many* diverse social, political, and religious communities concerned about human survival and a productive quality of life for the oppressed." She continues, "Multidialogical activity may, like a jazz symphony, communicate some of its most important messages in what the harmony-driven conventional ear hears as discord, as disruption of the harmony . . ."[65] This womanist approach should be embraced by all of us in our efforts to build truly inclusive collaborations.

There are bound to be differences and disagreements when people dialogue. When everyone is given a voice, a greater number of outlooks are laid out on the table. These are the moments that reveal whether our respect for the other person is genuine. For unity to be maintained, we must sincerely believe that people can disagree and still love Jesus. This can be healthy when there is a common commitment to the shared spiritual values of life's ultimate meaning in Christ. One of the most damaging things in the Christian community is the spirit of judgmentalism. This spirit creeps in when one professed believer doubts the faith of another professed believer because of a difference of opinion or belief on a particular issue. A spirit of community requires that we accept that each one is doing his or her best to understand and apply his or her faith in this complex world (and we leave the judging to God).

Worship has the potential to be an exceptionally powerful form of dialogue in the Christian community. In worship we are invited to interact with God and each other in ways that are reflective, emotive, and mystical. Therefore, our worship also needs to reflect a "multidialogical" intent. Some years ago I visited the Cathedral of St. John the Divine in New York City. It was a weekday, and the organist was there rehearsing for the Sunday mass. I was unfamiliar with the order of service, but the organist must have progressed to the point where Holy Communion would be served. All at once the antiphonal trumpets sounded forth with a majestic melody of praise to God. It was a glorious moment of worship! I also spent many Sundays at the Congregational Church of God, north of the cathedral in Harlem, listening as the choir would exuberantly sing the refrain "There is no power like the power of the risen Lord," and again I would feel caught up in a moment of praise to God.

I believe that anyone who focuses her or his attention on God can worship in any setting whose intent is to bring glory to the Almighty. We can worship God in a noisy celebration and in a silent meditation. We can worship God in the singing of gospel music and in the chanting of the Psalms. We can worship God in the quiet shedding of a tear and the loud shout of "hallelujah!" that all can hear. We can worship God when the preacher reads the sermon with little emotion while standing in the pulpit and when the preacher speaks extemporaneously in a voice filled with emotion as he or she walks back and forth on the platform. If we blend our various worship traditions into a beautiful harmony, the multicultural community can produce unique symphonies of praise unto God.

Multicultural Fluency

If we are to practice the discipline of dialogue in this diverse world, we must become fluent in cultures other than our own. This was the genius of the apostle Paul, who wrote:

> To the Jews I became as a Jew, in order to win Jews. . . . To those outside the law I became as one outside the law . . . so that I might win those outside of the law. To the weak I became weak, so that I might win the weak. I have become all things to all people, that I might by all means save some (1 Corinthians 9:20-22).

Paul had developed the ability to understand and communicate with people from different cultures and experiences. The widespread effects of racism require us to work through stereotypes and develop a sensitivity to cultural differences. This is particularly true for those who are isolated in culturally exclusive ghettos, suburbs, or rural areas. They may understand only their own cultural experience because they have no felt need to do otherwise. Of course, many people of color in places like the United States are, by necessity, fluent in their own culture and in mainstream culture because they live in two cultural experiences everyday. It is imperative that all of us become adept at understanding different cultures. We will never become "experts" on the lives of others, but we can become "fluent" in a variety of cultures. Some may choose to immerse themselves exclusively in another culture and become bicultural. But the mandate for most of us is to gain some expertise in the broad diversity of cultural experiences in our world. We are called to become "multicultural."

Dietrich Bonhoeffer, a German-Christian martyr during the Nazi regime, developed a way of seeing the world through the eyes of others he called "the view from below." He described it as follows:

> There remains an experience of incomparable value. We have for once learnt to see the great events of world history from below, from the perspective of the outcast, the suspects, the maltreated, the powerless, the oppressed, the reviled— in short, from the perspective of those who suffer.[66]

Bonhoeffer's commitment to be faithful to God's call on his life to work for reconciliation and social justice led him to understand the importance of solidarity with the oppressed. For Bonhoeffer, solidarity was not merely living with the oppressed; it was comprehending life from the perspective of the person who suffered. The "view from below" meant having the ability to see the world through the eyes of one who was being oppressed. Bonhoeffer allowed his life experience to mold his way of perceiving and thinking. As Geffrey Kelly states:

> This "view from below" was the perspective of a black preacher in Harlem, of a French pacifist, of pastors concerned about political idolatry creeping into their churches, of a fellow minister with Jewish blood, of inmates at Nazi prisons and death camps, of conspirators torn between loyalty to country and conscience. The circumstances of his life helped Bonhoeffer to see the problems of his people from the view of "the oppressed."[67]

The concept of viewing the world from the vantage point

of people who are suffering can be broadened to include the ability to understand life from the perspective of many other human beings. Not only do the powerful need to understand the experience of the oppressed, the powerless need to fathom empowerment. It is also important for the person who comes from a life of oppression to understand those who face injustice of a different sort (such as a person experiencing sexism seeking to become familiar with the suffering of racism). To live in community we need to develop the skill of comprehending the life experience of our brothers and sisters in the human family.

We can only fully appreciate what it means to be human when we welcome the viewpoints of another's culture. By interacting with people of other cultures, we learn more about ourselves as humans. When we are with people who are of African descent, a part of us is African. When we are with Native Americans, we learn about that part of us that is Native. When we are with Latinas/os, a part of us is Hispanic. When we are with Europeans, we understand better that part of us that is European. When we are with Asians, we gain a fuller comprehension of our "Asian-ness." All across the globe we are tied together by that God-created image we share. To fully understand our humanness, we must be multiculturally fluent. Also, as people who are created in the image of God, we gain a greater knowledge of our God when we understand the many cultural reflections of God's image.

How do we become fluent in other cultures? One way this happens is when we live outside of our comfort zones and relate in significant, ongoing ways to people who are different from us. Our fluency expands as we listen to and live with people from a diversity of settings. This helps us gain points of reference for communicating cross-culturally. If possible, we need to be mentored by persons who are from cultural or racial groups different from our own. Also men need to be mentored by women. Such an apprenticeship cannot be underestimated. Our ways of thinking and viewing the world will be radically altered because of this experience. It is also important to be in regular dialogue with those who are seasoned visionaries for unity and reconciliation.

As we struggle to become fluent in a multitude of cultural world-views, we will be called upon to use these sensitivities to heal and bring people together. Most adventures in community have individuals who serve in the role of catalyst. Martin Luther King, Jr., used his multicultural fluency as a reconciler in the cause of civil rights. This was particularly true of his preaching. He borrowed language and sources from the white liberal Protestant pulpit and fused them with the folk pulpit of the African American preaching tradition.[68] Keith Miller writes:

> King's unmatched words galvanized blacks and changed the minds of moderate and uncommitted whites. Others could embrace nonviolence, get arrested, and accept martyrdom. But only King could convince middle-of-the-road whites about the meaning of the revolutionary events they were witnessing on their television screens. . . . By persuading whites to accept the principle of racial equality, he made a monumental contribution to solving the nation's most horrific problem—racial injustice.[69]

Our Common Humanity

One of the results of multicultural fluency is a greater awareness of our similarities. As signaled at the outset of this book, while there are many cultural expressions, there is only one human family. It is necessary for us to be fluent in a diversity of cultural understandings. Yet there are times when our distinctive cultures must be worn like loose garments. We must be able to interact free from culture in a manner that is simply "human." When we come together, we need to remember that "ethnic, racial, and cultural differences are not to be viewed as a barrier to human community."[70]

I have a friend who was raised in Brazil, speaking German at home and Portuguese at school. When she moved to the United States as an adult, she acquired the ability to speak

English. She now teaches Spanish at a college. I once asked her in what language she thought. Her reply was that she does not think in any particular language but rather in concepts. We must have this same ability when relating to individuals and groups of people from other cultures. The freedom to interact as sisters and brothers in the family of God, liberated from the impediments of our differences (but not discounting our cultural uniqueness), may be the most important foundation for future community.

Questions for Discussion

1. Describe the many ways that people in our society are alienated from one another. What are the causes for this? Why are people of faith so segregated?

2. How would you define *community?* In addition to the images of community included in this chapter, what other biblical or cultural models of community come most readily to mind?

3. Which image of community—contrast community, household of God, *koinonia*, or the table fellowship of Jesus—do you find most appealing and compelling? Why?

4. In what ways have you personally experienced community? Cite some examples.

5. Why is "the discipline of dialogue" important to community? How can we ensure that everyone truly has a voice? What are some ways of addressing disagreements without manipulating or isolating someone?

6. In what ways can worship enhance our communication in community?

7. How can we improve our multicultural fluency? Why is this important?

8. After reading this chapter, how would you define what

it means to be created in the image of God?

9. What are some concrete ways you can strengthen the efforts at building community where you live?

10. In what ways in your life are you going to accept God's invitation to community?

Epilogue

Artisans of Reconciliation

Throughout the foregoing chapters, we have had the opportunity to reflect biblically on our fundamental oneness and our cultural diversity as a mandate for coming together as Christians. We observed very closely how Jesus entered history as a person living at the crossroads of many traditions and how, as the resurrected Christ, he can be a catalyst for blending our various cultural perspectives. These varied outlooks have also given us additional insight for understanding the majesty and mystery of God. We considered, at some length, how liberation and empowerment are key messages in God's self-revelation, challenging us to address injustice in its multiple forms, including racism, sexism, and classism. Finally, we envisioned new ways of understanding how we can come together as the community of God.

With this foundation, it is now time to take action. As people of faith, it is imperative that we heal the wounds of division in the household of God and reach out to a broken society.

Such a move toward reconciliation was occurring, in powerful ways, during the 1950s and 1960s in the United States. Those were days of great hope and idealism as many voices proclaimed the good news of unity. The possibility of coming together seemed almost within reach when, in 1963, Martin Luther King, Jr., spoke of his dream of a reconciled society. But then, in that same year, Medgar Evers and John F. Kennedy were shot to death. In 1964, James Chaney, Andrew Goodman, and Michael Schwerner were slain in Philadelphia, Mississippi. In 1965, Malcolm X, Jimmy Lee Jackson, and James Reeb were killed. In 1968, Martin Luther King, Jr., and Robert F. Kennedy were assassinated. The deaths of Martin Luther King, Jr., and Robert Kennedy, as the culmination of a season of murder, were a tragic blow for the United States. They were the last public figures in the United States who seemed able to unite people across racial and cultural lines to work for reconciliation and social justice. In the final year of their lives, they were in the midst of bringing together African Americans, European Americans, Native Americans, and Latinas/os. When King and Kennedy were killed, within two months of each other, something died in the spirit of many people. In our collective grief we gave up on idealism and the possibility of positive change. In the years since the sixties' killings, the United States has become a much more fragmented and polarized country, emphasizing self-interest rather than self-sacrifice. A whole generation has grown to adulthood struggling to find an ever-elusive reason to hope. Voices of hope are rarely heard anymore above the shouts of gloom and doom.

But quite suddenly a vision for reconciliation and social justice was resurrected, with a new sense of energy, in many parts of the world during the final days of the 1980s and the early 1990s. The images were powerful: the Berlin Wall being torn down, a Chinese dissident placing his body in front of a tank, Yitzhak Rabin and Yasser Arafat shaking hands in peace, and Nelson Mandela walking to freedom (on his way to becoming president of South Africa). These brief interludes of hope and joy were soon overshadowed by renewed hatred and oppression, and the images that ensued were equally as powerful: ethnic and religious cleansing in Europe, mosques and temples burning in India, swastikas carried by neo-Nazis in a reunited Germany, the beating of Rodney King in Los Angeles, and civil war in Rwanda.

Are we living in days when hope is a rare commodity and idealism a lost art? Perhaps we have grown traumatized by the daily tragedies in our world—ethnic cleansing, religious bigotry, neo-Nazism, anti-Semitism, sexual harassment, entrenched racism, brutal acts of violence—and feel powerless as we watch the human family become further partitioned and polarized. Many people have come to believe that our problems are too big, and therefore solutions cannot be found. People are coping in a variety of ways by focusing on day-to-day survival, feeding on the misery of others, or resigning themselves to the belief that the great injustices of our world are here to stay. Has a spirit of despair and hopelessness settled over planet Earth?

Too few Christians are honestly attempting to envision a world where reconciliation is pursued and social justice is valued. Where are the new visions of hope? Can unity still capture our imagination? We need to ask, in the midst of hopelessness and fragmentation, how we, as people of faith, can be catalysts in the pursuit of reconciliation. As we approach and enter the twenty-first century, we must also discover how to sustain these efforts at reconciliation. Cornel West reminds us: "For as long as hope remains and meaning is preserved, the possibility of overcoming oppression stays alive."[1] Nearly two thousand years ago the apostle Paul summed up our task for today:

> So if anyone is in Christ, there is a new creation: everything old has passed away; see, everything has become new! All this is from God, who reconciled us to himself through Christ, and has given us the ministry of reconciliation; that is, in Christ God was reconciling the world to himself, not counting their trespasses against them, and entrusting the message of reconciliation to us. So we are ambassadors for Christ, since God is making his appeal through us; we entreat you on behalf of Christ, be reconciled to God (2 Corinthians 5:17-20).

It is clear from this passage that we are to be Christ's ambassadors for reconciliation in a world that is alienated from itself. The Greek term for reconciliation (katalage) literally means, "becoming friends." As reconciled people, we are to become "friends" with God and with one another.

Perhaps in a world where people are "friends," war and injustice beome obsolete.

The *Christian Community Bible* captures an additional insight in the interpretation of this text when it comments that "what Paul sees in Christ is the great messenger and artisan of reconciliation."[2] An artisan is a person who is highly skilled at a craft and commits her or his life to excelling at this proficiency. We need artisans of reconciliation who are highly skilled at the craft of bringing people together across the lines that divide us. These are people who are intensely devoted to sharpening and shaping their reconciling skills. Such persons, accomplished at persuading people to come together, "no longer live by other people's expectation."[3] Artisans of reconciliation live as though unity is already a reality. In a real sense, we are already one through our shared humanity and through Jesus Christ. The coming of Jesus Christ ushered in a new world. A new age was born. Contrary to the statements of political leaders, the new world order is not just beginning. The new world order was born in the life, death, and resurrection of Jesus Christ. New possibilities for relating to each other were created. New power for transformation was made available. New passion for reconciliation was released. So when our differences take precedent over our oneness, artisans emerge with inspired ideas for promoting unity and creating community.

Artisans of reconciliation are visionaries who have the ability to see and understand clearly what causes injustice and how injustice gives birth to oppressive social conditions. But they also have an equal ability to see and understand clearly what creates a just society (and sincerely believe in the possibility of achieving this). Robert Kennedy's famous paraphrase of the words of George Bernard Shaw captures the essence of the visionary, "Some [people] see things as they are, and say why; I dream of things that never were, and say why not?"[4] Artisans of reconciliation are individuals whose visions of reconciliation and social justice emerge from their faith experience. Their faith is like that which is described by the author of Hebrews: "Now faith is the assurance of things hoped for, the conviction of things not seen" (11:1). The hope of the reconciler is not in individuals who may symbolize the cause (such as King and Kennedy). Rather it is in the faith that the symbols point to, the resurrection of Jesus Christ. Therefore, hope does not die when the "symbols of hope" die. Because Jesus Christ lives, hope still lives. This is the Good News that must be announced to our world.

In addition to being visionaries, artisans of reconciliation are also activists. They recognize injustice and can envision a just world, but they also design and implement methods for moving from the way things are to how things should be. They "establish beachheads of caring and concern in a world that seems so unredeemed and so cruel."[5] They are not afraid of adapting or changing their ways of thinking or plans of action if it brings them closer to the goal of reconciliation and social justice. Artisans of reconciliation motivate other people to work for change because of their sincere belief that things really can change for the better. As Cornel West states:

> To talk about human hope is to engage in an audacious attempt to galvanize and energize, to inspire and to invigorate world-weary people. . . . we have given up on the capacity of human beings to do *anything* right. The capacity of human communities to solve any problem. . . . If you don't think what you think and what you do can make a difference, then the possibility of human hope wanes.[6]

As visionary-activists, they are the type of leaders needed for the twenty-first century.

We live in a world where the need for reconciliation and social justice has never been greater. We need visionary-activists who will guide us in our search for a more just world. In order to sustain efforts at reconciliation, the cadre of artisans must multiply beyond a few "called" individuals. The urgency of this task is great![7] We must not let that powerful flame of unity and reconciliation, set ablaze by the hope of the 1950s and 1960s, become an intermittent flicker as we enter the twenty-first century. The Bible's message, in this age of diversity, is an invitation to come together at God's table of fellowship and to go forth into all the world as God's artisans of reconciliation. Steve Charleston predicts that

> In the next century, the Christian church is going to experience a second major reformation. It will be far more powerful than the one we knew in sixteenth century Europe. For one thing, it will be international, not just regional. It will cross over not only denominational lines, but also over lines of color, class, gender, and age. It will be more important than the last reformation because it will change the way people think and feel about themselves. While the West will participate in this reformation, it will not play a dominant role. The leaders of the coming reformation will be women. They will be from Africa, Asia, Latin America, and Native America. They are being born right now.[8]

Each of us must accept the challenge to stand up in a world estranged from itself and carry the banner of reconciliation.

> Nothing that is worth doing can be achieved in a lifetime; therefore we must be saved by hope. Nothing which is true or beautiful or good makes complete sense in any immediate context of history; therefore we must be saved by faith. Nothing we do, however virtuous, can be accomplished alone; therefore we are saved by love.[9]

Appendix

Identification of Sources by Culture

This list does not include all of the people quoted. The people listed here identified themselves in the source material utilized (or the editor of the volume identified them) or I am personally aware of this information. This should be considered as an attempt at identification. Cultural designations are not always completely accurate and sometimes the designations used change over the course of time (such as "colored" to "Negro" to "black" to "African American").

Name	Country of Origin or Cultural Designation
Heribert Adam	South Africa
David Tuesday Adamo	Kenya
Naim Stifan Ateek	Palestine
Randall C. Bailey	African American
Tissa Balasuriya	Sri Lanka
James Baldwin	African American
James Banks	African American
Joseph Barndt	United States White
Eberhard Bethge	Germany
Allan Boesak	South Africa
Dietrich Bonhoeffer	Germany
Deacon Boniface	Aboriginal—Australia
José Míguez Bonino	Argentina

Marcus J. Borg	United States White
Taylor Branch	United States White
Byung Mu Ahn	Korea
Steve Charleston	Choctaw Nation—Native America
Chung Hyun Kyung	Korea
Albert Cleage	African American
Charles B. Copher	African American
James H. Cone	African American
Nicholas Cooper-Lewter	African American
Orlando Costas	Puerto Rica
J. Severino Croatto	Argentina
Donald Dayton	United States White
Vine Deloria, Jr.	Sioux Nation—Native America
Kelly Brown Douglas	African American
Ruben Dri	Costa Rica
Alfred G. Dunston	African American
Virgilio Elizondo	Mexican American
Ignacio Ellacuría	Spain/El Salvador
Virginia Fabella	Philippines
Cain Hope Felder	African American
Charles Finney	United States White
S. D. Gaede	United States White
Aaron Gallegos	Hispanic American
David Garrow	United States White
Ivone Gebara	Brazil
Djiniyini Gondarra	Aboriginal—Australia
Justo González	Cuba
Leonard Goppelt	German
Billy Graham	United States White
Jacquelyn Grant	African American
Andrew Hacker	United States White
Vincent Harding	African American
Samuel Hines	Jamaica
Elizabeth Hooten	England
Ada María Isasi-Díaz	Cuba

Joachim Jeremias	Germany
John L. Johnson	African American
E. Stanley Jones	United States White
François Kabasélé	Zaire
Stetson Kennedy	United States White
Kim Chi Ha	Korea
Stephen S. Kim	Korea
Martin Luther King, Jr.	African American
Cécé Kolié	Guinea
Kosuke Koyama	Japan
Kwok Pui Lan	Hong Kong
Doug LaFriniere	Ojibwe Nation—Native America
Mary John Mananzan	Philippines
Willi Marxsen	Germany
James Earl Massey	African American
Rigoberta Menchú	Native American Indian— Guatemala
Keith Miller	United States White
Henry Mitchell	African American
Elisabeth Moltmann-Wendel	Germany
William Mosley	African American
Kogila Moodley	South Africa
Cyrus H. S. Moon	Korea
Calvin Morris	African American
Anne Nasimiyu-Wasike	Kenya
Reinhold Niebuhr	United States White
Albert Nolan	South Africa
Homer Noley	Choctaw Nation— Native America
Mercy Amba Oduyoye	Ghana
Sun Ai Park	Korea
Efoé Julien Pénoukou	Benin
George Pixley	Nicaragua
Sharon Ringe	United States White
Lydia E. Lebrón Rivera	Puerto Rico

Oscar Romero	El Salvador
Stanley J. Samartha	India
Cheryl Sanders	African American
Anselme T. Sanon	Burkina Faso
A. H. Sayce	England
Ronald Sider	United States White
George M. Soares-Prabhu	India
Jon Sobrino	Spain/El Salvador
C. S. Song	Taiwan
Naomi P. F. Southard	Asian American
Marie Strong	United States White
R. S. Sugirtharajah	Sri Lanka
Elsa Tamez	Costa Rica
Kuribayashi Teruo	Burakumin—Japan
Howard Thurman	African American
George Tinker	Osage/Cherokee Nation— Native America
Saúl Trinidad	Peru
Jose Vasconcelos	Mexico
Raul Vidáles	Mexico
Lloyd K. Wake	Japanese American
John M. Waliggo	Uganda
Robert Allen Warrior	Osage Nation—Native America
Renita J. Weems	African American
Anton Wessels	Netherlands
Cornel West	African American
Amos Niven Wilder	United States White
Delores S. Williams	African American
Gayraud S. Wilmore	African American

Notes

Introduction

1. Frank Feather, *G-Forces: Reinventing the World* (Toronto: Summerhill Press, Ltd., 1989), 81-82.

2. Brad Edmondson, "The Big Picture," *American Demographics Desk Reference Series* (no. 1), July 1991, 5.

3. Cornel West, *Race Matters* (Boston: Beacon Press, 1993), 6.

4. Designating groups of people by culture, race, geographic location, and so on is always a tentative task. This book uses terminology that reflects the predominant usage at the time of writing. A few years from now these designations may change. Of course, each of these classifications includes a broad range of cultural expressions. For example, "Asian" would include people from China, Iran, Japan, India, Laos, and the like. The terms "Latino" and "Hispanic" are used interchangeably in the book since both are currently in use and with strong preferences for each, neither has emerged as a singularly representative term. Gender-inclusive language is used except when quoting sources. The word "Latino," which in Spanish is masculine, is considered by many to be an inclusive term. This is similar to English words once considered to be inclusive, such as "mankind" (now "humankind"). In the spirit of inclusiveness, the term "Latina/o" will be used in this book.

5. See chapter six, section entitled "Everyone Has a Voice."

Chapter One

1. Title of lecture by Cain Hope Felder on October 23, 1992, at the conference, "The Bible in an Age of Multiculturalism" in St. Paul, Minnesota, sponsored by TURN Leadership Founda-

tion and Biblical Institute for Social Change.

2. Cain Hope Felder, "Out of Africa I Have Called My Son," in *The Other Side*, (vol. 28, no. 6), November-December 1992, 10.

3. Charles B. Copher, *Black Biblical Studies: An Anthology of Charles B. Copher* (Chicago: Black Light Fellowship, 1993), 133.

4. Cain Hope Felder, "Afrocentric Biblical Interpretation," in *The BISC Quarterly*, (vol. 3, no. 1), 2.

5. Felder, "Out of Africa," 11.

6. Calvin S. Morris, "We, the [White] People: A History of Oppression," in *America's Original Sin: A Study Guide on White Racism* (Washington: Sojourners, 1992), 12-15.

7. A. H. Sayce, *The Races of the Old Testament* (New York: Fleming H. Revell Company, 1891), 174.

8. William F. Albright, "The Old Testament World," in George Arthur Buttrick, ed., *The Interpreter's Bible*, Volume 1 (New York: Abingdon Press, 1952), 238-239.

9. For an overview of the various views regarding the location of Eden, see David Tuesday Adamo, "Ancient Africa and Genesis 2:10-14" in *The Journal of Religious Thought*, (vol. 49, no. 1), Summer-Fall, 1992, 38-43. At times the issue is avoided, such as in Terrance E. Fretheim, "The Book Of Genesis," in Leander E. Keck, convening ed., *The New Interpreter's Bible*, Volume 1 (Nashville: Abingdon Press, 1994), 351, where it refers to the Pishon, Gihon, Havilah and Cush as "rivers and places no longer known to us." There is no acknowledgment of the research of scholars, such as Charles Copher and Cain Hope Felder, who argue that these rivers and places can be known and they are in Africa.

10. Cuthbert A. Simpson, "The Book of Genesis: Introduction and Exegesis," in George Arthur Buttrick, ed., *The Interpreter's Bible*, Volume 1 (New York: Abingdon Press, 1952), 495.

11. Cain Hope Felder, "Introduction," in Cain Hope Felder, gen. ed., *The Original African Heritage Study Bible* (Nashville: The James C. Winston Publishing Company, 1993), ix. Also, Felder, "Afrocentric Biblical Interpretation," 5.

12. Cain Hope Felder, "Recovering Multiculturalism in Scripture," in Cain Hope Felder, gen. ed., *The Original African Heritage Study Bible* (Nashville: The James C. Winston Publishing Company, 1993), 99.

13. Cain Hope Felder, *Troubling Biblical Waters: Race, Class*

and Family (Maryknoll: Orbis Books, 1989), 37.

14. Felder, "Out of Africa," 10.

15. Alfred G. Dunston, Jr., *The Black Man in the Old Testament and Its World* (Philadelphia: Dorrance & Company, 1974), 58-69. See also Copher, 138.

16. Cain Hope Felder, "Introduction," in *The Original African Heritage Study Bible* , xi.

17. Dunston, 82-86.

18. Felder, "Out of Africa," 10.

19. In this section we will address the African presence in the Bible rather than the black presence which is discussed in the works of Charles B. Copher, Alfred G. Dunston, Jr., John L. Johnson, Walter Arthur McCray, William Dwight McKissic, Sr., Daud Malik Watts and others.

20. Copher, 135.

21. John M. Waliggo, "African Christology in a Situation of Suffering," Robert J. Schreiter, ed., *Faces of Jesus in Africa* (Maryknoll: Orbis Books, 1991), 171, 173.

22. Felder, "Out of Africa," 10.

23. Robert J. Schreiter, "Jesus Christ in Africa Today," Robert J. Schreiter, ed., *Faces of Jesus in Africa* (Maryknoll: Orbis Books, 1991), viii.

24. For a detailed discussion on the history and various interpretations of the curse of Cain and Ham as "blackness," see Cain Hope Felder, "Race, Racism, and the Biblical Narratives," and Charles B. Copher, "The Black Presence in the Old Testament," Cain Hope Felder, ed., *Stony the Road We Trod: African American Biblical Interpretation* (Minneapolis: Fortress, 1991), 129-132, 146-153.

25. David Roberts, "Out of Africa: the superb artwork of ancient Nubia," *Smithsonian*, June 1993, 91.

26. Ibid.

27. Felder, *Troubling Biblical Waters*, 42.

28. Randall C. Bailey, "Africans in Old Testament Poetry and Narratives," Cain Hope Felder, ed., *Stony the Road We Trod: African American Biblical Interpretation* (Minneapolis: Fortress Press, 1991), 179-180. See also Cain Hope Felder, "Race, Racism, and the Biblical Narratives," Cain Hope Felder, ed., *Stony the Road We Trod: African American Biblical Interpretation* (Minneapolis: Fortress Press, 1991), 135-136.

29. Charles Copher, "The Black Presence in the Old Testa-

ment," Cain Hope Felder, ed., *Stony the Road We Trod: African American Biblical Interpretation* (Minneapolis: Fortress Press, 1991), 157, 161.

30. Felder, *Troubling Biblical Waters*, 22-28.

31. This is the preference of Hebrews' scholar James Earl Massey as stated at the 1986 Newell Lectureship in Biblical Studies, Anderson School of Theology, Anderson, Indiana, June 18, 1986.

32. R. S. Sugirtharajah, "Prologue and Perspective," in R. S. Sugirtharajah, ed., *Asian Faces of Jesus* (Maryknoll: Orbis Books, 1993), viii.

33. J. C. Greenfield, "Cherethites and Pelethites," in George Arthur Buttrick, ed., *The Interpreter's Dictionary of the Bible*, Volume 1 (Nashville: Abingdon Press, 1962), 557.

34. Greece is also mentioned in Joel 3:6 and Zechariah 9:13.

35. Tarshish is mentioned elsewhere as a sea power in Isaiah 23:1, Jeremiah 10:9, and Ezekiel 27:12, 25.

36. C. H. Gordon, "Tarshish," in George Arthur Buttrick, ed., *The Interpreter's Dictionary of the Bible*, Volume 4 (Nashville: Abingdon Press, 1962), 517.

37. E. P. Blair, "Luke (Evangelist)," in George Arthur Buttrick, ed., *The Interpreter's Dictionary of the Bible*, Volume 2 (Nashville: Abingdon Press, 1962), 179.

38. Cain Hope Felder, from lectures on October 23-24, 1992 at the conference, "The Bible in an Age of Multiculturalism" in St. Paul, Minnesota, sponsored by TURN Leadership Foundation and Biblical Institute for Social Change.

39. Clement of Rome in Maxwell Staniforth, trans., *Early Christian Writings: The Apostolic Fathers* (New York: Dorset Press, 1968), 25.

40. Arthur A. Rupprecht, "The Cultural and Political Setting of the New Testament," *The Expositor's Bible Commentary*, Volume 1, (Grand Rapids: Zondervan Publishing House, 1979), 485.

41. Justo L. González, *Mañana: Christian Theology from a Hispanic Perspective* (Nashville: Abingdon Press, 1990), 77.

42. Jose Vasconcelos quoted in Aaron Gallegos, "Mestizo Popular Religion", *America's Original Sin: A Study Guide on White Racism* (Washington: Sojourners, 1992), 148.

43. Orlando Costas, "Liberation Theologies in the Americas: Common Journeys and Mutual Challenges" in Mar Peter-Raoul,

Linda Rennie Forcey and Robert Fredrick Hunter, Jr., eds., *Yearning to Breathe Free: Liberation Theologies in the U. S.* (Maryknoll: Orbis Books, 1990), 37.

44. Virgilio Elizondo, *Galilean Journey: The Mexican-American Promise* (Maryknoll: Orbis Books, 1983), 51.

45. Ibid., 52.

46. Fernando F. Segovia, "Reading the Bible As Hispanic Americans," in Leander E. Keck, convening ed., *The New Interpreter's Bible*, Volume 1 (Nashville: Abingdon Press, 1994), 169.

47. Ibid., 49-50.

48. Cain Hope Felder, "The Bible in an Age of Multiculturalism" conference.

49. Robert Allen Warrior, "A Native American Perspective: Canaanites, Cowboys, and Indians," in R. S. Sugirtharajah, ed., *Voices from the Margin: Interpreting the Bible in the Third World* (Maryknoll: Orbis Books, 1991), 289.

50. John L. Johnson, *The Black Biblical Heritage* (Nashville: Winston-Derek Publishers, Inc., 1991), 209.

51. Elizondo, 85.

Chapter Two

1. Columbus Salley and Ronald Behm, *What Color Is Your God?: Black Consciousness and the Christian Faith* (Downers Grove, Illinois: InterVarsity Press, 1981).

2. Vine Deloria, Jr., *God Is Red* (New York: Grosset and Dunlap, 1973).

3. Albert Cleage, *The Black Messiah* (Kansas City: Sheed and Ward, 1969), 42-43, quoted in Kelly Brown Douglas, *The Black Christ* (Maryknoll: Orbis Books, 1994), 56.

4. William Mosley, *What Color Was Jesus?* (Chicago: African American Images, 1987), 34.

5. Anton Wessels, *Images of Jesus: How Jesus Is Perceived and Portrayed in Non-European Cultures* (Grand Rapids: William B. Eerdmans Publishing Company, 1990), 179.

6. Cain Hope Felder, "The Challenges and Implications of Recovering the Afro-Asiatic Identity of Jesus of Nazareth," *The BISC Quarterly* (vol. 4, no. 1), 1993, 1.

7. Footnote 6 in the "Book of Revelation" Cain Hope Felder, gen. ed., *The Original African Heritage Bible* (Nashville: The James C. Winston Publishing Company, 1993), 1783, says,

"European and American white Bible translators have intentionally rendered this description in a manner to minimize the Negroid features clearly evident in the original Old Testament Hebrew and New Testament Greek texts."

8. Cain Hope Felder, "Out of Africa I Have Called My Son," *The Other Side*, November-December 1992, 10.

9. R. S. Sugirtharajah, ed., *Asian Faces of Jesus* (Maryknoll: Orbis Books, 1993), viii.

10. There may have been others. Such a possibility is that the mother of Rehoboam could have been Solomon's Egyptian wife, the daughter of Pharaoh. She seemed to be Solomon's favorite wife.

11. Mosley, 5-6.

12. Felder, *BISC Quarterly,* 1,3,5,8.

13. Stetson Kennedy, *Jim Crow Guide: The Way It Was* (Boca Raton, Florida: Florida Atlantic University Press, 1970), 47.

14. Wessels, 3.

15. Ibid., 3-5.

16. Ibid., 6.

17. James Burns, *The Christ Face in Art* (New York: E. P. Dutton and Co., 1907), xx.

18. Ibid., xviii.

19. J. A. Mackay, quoted in Saúl Trinidad, "Christology, Conquista, Colonization," José Míguez Bonino, ed., *Faces of Jesus: Latin American Christologies*, trans. Robert R. Barr (Maryknoll: Orbis Books, 1984), 62.

20. Sugirtharajah, *Asian Faces of Jesus,* viii.

21. Aaron Gallegos, "Mestizo Popular Religion," *America's Original Sin: A Study Guide on White Racism* (Washington: Sojourners, 1992), 148.

22. Virgilio Elizondo, *Galilean Journey: The Mexican-American Promise* (Maryknoll: Orbis Books, 1983), 11.

23. Gallegos, 149.

24. Elizondo, 12.

25. Ibid.

26. Ibid.

27. Chung Hyun Kyung, "Who Is Jesus for Asian Women?" Sugirtharajah, *Asian Faces of Jesus*, 225.

28. Douglas, 9.

29. Mosley, 36.

30. Efoé Julien Pénoukou, "Christology in the Village," Robert J. Schreiter, C.P.P.S., ed., *Faces of Jesus in Africa* (Maryknoll:

Orbis Books, 1991), 47.

31. Kosuke Koyama, "The Crucified Christ Challenges Human Power," Sugirtharajah, *Asian Faces of Jesus*, 155-156.

32. Susan Bogg, in John W. Blassingame, ed., *Slave Testimony* (Baton Rouge: Louisiana State University Press, 1977), 420, quoted in Douglas, 18.

33. Douglas, 12.

34. Douglas, 13-18.

35. Ibid., 13-17.

36. Nicholas C. Cooper-Lewter, "My Jesus Was Jim Crowed!" *Colors*, May-June 1994, 18.

37. Douglas, 29.

38. Mosley, 42.

39. Steve Charleston, "The Old Testament of Native America," Susan Brooks Thistlethwaite and Mary Potter Engel, eds., *Lift Every Voice: Constructing Christian Theologies from the Underside* (San Francisco: HarperSanFrancisco, 1990), 59.

40. J. N. Sanders, "Gospel of John", vol. 2, George Arthur Buttrick, gen. ed., *The Interpreter's Dictionary of the Bible* (Nashville: Abingdon Press, 1962), 944.

41. Charleston, 59.

42. Sugirtharajah, *Asian Faces of Jesus*, 260.

43. François Kabasélé, "Christ as Chief," Schreiter, 125.

44. Raúl Vidales, "How Should We Speak of Christ Today?" Bonino, 140.

45. Sugirtharajah, *Asian Faces of Jesus*, x.

46. Kim Chi Ha, *The Gold-Crowned Jesus and Other Writings* (Maryknoll: Orbis Books, 1978), 85-131.

47. C. S. Song, "Oh, Jesus, Here with Us!" Sugirtharajah, *Asian Faces of Jesus,* 133.

48. Kim Chi Ha, 121-23.

49. Byung Mu Ahn, "Jesus and People (Minjung)," Sugirtharajah, *Asian Faces of Jesus*, 165.

50. Song, 146.

51. Byung Mu Ahn, 165.

52. Song, 133.

53. Orlando E. Costas, "Liberation Theologies in the Americas: Common Journeys and Mutual Challenges," Mar Peter-Raoul, Linda Rennie Forcey, and Robert Frederick Hunter, Jr., eds., *Yearning to Breathe Free: Liberation Theologies in the United States* (Maryknoll: Orbis Books, 1990), 42-43.

54. Elizondo, 54.

55. Justo L. González, *Mañana: Christian Theology from a Hispanic Perspective* (Nashville: Abingdon Press, 1990), 78.

56. Elizondo, 56.

57. Ibid., 94.

58. Kuribayasha Teruo, "Recovering Jesus for Outcasts in Japan," R. S. Sugirtharajah, ed., *Frontiers in Asian Christian Theology: Emerging Trends* (Maryknoll: Orbis Books, 1994), 11-26.

59. Ibid., 15.

60. Ibid., 16-17.

61. Ibid., 15.

62. Ibid.

63. Rigoberta Menchú, *I Rigoberta Menchú: An Indian Woman in Guatemala* (London: Verso, 1984), 130-35, 245-46.

64. Teruo, *Frontiers,* 19.

65. Anselme T. Sanon, "Jesus, Master of Initiation," Schreiter, 90.

66. Cécé Kolié, "Jesus as Healer?" Schreiter, 128.

67. Anne Nasimiyu-Wasike, "Christology and an African Woman's Experience," Schreiter, 80.

68. Kolié, 128.

69. Ibid., 131.

70. Ibid., 145.

71. Douglas, 20-24.

72. James H. Cone, "Jesus Christ in Black Theology," Curt Cadorette, et al., *Liberation Theology: An Introductory Reader* (Maryknoll: Orbis Books, 1992), 143, 148.

73. Cooper-Lewter, 18-19.

74. Ibid., 19.

75. Ibid.

76. While it could have been any religion, it was Christianity.

77. Ada María Isasi-Díaz, "Solidarity: Love of Neighbor in the 1980s," Thistlethwaite and Engel, 37.

78. Ibid., 37-38.

79. James Baldwin, "Martin and Malcolm," David Gallen, *Malcolm X As They Knew Him* (New York: Carroll and Graf Publishers, Inc., 1992), 277.

80. Andrew Hacker, *Two Nations: Black And White, Separate, Hostile, Unequal* (New York: Charles Scribner's Sons, 1992), 60.

Chapter Three

1. Justo L. González, *Out of Every Tribe and Nation: Christian Theology at the Ethnic Roundtable* (Nashville: Abingdon Press, 1992), 18-29.

2. James Earl Massey, "Reading the Bible from Particular Social Locations," Leander Keck, convening ed., *The New Interpreter's Bible,* Volume 1 (Nashville: Abingdon Press, 1994), 151.

3. Tissa Balasuriya, "Toward the Liberation of Theology in Asia," Curt Cadorette, et al., eds., *Liberation Theology: An Introductory Reader* (Maryknoll: Orbis Press, 1992), 33.

4. George Tinker, "With Drum and Cup: White Myths and Indian Spirituality," *America's Original Sin: A Study Guide on White Racism* (Washington: Sojourners, 1992), 133.

5. Lydia E. Lebrón Rivera, "Response to the Paper Presented by Justo González," *Uncover the Myths*: *Proceedings of the Roundtable of Ethnic Theologians of the United Methodist Church,* October 20-23, 1988, Des Plaines, Illinois), 15.

6. Massey, 152.

7. Justo L. González and Catherine G. González, *Liberation Preaching: The Pulpit and the Oppressed* (Nashville: Abingdon, 1980), 50.

8. See Massey, 150-53.

9. Elsa Tamez, "Women's Rereading of the Bible," R. S. Sugirtharajah, ed., *Voices from the Margin: Interpreting the Bible in the Third World* (Maryknoll: Orbis Books, 1991), 61-70. See also Ada María Isasi-Díaz, "Solidarity: Love of Neighbor in the 1980s," and "The Bible and *Mujerista* Theology," Susan Brooks Thistlethwaite and Mary Potter Engel, eds., *Lift Every Voice: Constructing Christian Theologies from the Underside* (San Francisco: Harper Collins, 1990), 31-40, 261-269; and "*Mujeristas*: A Name of Our Own," Mar Peter-Raoul, Linda Rennie Forcey, and Robert Fredrick Hunter, Jr., eds., *Yearning to Breathe Free: Liberation Theologies in the United States* (Maryknoll: Orbis Books, 1990), 121-28. Of related interest are Fernando F. Segovia, "Reading the Bible As Hispanic Americans," and Carolyn Osiek, "Reading the Bible As Women" Leander Keck, convening ed., *The New Interpreter's Bible,* Volume 1 (Nashville: Abingdon Press, 1994), 167-73, 181-87.

10. Stanley J. Samartha, "The Asian Context: Sources and Trends," Sugirtharajah, *Voices from the Margin,* 36-49.

11. Tamez, in Sugirtharajah, *Voices from the Margin,* 64.

12. Ibid., 67-68.

13. Ibid., 68.

14. Renita J. Weems, "Reading Her Way through the Struggle: African American Women and the Bible," Cain Hope Felder, ed., *Stony the Road We Trod: African American Biblical Interpretation* (Minneapolis: Fortress, 1991), 59.

15. Samartha, 37.

16. Balasuriya, 34.

17. R. S. Sugirtharajah, ed., *Asian Faces of Jesus* (Maryknoll: Orbis Books, 1993), x.

18. Samartha, 43.

19. Kwok Pui Lan, "Discovering the Bible in the Non-biblical World," Sugirtharajah, *Voices from the Margin,* 303.

20. See Cain Hope Felder, *Troubling Biblical Waters: Race, Class, and Family* (Maryknoll: Orbis Books, 1989), 79-101, for rules of interpretation used in the African American church.

21. George Tinker, "Reading the Bible As Native Americans" Leander Keck, convening ed., *The New Interpreter's Bible,* Volume 1 (Nashville: Abingdon Press, 1994), 174-180; "Native Americans and the Land: 'The End of Living, and the Beginning of Survival,'" Thistlethwaite and Engel, 141-151; "The Full Circle of Liberation," *Sojourners,* October 1992, 12-17; and "With Drum and Cup" and "For All My Relations," *America's Original Sin,* 130-37.

22. Tinker, "The Full Circle of Liberation," 15.

23. Tinker, "Native Americans and the Land," 149.

24. Ibid., 145.

25. Tinker, "For All My Relations," 136-37, and "Reading the Bible As Native Americans," 176-80.

26. Tinker, "Reading the Bible As Native Americans," 174.

27. Tinker, "For All My Relations," 136.

28. Tinker, "Reading the Bible As Native Americans," 179.

29. Ibid., 176.

30. Homer Noley, "Native Americans and the Hermeneutical Task," *Uncover the Myths,* 2.

31. Tinker, "Reading the Bible As Native Americans," 176.

32. See James Earl Massey, "Reading the Bible As African Americans" *The New Interpreter's Bible,* Volume 1, 154-155, and Gayraud S. Wilmore, *Last Things First* (Philadelphia: The Westminster Press, 1982), 72-73.

33. Wilmore, 79-81.

34. Massey, "Reading the Bible As African Americans," 157.

35. Nicholas Cooper-Lewter and Henry Mitchell, *Soul Theology: The Heart of American Black Culture* (San Francisco: Harper and Row, 1986), 2-3. For an overview of the perspective of African Americans on the Bible, see Massey, "Reading the Bible As African Americans," 154-60.

36. Ibid., 6.

37. Nicholas Cooper-Lewter, "Fishin 4 Religion," *Colors,* May-June 1993, 13.

38. James A. Banks, "Integrating the Curriculum with Ethnic Content: Approaches and Guidelines," James A. Banks and Cherry A. McGee Banks, eds., *Multicultural Education: Issues and Perspectives* (Boston: Allyn and Bacon, 1989), 196-98.

39. Ibid., 196.

40. Kwok Pui Lan, 304-8.

41. Ibid., 304.

42. This story has often been used to encourage middle-class whites to help impoverished people of color in urban slums. While this might be a noble use of the passage, what we have here are two people of color (see chapters one and two) who were both under the domination of Roman colonial rule. It is true that the Jews were a step above the Samaritans on the Roman social ladder.

43. T. H. Gaster, "Samaritans," George Arthur Buttrick, ed., *The Interpreter's Dictionary of the Bible,* Volume 4 (Nashville: Abingdon Press, 1962), 190-92.

44. Joachim Jeremias, *Jerusalem in the Time of Jesus* (Philadelphia: Fortress Press, 1969), 353.

45. Ibid., 356-57.

46. George R. Beasley-Murray, *Word Biblical Commentary,* Volume 36 (Waco: Word Books, 1987), 62-63.

47. Amos Niven Wilder, *Theopoetic: Theology and the Religious Imagination* (Philadelphia: Fortress Press, 1976), 26.

48. G. H. C. Macgregor, "The Acts of the Apostles," *The Interpreter's Bible,* Volume 9, 231.

49. Robert A. Spivey and D. Moody Smith, *Anatomy of the New Testament: A Guide to Its Structure and Meaning,* 3d ed. (New York: Macmillan Publishing Co., Inc., 1982), 298.

50. I. Howard Marshall, *The Acts of the Apostles: An Introduction and Commentary* (Grand Rapids: William B. Eerdmans

Publishing Company, 1980), 282.

51. See chapter one for discussion on Afro-Asiatic Hebrews and biblical people born in Asia.

52. Don Richardson, *Eternity in Their Hearts,* Revised (Ventura: Regal Books, 1984).

53. Steve Charleston, "The Old Testament of Native America," Thistlethwaite and Engel, 49-61.

54. Ibid., 54.

55. Tinker, "Reading the Bible As Native Americans," 175.

56. Charleston, 55.

57. Ibid., 59.

58. Ibid., 58.

59. Doug LaFriniere, from "Cultural Keys for Evangelism: An Ojibwa (Native American) Model," lecture at the TURN Dialogue, Minneapolis, October 14, 1992.

60. Djiniyini Gondarra, "For Us, Everything Is Life," *Sojourners,* May 1992, 27.

61. Deacon Boniface, quoted by Gondarra, 26.

62. This is a condensed version of the story as recited by Doug LaFriniere at the conference, "The Bible in an Age of Multiculturalism," hosted by TURN Leadership Foundation (Minneapolis) and Biblical Institute for Social Change (Washington, D.C.) in St. Paul, Minnesota, on October 24, 1992. LaFriniere first learned of the story in George Copway, *Indian Life and Indian History* (Boston: Albert Colby Company, 1860), 163-169. He has also discovered that the story remains in the oral tradition of some of the Ojibwe people. LaFriniere hopes to publish his research in an upcoming book, tentatively titled *The Vine Speaks.*

Chapter Four

1. Howard Thurman, *Jesus and the Disinherited* (New York: Abingdon-Cokesbury Press, 1949), 13.

2. George Tinker, "With Drum and Cup: White Myths and Indian Spirituality," *America's Original Sin: A Study Guide on White Racism* (Washington: Sojourners, 1992), 132.

3. Ruben Dri, "Theology of Domination," Philip E. Wheaton, ed., *500 Years: Domination or Liberation? Theological Alternatives for the Americas in the 1990s* (Managua, Nicaragua, and Ocean City, Maryland: Ediciones Nicaro and Skipjack Press,

Inc., 1992), 23-56.

4. From a speech given by Allan Boesak on April 21, 1993, at Luther Seminary in St. Paul, Minnesota.

5. Orlando Costas, "Liberation Theologies in the Americas: Common Journeys and Mutual Challenges," Mar Peter-Raoul, Linda Rennie Forcey, and Robert Frederick Hunter, Jr., eds., *Yearning to Breathe Free: Liberation Theologies in the United States* (Maryknoll: Orbis Books, 1990), 29.

6. Elsa Tamez, *Bible of the Oppressed*, trans. Matthew J. O'Connell (Maryknoll: Orbis Press, 1982), 60.

7. George V. Pixley, "A Latin American Perspective: The Option for the Poor in the Old Testament," R. S. Sugirtharajah, ed., *Voices from the Margin: Interpreting the Bible in the Third World* (Maryknoll: Orbis Books, 1991), 229.

8. Ibid., 230-231.

9. Cyris H. S. Moon, *A Korean Minjung Theology—An Old Testament Perspective* (Kowloon, Hong Kong, and Maryknoll: Plough Publications and Orbis Books, 1985), 7.

10. Tamez, 62.

11. Bernard W. Anderson, *Understanding the Old Testament* (Englewood Cliffs: Prentice-Hall, Inc., 1975), 9.

12. Sharon H. Ringe, *Jesus, Liberation, and the Biblical Jubilee: Images for Ethics and Christology* (Philadelphia: Fortress Press, 1985), 16-17, 25-28, 32.

13. See discussion on biblical images of freedom and the Galatians struggle to incorporate freedom into their lifestyles in Cain Hope Felder, *Troubling Biblical Waters: Race, Class, and Family* (Maryknoll: Orbis Books, 1989), 104-9.

14. Ringe, 29-32.

15. Ibid., 32.

16. Moon, 5.

17. Ibid.

18. Mar Peter-Raoul, "South Bronx to South Africa: Prayer, Praxis, Song," Peter-Raoul, Forcey, and Hunter, 12.

19. Thurman, 33.

20. J. Severino Croatto, "The Political Dimension of Christ the Liberator," José Míguez Bonino, ed., *Faces of Jesus: Latin American Christologies* (Maryknoll: Orbis Books, 1984), 104.

21. I heard Samuel G. Hines, former pastor of Third Street Church of God in Washington, D.C., make this statement on numerous occasions.

22. Virginia Fabella, "Christology from an Asian Woman's Perspective," R. S. Sugirtharajah, ed., *Asian Faces of Jesus* (Maryknoll: Orbis Books, 1993), 219.

23. See common themes in these passages: James 2:14-26; Philippians 2:12-13; Hebrews 11; 1 John 3:16-17.

24. Ignacio Ellacuría, "The Political Nature of Jesus' Mission," Bonino, 90-91.

25. Pheme Perkins, *Resurrection: New Testament Witness and Contemporary Reflection* (Garden City: Doubleday and Company, Inc., 1984), 441.

26. Tamez, 67.

27. Tissa Balasuriya, "Toward the Liberation of Theology in Asia" Curt Cadorette, et al., eds., *Liberation Theology: An Introductory Reader* (Maryknoll: Orbis Books, 1992), 31-41.

28. Ibid., 35.

29. George E. Tinker, *Missionary Conquest: The Gospel and Native American Cultural Genocide* (Minneapolis: Fortress Press, 1993), 9.

30. Balasuriya, 33.

31. Ibid., 37.

32. Ibid., 39.

33. Jacquelyn Grant, *White Women's Christ and Black Women's Jesus: Feminist Christology and Womanist Response* (Atlanta: Scholars Press, 1989), 211, quoted in Justo L. González, *Out of Every Tribe and Nation: Christian Theology at the Ethnic Roundtable* (Nashville: Abingdon Press, 1992), 45.

34. Cain Hope Felder, gen. ed., *The Original African Heritage Study Bible* (Nashville: The James C. Winston Publishing Company, 1993).

35. *Christian Community Bible,* 2d ed. (Quezon City; Makati; Manila, Philippines: Claretian Publications, Saint Paul Publications, Divine Word Publications, 1988).

36. Robert Allen Warrior, "A Native American Perspective: Canaanites, Cowboys, and Indians," Sugirtharajah, *Voices from the Margin,* 288.

37. Ibid., 289.

38. Arthur Lewis, "Introduction: Joshua," Kenneth L. Barker, gen. ed., *The NIV Study Bible* (Grand Rapids: Zondervan Bible Publishers, 1985), 290. For a different approach for appropriating these texts, see Chan-Hie Kim, "Reading the Bible As Asian Americans," Leander Keck, convening ed., *The New Interpreter's*

Bible, Volume 1 (Nashville: Abingdon Press, 1994), 165-66.

39. Warrior, 292.

40. Ibid.

41. Naim Stifan Ateek, "A Palestinian Perspective: The Bible and Liberation," Sugirtharajah, *Voices from the Margin,* 283.

42. Amos Niven Wilder, *Theopoetic: Theology and the Religious Imagination* (Philadelphia: Fortress Press, 1976), 29.

43. Ibid., 27.

44. These ideas were developed in conversations with Nicholas Cooper-Lewter.

45. Warrior, 294.

46. Vine Deloria, Jr., "Vision and Community: A Native-American Voice," Peter-Raoul, Forcey, and Hunter, 78.

47. David J. Garrow, *Bearing the Cross: Martin Luther King, Jr., and the Southern Christian Leadership Conference* (New York: William Morrow and Company, Inc., 1986), 57-58.

48. Keith D. Miller, *Voice of Deliverance: The Language of Martin Luther King, Jr. and Its Sources* (New York: The Free Press, 1992), 138.

49. In many African American churches, the older members of the congregation are esteemed for the wisdom that comes with a long experience in the faith, and they can speak when they feel so moved.

50. Taylor Branch, *Parting the Waters: America in the King Years 1954-63* (New York: Simon and Schuster, 1988), 164.

51. Ibid., 166.

52. Lloyd K. Wake, "Salvation, Struggle, and Survival: An Asian-American Reflection," *Proceedings* (Nashville: Division of Ordained Ministry of the Board of Higher Education and Ministry, The United Methodist Church, 1989), 31, quoted in González, 92.

53. Donald W. Dayton, *Discovering an Evangelical Heritage* (1976; reprint, Peabody, Massachusetts: Hendrickson Publishers, 1992), 7-119.

54. Ibid., 18-19.

55. Ibid., 73-84, 91-92.

56. Ibid., 102, 112.

57. Ibid., 113.

58. Ibid., 97-98, 113-14.

59. John W. V. Smith, *The Quest for Holiness and Unity* (Anderson, Indiana: Warner Press, 1980), 162-69, and Dayton, 97.

60. Dayton, 7-14, 35-62, 88-89.

61. Branch, 227-28.

62. Kosuke Koyama, "Union of Ethical Walking and Theological Beholding: Reflections from an Asian American," Peter-Raoul, Forcey, and Hunter, 111-19.

63. Ibid., 111.

64. James H. Cone, *Martin and Malcolm and America: A Dream or a Nightmare* (Maryknoll: Orbis Press, 1991), 164-65.

Chapter Five

1. Rigoberta Menchú, *I, Rigoberta Menchú: An Indian Woman in Guatemala* (New York: Verso, 1984), 245.

2. David J. Garrow, *Bearing the Cross: Martin Luther King, Jr., and the Southern Christian Leadership Conference* (New York: William Morrow and Company, 1986), 58.

3. Mary John Mananzan and Sun Ai Park, "Emerging Spirituality of Asian Women," Curt Cadorette, et al., eds., *Liberation Theology: An Introductory Reader* (Maryknoll: Orbis Books, 1992), 245.

4. Eberhard Bethge, *Dietrich Bonhoeffer* (New York: Harper and Row, 1970), 155.

5. Archbishop Oscar Romero, *Voice of the Voiceless: The Four Pastoral Letters and Other Statements,* trans. Michael J. Walsh (Maryknoll: Orbis Books, 1985), 193.

6. Justo L. González, "Hermeneutics: A Hispanic Perspective," *Uncover the Myths: Proceedings of the Roundtable of Ethnic Theologians of the United Methodist Church,* October 20-23, 1988, Des Plaines, Illinois, 11.

7. Steve Charleston, "Victims of an American Holocaust: Genocide of Native People," *America's Original Sin: A Study Guide on White Racism* (Washington: Sojourners, 1992), 47.

8. S. D. Gaede, *When Tolerance Is No Virtue: Political Correctness, Multiculturalism and the Future of Truth and Justice* (Downers Grove, Illinois: InterVarsity Press, 1993), 42.

9. E. Stanley Jones, *Mahatma Gandhi: An Interpretation* (New York: Abingdon-Cokesbury Press, 1948), 55.

10. Cain Hope Felder, *Troubling Biblical Waters: Race, Class, and Family* (Maryknoll: Orbis Books, 1989), 37.

11. For an extended discussion on these various forms of racism and their affect on the church, see Joseph Barndt,

Dismantling Racism: The Continuing Challenge to White America (Minneapolis: Augsburg, 1991), 51-154.

12. For an extended treatment of the so-called curses of Cain and Ham, see Charles B. Copher, "The Black Presence in the Old Testament," Cain Hope Felder, ed., *Stony the Road We Trod: African American Biblical Interpretation* (Minneapolis: Fortress Press, 1991), 146-64.

13. John M. Waliggo, "African Christology in a Situation of Suffering," Robert J. Schreiter, ed., *Faces of Jesus in Africa* (Maryknoll: Orbis Books, 1991), 172.

14. Virgilio Elizondo, *Galilean Journey: The Mexican-American Promise* (Maryknoll: Orbis Books, 1983), 7,8-9.

15. Ibid., 2.

16. Gaede, 64.

17. Heribert Adam and Kogila Moodley, *South Africa without Apartheid: Dismantling Racial Domination* (Berkeley: University of California Press, 1986), 198, 200.

18. E. Stanley Jones, *The Reconstruction of the Church—On What Pattern?* (Nashville: Abingdon Press, 1970), 166.

19. For a detailed description of the experience of women in biblical times, see Joachim Jeremias, *Jerusalem in the Time of Jesus* (Philadelphia: Fortress Press, 1969), 359-76.

20. There are no books of the Bible attributed to women. Some scholars, however, have suggested that Hebrews could have been written by Prisca.

21. For an overview of the perspectives of women scholars on the Bible, see Carolyn Osiek, "Reading the Bible As Women," Leander Keck, convening ed., *The New Interpreter's Bible,* Volume 1 (Nashville: Abingdon Press, 1994), 181-87.

22. Renita J. Weems, "Reading Her Way through the Struggle: African American Women and the Bible," Felder, *Stony the Road We Trod,* 57.

23. Elsa Tamez, "Women's Rereading of the Bible," R. S. Sugirtharajah, ed., *Voices from the Margin: Interpreting the Bible in the Third World* (Maryknoll: Orbis Books, 1991), 62.

24. Elisabeth Moltmann-Wendel, *The Women around Jesus* (New York: Crossroad, 1982), 7.

25. Marie Strong, "The Biblical Vision: An Interpretation of Acts 2:17-18," Juanita Evans Leonard, ed., *Called to Minister . . . Empowered to Serve* (Anderson, Indiana: Warner Press, 1989), 7.

26. Elaine C. Huber, "'A Woman Must Not Speak': Quaker Women in the English Left Wing," Rosemary Ruether and Eleanor McLaughlin, eds., *Women of Spirit: Female Leadership in the Jewish and Christian Traditions* (New York: Simon and Schuster, 1979), 168.

27. Emily Manners, *Elizabeth Hooton: First Quaker Woman Preacher* (London: Headley Brothers, 1914), 6, quoted in Huber, 168.

28. Renita J. Weems, *Just a Sister Away: A Womanist Vision of Women's Relationships in the Bible* (San Diego: LuraMedia, 1988), viii.

29. Cheryl Sanders, "Ethics of Holiness and Unity in the Church of God," Leonard, 143.

30. Ibid.

31. Elaine Storkey, *What's Right with Feminism* (Grand Rapids: William B. Eerdmans Publishing Company, 1985), 154.

32. Strong, 5.

33. See Barbara J. MacHaffie, *Her Story: Women in Christian Tradition* (Philadelphia: Fortress Press, 1986), 10-11.

34. Anne Nasimiyu-Wasike, "Christology and an African Woman's Experience," Schreiter, 73.

35. MacHaffie, 15.

36. Jeremias, 376.

37. MacHaffie, 15.

38. Mary J. Evans, *Woman in the Bible* (Downers Grove, Illinois: InterVarsity Press, 1983), 46.

39. Moltmann-Wendel, 5.

40. These examples are found in Nasimiyu-Wasike, 73-74, and MacHaffie, 15-16.

41. Jeremias, 370.

42. Virginia Fabella, "Christology from an Asian Woman's Perspective," Sugirtharajah, *Asian Faces of Jesus*, 212.

43. Kelly Brown Douglas, *The Black Christ* (Maryknoll: Orbis Books, 1994), 91.

44. Jacquelyn Grant, "Subjectification as a Requirement for Christological Construction," Susan Brooks Thistlethwaite and Mary Potter Engel, eds., *Lift Every Voice: Constructing Christian Theologies from the Underside* (San Francisco: Harper, 1990), 213.

45. MacHaffie, 24.

46. The "elect lady" of 2 John 1 could be another reference to

a woman leading a house church, or it could be a reference to the church itself.

47. Evans, 123.

48. Elisabeth Schussler Fiorenza, "Word, Spirit and Power: Women in Early Christian Communities," Ruether and McLaughlin, 34.

49. John Chrysostom, *The Homilies of St. John Chrysostom,* Volume 11, 555, quoted in Evans, 124.

50. Fabella, fn. 6, 221.

51. MacHaffie, 19.

52. Osiek, 186.

53. Ibid., 187.

54. For extended discussions on social and economic classism, see Jeremias, 87-376; Felder, *Troubling Biblical Waters,* 51-78, 102-134; and George M. Soares-Prabhu, "Class in the Bible: The Biblical Poor a Social Class?" Sugirtharajah, *Voices from the Margin,* 147-71.

55. Ronald J. Sider, *Cry Justice: The Bible on Hunger and Poverty* (New York:

Paulist Press, 1980), 3.

56. Soares-Prabhu, 149-51.

57. Ibid., 151.

58. Ibid., 157-58.

59. Felder, *Troubling Biblical Waters,* 59.

60. John R. Donahue, "Biblical Perspectives on Justice," John C. Haughey, ed., *The Faith That Does Justice: Examining the Christian Sources for Social Change* (New York: Paulist Press, 1977), 78.

61. Soares-Prabhu, 158.

62. James H. Cone, "Jesus Christ in Black Theology," Cadorette, et al., 143-44.

63. John C. Haughey, "Jesus as the Justice of God," Haughey, 271.

64. Mercy Amba Oduyoye, "The Empowering Spirit of Religion," Thistlethwaite and Engel, 246.

Chapter Six

1. Martin Luther King, Jr., *Where Do We Go from Here: Chaos or Community?* (New York: Harper and Row, 1967), 190.

2. Curtiss Paul DeYoung, *Milwaukee's Faith Community*

Speaks (Milwaukee: Social Development Commission, 1991).

3. These men and women represented over twelve Protestant denominations as well as Roman Catholic, Greek Orthodox, Orthodox Judaism, Conservative Judaism, Reform Judaism, Nation of Islam, Baha'i, Buddhist, Native American Church, and several independent Protestant congregations. They were African American, Asian, Latina, Native American, and white.

4. DeYoung, 21.

5. Luther E. Smith, Jr., "Community: Partnership of Friendship and Responsibility," Henry J. Young, ed., *God and Human Freedom: A Festschrift in Honor of Howard Thurman* (Richmond: Friends United Press, 1983), 24.

6. Howard Thurman, *Meditations of the Heart* (Richmond: Friends United Press, 1976), 121-22.

7. Willi Marxsen, *The Lord's Supper as a Christological Problem* (Philadelphia: Fortress Press, 1970), 23.

8. Dietrich Bonhoeffer, *Life Together* (New York: Harper and Row, Publishers, 1954), 21.

9. Leonard Goppelt, *Theology of the New Testament Volume 2: The Variety and Unity of the Witness to Christ* (Grand Rapids: Wm. B. Eerdmans Publishing Co., 1982), 10-11.

10. Ibid., 143-44.

11. Justo L. González, *Out of Every Tribe and Nation: Christian Theology at the Ethnic Roundtable* (Nashville: Abingdon Press, 1992), 102.

12. Cain Hope Felder, quoted in González, 106.

13. Similar to the dichotomy between white Christ and black Christ described in chapter two.

14. Paul S. Minear, *Images of the Church in the New Testament* (Philadelphia: The Westminster Press, 1960), 211.

15. George M. Soares-Prabhu, "Class in the Bible: The Biblical Poor a Social Class?" R. S. Sugirtharajah, ed., *Voices from the Margin: Interpreting the Bible in the Third World* (Maryknoll: Orbis Books, 1991), 163-164. He borrowed the idea of "contrast community" from Norbert Lohfink (see fn. 5, 171).

16. Ibid., 164.

17. Ibid., 163.

18. Ibid.

19. Steve Charleston, "Victims of an American Holocaust: Genocide of Native People," *America's Original Sin: A Study Guide on White Racism* (Washington: Sojourners, 1992), 48.

20. Ibid. Charleston's contention regarding the tribe is being tested by the effect of the material prosperity created by casinos on many reservations.

21. Soares-Prabhu, 164.

22. Ibid.

23. Charleston, 48.

24. Cain Hope Felder, *Troubling Biblical Waters: Race, Class, and Family* (Maryknoll: Orbis Books, 1989), 157.

25. Ibid., 158.

26. Ibid., 163.

27. Anselme T. Sanon, "Jesus, Master of Initiation," Robert J. Schreiter, ed., *Faces of Jesus in Africa* (Maryknoll: Orbis Books, 1991), 85.

28. C. Daniel Harden, "Kendall Community Church of God—Miami, Florida," *The Shining Light,* January/February 1994, 3,6. In 1994, the people in this unique congregation were 38 percent from the West Indies, 35 percent Anglo, 10 percent Hispanic, 8 percent African American, 6 percent Haitian, 2 percent Asian, and 1 percent Jewish—a truly multicultural and multilingual community of faith.

29. Minear, 141.

30. Marilyn J. Legge, "The Church in Solidarity: Liberation Ecclesiology—Introduction," Curt Cadorette, et al., eds., *Liberation Theology: An Introductory Reader* (Maryknoll: Orbis Books, 1992), 162.

31. George E. Tinker, "Native Americans and the Land: 'The End of Living, and the Beginning of Survival,'" Susan Brooks Thistlethwaite and Mary Potter Engel, eds., *Lift Every Voice: Constructing Christian Theologies from the Underside* (San Francisco: Harper Collins, 1990), 149.

32. George Tinker, "The Full Circle of Liberation: An American Indian Theology of Place," *Sojourners,* October 1992, 16.

33. Albert Nolan, *Jesus before Christianity* (Maryknoll: Orbis Books, 1976), 37.

34. Marcus J. Borg, *Jesus a New Vision: Spirit, Culture, and the Life of Discipleship* (San Francisco: Harper and Row, 1987), 101-102.

35. Nolan, 117-18.

36. Ibid., 39.

37. Borg, 133.

38. James D. G. Dunn, "Jesus, Table-Fellowship, and Qum-

ran," James H. Charlesworth, ed., *Jesus and the Dead Sea Scrolls* (New York: Doubleday, 1992), 268.

39. Virginia Fabella, "Christology from an Asian Woman's Perspective," R. S. Sugirtharajah, ed., *Asian Faces of Jesus* (Maryknoll: Orbis Books, 1993), 213.

40. Jerome H. Neyrey, "Ceremonies in Luke-Acts: The Case of Meals and Table Fellowship," Jerome H. Neyrey, ed., *The Social World of Luke-Acts: Models for Interpretation* (Peabody, Massachusetts: Hendrickson Publishers, 1991), 361.

41. Jon Sobrino, "Jesus and the Kingdom of God," Cadorette, 114.

42. Richard A. Horsley, *Jesus and the Spiral of Violence: Popular Jewish Resistance in Roman Palestine* (San Francisco: Harper and Row, 1987), 178-79.

43. Borg, 131.

44. C. S. Song, "Oh, Jesus, Here with Us!" Sugirtharajah, *Asian Faces of Jesus*, 144.

45. Stephen S. Kim, "From I-Hermeneutics to We-Hermeneutics: Prolegomenon to Theology of Community from an Asian-American Perspective," *Uncover the Myths: Proceedings of the Roundtable of Ethnic Theologians of the United Methodist Church,* October 20-23, 1988, Des Plaines, Illinois, 55.

46. Howard Thurman, *The Search for Common Ground: An Inquiry into the Basis of Man's Experience of Community* (New York: Harper and Row, 1971), 103.

47. Ivone Gebara, "Women Doing Theology in Latin America," Cadorette, 63.

48. Vincent Harding was paraphrased by George Tinker, "With Drum and Cup: White Myths and Indian Spirituality," *America's Original Sin*, 133.

49. Tinker, "With Drum and Cup," 133.

50. Naomi P. F. Southard, "Response to the Paper Presented by Stephen Kim," *Uncover the Myths*, 64. She uses imagery from Audre Lorde, *Sister Outsider* (Trumansburg, New York: The Crossing Press, 1984), 110-14.

51. Bonhoeffer, *Life Together,* 26.

52. Howard Thurman, *The Luminous Darkness: A Personal Interpretation of the Anatomy of Segregation and the Ground of Hope* (New York: Harper and Row, 1965), 112.

53. Ibid., 113.

54. Walter E. Fluker, *They Looked for a City: A Comparative*

Analysis of the Ideal of Community in the Thought of Howard Thurman and Martin Luther King, Jr. (Lanham: University Press of America, 1989), 174.

55. The Covenant House Faith Community, a group of people who volunteer a year of their life or longer to prayer, community, and service, was created to provide a spiritual core for the work of Covenant House, an outreach to runaway and homeless youth in several cities. In February 1990, Father Bruce Ritter, the founder of Covenant House, left the agency due to alleged financial and sexual impropriety. The "faith community" became an important foundation in the rebuilding process.

56. Howard Thurman, *With Head and Heart* (New York: Harper and Row, 1963), 9, quoted in Luther E. Smith, Jr., "Community: Partnership of Friendship and Responsibility," Henry James Young, ed., *God and Human Freedom: A Festschrift in Honor of Howard Thurman* (Richmond: Friends United Press, 1983), 28.

57. Kim, *Uncover the Myths,* 45.

58. Dwight N. Hopkins, "Columbus, the Church, and Slave Religion," *The Journal of Religious Thought*, Winter-Spring, 1992-93, 35.

59. Southard, *Uncover the Myths,* 61.

60. González, *Out of Every Tribe and Nation,* 54.

61. James Earl Massey, *Spiritual Disciplines* (Grand Rapids: Francis Asbury Press, 1985), 71-87.

62. Ibid., 87.

63. Ibid., 72.

64. Thistlethwaite and Engel, "Conclusion: Directions for the Future," Thistlethwaite and Engel, 295.

65. Delores S. Williams, "Womanist Theology: Black Women's Voices," Mar Peter-Raoul, Linda Rennie Forcey, and Robert Frederick Hunter, Jr., eds., *Yearning to Breathe Free: Liberation Theologies in the United States* (Maryknoll: Orbis Books, 1990), 67.

66. Dietrich Bonhoeffer, *Letters and Papers from Prison: The Enlarged Edition* (New York: Macmillan Publishing Co., Inc., 1971), 17.

67. Geffrey B. Kelly, *Liberating Faith: Bonhoeffer's Message for Today* (Minneapolis: Augsburg Publishing House, 1984), 156.

68. Keith D. Miller, *Voice of Deliverance: The Language of Martin Luther King, Jr. and Its Sources* (New York: The Free

Press, 1992), 7-8, 155-56.

69. Ibid., 10-11.

70. James Earl Massey, *Concerning Christian Unity* (Anderson: Warner Press, 1979), 59.

Epilogue

1. Cornel West, *Race Matters* (Boston: Beacon Press, 1993), 15.

2. *Christian Community Bible,* 2d ed. (Quezon City; Makati; Manila, Philippines: Claretian Publications, Saint Paul Publications, Divine Word Publications, 1988), 369.

3. Samuel Hines, "Reconciliation," *Expand Your Horizon* (New Wilmington, Pennsylvania: Son-Rise Publications, 1985), 172.

4. Jules Witcover, *85 Days: The Last Campaign of Robert Kennedy* (New York: William Morrow, 1988), 8.

5. Cain Hope Felder, "The Troubler of Biblical Waters," interviewed in William H. Myers, *The Irresistible Urge to Preach: A Collection of African American "Call" Stories* (Atlanta: Aaron Press, 1992), 110.

6. Cornel West, *Prophetic Thought in Postmodern Times* (Monroe, Maine: Common Courage Press, 1993), 6.

7. Many of our brightest lights for unity have died. A number of these have been martyred. Others have fallen prey to illness at the prime of their reconciling efforts, such as Tom Skinner, who died of cancer during the writing of this book. Some have died in tragic accidents just as they were embarking on their journey, such as Rachel Morris, who died in a car accident while in her early twenties, also as this book was being written. Rachel was already proving to be a force for reconciliation. She was following in the footsteps of her father, Calvin S. Morris, an artisan of reconciliation shaped by the 1960s civil rights movement in the United States. Also, many of the leading artisans of reconciliation today are of the same generation as King and Kennedy. Many of the leaders in South Africa, such as Nelson Mandela, Desmond Tutu, and Allan Boesak, are of that generation. Two of my mentors, James Earl Massey and Samuel G. Hines, are of that generation. Hines died just prior to publication of this book. We must be ready as the mantle passes.

8. Steve Charleston, "The Old Testament of Native America,"

Susan Brooks Thistlethwaite and Mary Potter Engel, eds., *Lift Every Voice: Constructing Christian Theologies from the Underside* (San Francisco: Harper Collins, 1990), 60.

9. Reinhold Niebuhr in Ursula M. Niebuhr, ed., *Justice and Mercy* (New York: Harper and Row, 1974), v, quoted in Luther E. Smith, Jr., "Community: Partnership of Friendship and Responsibility," Henry J. Young, ed., *God and Human Freedom: A Festschrift in Honor of Howard Thurman* (Richmond: Friends United Press, 1983), 29.